SENSORDEVICES 2021

The Twelfth International Conference on Sensor Device Technologies and Applications

November 14 - 18, 2021

Athens, Greece

SENSORDEVICES 2021 Editors

Antonio L. L. Ramos, PhD, University of South-Eastern Norway (USN), Norway
Cosmin Dini, IARIA, USA/EU
Manuela Vieira, CTS-ISEL, Portugal

Printed from e-media with permission by:

Curran Associates, Inc.
57 Morehouse Lane
Red Hook, NY 12571

International Academy, Research, and Industry Association (IARIA)
412 Derby Way
Wilmington, DE 19810

Phone: (408) 893-6407
Fax: (408) 527-6351

petre@iaria.org

Additional copies of this publication are available from:

Curran Associates, Inc.
57 Morehouse Lane
Red Hook, NY 12571 USA
Phone: 845-758-0400
Fax: 845-758-2633
Email: curran@proceedings.com
Web: www.proceedings.com

Table of Contents

Data-driven Detection and Identification of Undesirable Events in Subsea Oil Wells 1
Chrisander Bronstad, Sergio L. Netto, and Antonio L.L Ramos

Small Scale Unmanned Aircraft System and Photogrammetry Applied for 3D Modeling of Historical Buildings 7
Alexandre Boente, Thiago Baldivieso, Thiago Oliveira, Vinicius Fonseca, and Paulo Rosa

Drones Operations and Communications in an Urban Environment 13
Sandeep Shivakoti, Aurelie Aurilla Arntzen bechina, Serkan Guldal, and Esther Nistal Cabanas

Tracking Suspicious Entities Using UAVs in Critical Urban Areas: A R-CNN Approach 19
Mathias Afonso Guedes de Menezes, Paulo Fernando Ferreira Rosa, and Erick Menezes Moreira

A UAV-based Infrared Small Target Detection System for Search and Rescue Missions 25
Victor J. Hansen, Antonio L. L. Ramos, and Jose A. Apolinario Jr.

3D Reconstruction with Drone Images: Optimization by Reinforcement Learning 31
Thiago Joao Miranda Baldivieso, Taise Grazielle da Silva Batista, Luiz Carlos Pacheco Rodrigues Velho, and Paulo Fernando Ferreira Rosa

Influences on the Detection Probability of Ferromagnetic Objects 35
Lukas Heindler, Ruben Piepgras, and Bernhard G. Zagar

Environmental Monitoring in Built Environment Through Wearable Devices: a Bibliometric Review 41
Francesco Salamone, Sergio Sibilio, and Massimiliano Masullo

Design, Fabrication and Characterization of a Novel Piezoresistive Pressure Sensor for Blast Waves Monitoring 47
Kevin Sanchez, Bilel Achour, Jerome Riondet, Laurene Anglade, Miguel Carrera, Anthony Coustou, Aurelie Lecestre, Samuel Charlot, Herve Aubert, Maylis Lavayssiere, Alexandre Lefrancois, Jerome Luc, and Patrick Pons

HCI Preliminary Study and Implementation for a LoRa based SAR System 53
Christos Bouras, Apostolos Gkamas, and Spyridon Aniceto Katsampiris Salgado

Study on the Performance of Sensitive Part of Bridge Type Ultra-Thin Film Hydrogen Sensor 59
Takahiro Mori, Shoki Wakabayashi, Kenji Kondoh, Takuya Takahashi, Makoto Nakagawa, Naohiro Ueda, Jin Wang, Kenji Sakai, Keiji Tsukada, and Toshihiko Kiwa

Vehicular Visible Light Communication in a Two-Way-Two-Way Traffic Light Controlled Crossroad 61
Manuel Vieira, Manuela Vieira, Paula Louro, Pedro Vieira, and Mirtes de Lima

Indoor Self-localization and Wayfinding Services using Visible Light Communication: A model 67

Manuela Vieira, Manuel Vieira, Paula Louro, Pedro Vieira, and Joao Rodrigues

A Wearable Internet of Things Device for Bio-signals Real Time Monitoring of Elderly People 73
Panagiotis Pikasis and Grigoris Kaltsas

PdAu Based Resistive Hydrogen Sensor in Anaerobic Environment 77
Clement Occelli, Tomas Fiorido, Carine Perrin-Pellegrino, and Jean-Luc Seguin

Signal Accuracy of Terahertz Chemical Microscope for Lung Cancer Cell Detection 82
Yuichi Yoshida, Xue Ding, Kohei Iwatsuki, Sayaka Tsuji, Hirofumi Inoue, Jin Wang, Kenji Sakai, and Toshihiko Kiwa

Detection of Proteins Associated with Alzheimer's Disease using a Terahertz Chemical Microscope 84
Kohei Iwatsuki, Yuichi Yoshida, Xue Ding, Sayaka Tsuji, Jin Wang, Kenji Sakai, and Toshihiko Kiwa

A Method to Minimize Resonant Frequency Drift of CMUTs Due to Fluid Loading 86
Thasnim Mohammed and Sazzadur Chowdhury

Footprint Model in a Navigation System Based on Visible Light Communication 92
Paula Louro, Manuela Vieira, Manuel A. Vieira, Mirtes de Lima, Joao Rodrigues, and Pedro Vieira

High-precision Time Synchronization Digital Sensing Platform Enabling Connection of a Camera Sensor 98
Narito Kurata

Triboelectric-based energy harvesting face mask using recyclable materials 105
Brady Miller, Samantha Barker, and Reza Rashidi

SENSORDEVICES 2021

Forward

The Twelfth International Conference on Sensor Device Technologies and Applications (SENSORDEVICES 2021), held on November 14-18, 2021, continued a series of events focusing on sensor devices themselves, the technology-capturing style of sensors, special technologies, signal control and interfaces, and particularly sensors-oriented applications. The evolution of the nano-and microtechnologies, nanomaterials, and the new business services make the sensor device industry and research on sensor-themselves very challenging.

Most of the sensor-oriented research and industry initiatives are focusing on sensor networks, data security, exchange protocols, energy optimization, and features related to intermittent connections. Recently, the concept of Internet-of-things gathers attention, especially when integrating IPv4 and IIPv6 networks. We welcomed technical papers presenting research and practical results, position papers addressing the pros and cons of specific proposals, such as those being discussed in the standard fora or in industry consortia, survey papers addressing the key problems and solutions on any of the above topics short papers on work in progress, and panel proposals.

We take here the opportunity to warmly thank all the members of the SENSORDEVICES 2021 technical program committee, as well as all the reviewers. The creation of such a high quality conference program would not have been possible without their involvement. We also kindly thank all the authors who dedicated much of their time and effort to contribute to SENSORDEVICES 2021. We truly believe that, thanks to all these efforts, the final conference program consisted of top quality contributions.

We also thank the members of the SENSORDEVICES 2021 organizing committee for their help in handling the logistics and for their work that made this professional meeting a success.

We hope that SENSORDEVICES 2021 was a successful international forum for the exchange of ideas and results between academia and industry and to promote further progress in the area of sensor devices technologies and applications.

SENSORDEVICES 2021 Chairs

SENSORDEVICES 2021 Steering Committee

Arcady Zhukov, University of Basque Country (UPV/EHU), San Sebastian / Ikerbasque, Basque Foundation for Science, Bilbao, Spain
Narito Kurata, Tsukuba University of Technology, Japan
Sazzadur Chowdhury. University of Windsor, Canada
Manuela Vieira, CTS/ISEL/IPL, Portugal

SENSORDEVICES 2021 Publicity Chair

Mar Parra Boronat, Universitat Politecnica de Valencia, Spain
Sandra Viciano Tudela, Universitat Politecnica de Valencia, Spain

SENSORDEVICES 2021

Committee

SENSORDEVICES 2021 Steering Committee

Arcady Zhukov, University of Basque Country (UPV/EHU), San Sebastian / Ikerbasque, Basque Foundation for Science, Bilbao, Spain
Narito Kurata, Tsukuba University of Technology, Japan
Sazzadur Chowdhury. University of Windsor, Canada
Manuela Vieira, CTS/ISEL/IPL, Portugal

SENSORDEVICES 2021 Publicity Chair

Mar Parra Boronat, Universitat Politecnica de Valencia, Spain
Sandra Viciano Tudela, Universitat Politecnica de Valencia, Spain

SENSORDEVICES 2021 Technical Program Committee

Ahmed Alfadhel, Rochester Institute of Technology, USA / Research Products Development Company, Saudi Arabia
Jesús B. Alonso Hernández, Institute for Technological Development and Innovation in Communications (IDeTIC) | University of Las Palmas de Gran Canaria (ULPGC), Spain
Sebastian Anand Alphonse, LivaNova PLC, Houston, USA
Ismael Andrade Pimentel, Pontifical Catholic University of Rio de Janeiro. Brazil
Darius Andriukaitis, Kaunas University of Technology (KTU), Lithuania
Francisco Arcega, University of Zaragoza, Spain
Herve Aubert, Laboratory for Analysis and Architecture of Systems (LAAS-CNRS), Toulouse, France
Ripendra Awal, Prairie View A&M University, USA
Valerio Baiocchi, "Sapienza" University of Rome, Italy
Camelia Bala, University of Bucharest, Romania
Jose Barata, NOVA University of Lisbon, Portugal
Yoseph Bar-Cohen, Jet Propulsion Laboratory | NASA, USA
Michal Borecki, Warsaw University of Technology | Institute of MIcroelectronics and Optoelectronics, Poland
Manuel José Cabral dos Santos Reis, IEETA / University of Trás-os-Montes e Alto Douro, Portugal
Luigi Campanella, Sapienza University of Rome, Italy
Juan-Carlos Cano, Universitat Politecnica de Valencia, Spain
Nicola Carbonaro, Research Centre "E. Piaggio" | University of Pisa, Italy
Vítor Carvalho, 2Ai Lab- School of Technology - IPCA / Algoritmi Research Center - Minho University, Portugal
Paula María Castro Castro, University of A Coruña, Spain
Fulvio Re Cecconi, Politecnico di Milano, Italy
Diliang Chen, University of New Hampshire, USA
Irinela Chilibon, National Institute of Research and Development for Optoelectronics - INOE-2000, Romania
Raad Farhood Chisab, Middle Technical University, Baghdad, Iraq
Nan-Fu Chiu, National Taiwan Normal University, Taiwan

Joo Yeon Cho, ADVA Optical Networking, Munich, Germany
Chi-Wai Chow, National Chiao Tung University, Hsinchu, Taiwan
Sazzadur Chowdhury, University of Windsor, Canada
Juan M. Corchado, University of Salamanca, Spain
Marco Crescentini, University of Bologna, Italy
Francesco G. Della Corte, Università degli Studi Mediterranea, Italy
Emiliano Descrovi, Norwegian University of Science and Technology (NTNU), Trondheim, Norway / Polytechnic University of Turin, Torino, Italy
Abdou Karim Diallo,Gaston Berger University, Senegal
Dermot Diamond, Dublin City University, Ireland
Amad Ud Din, Fatima Jinnah Women University, Pakistan
Toan Dinh, University of Southern Queensland, Australia
René Domínguez-Cruz, Universidad Autónoma de Tamaulipas, Mexico
Jimmy T. Efird, CSPEC/DVAHCS/HSR&D (Duke University Affiliated Center), Durham, USA
Eugenia Fagadar-Cosma, Institute of Chemistry "Coriolan Dragulescu", Timisoara, Romania
Francisco Falcone, UPNA-ISC, Spain
Rui Fonseca-Pinto, Polytechnic of Leiria, Portugal
Óscar Fresnedo Arias, University of A Coruña, Spain
Mounir Gaidi, University of Sharjah, UAE
Juan Carlos García, University of Alcala, Spain
Francesca Giannone, Niccolò Cusano University, Rome, Italy
Jan Havlík, Czech Technical University in Prague, Czech Republic
Eiji Higurashi, National Institute of Advanced Industrial Science and Technology (AIST), Japan
Johan Holmgren, Malmö University, Sweden
M. Carmen Horrillo Güemes, Group of Technology of Advanced Sensors (SENSAVAN)-ITEFI-CSIC, Spain
Wen-Jyi Hwang, National Taiwan Normal University, Taipei, Taiwan
Mohamed Ichchou, Ecole Centrale de Lyon, France
Raul Igual, EUP Teruel | University of Zaragoza, Spain
Illyas Md Isa, Universiti Pendidikan Sultan Idris, Malaysia
Kh Tohidul Islam, The University of Melbourne | Melbourne Medical School, Australia
Rajesh Khanna, Thapar Institute of Engineering and Technology, India
Ahmed Khorshid, Advanced Micro Devices (AMD), USA
Hyunook Kim, University of Seoul, Korea
Farzana Kulsoom, University of Engineering and Technology, Taxila, Pakistan
Narito Kurata, Tsukuba University of Technology, Japan
José Luis Lázaro-Galilea, University of Alcalá, Spain
Ching-Ting Lee, Yuan Ze University / National Cheng-Kung University, Taiwan
Gyu Myoung Lee, Liverpool John Moores University, UK
Kevin Lee, School of InformationTechnology | Deakin University, Melbourne, Australia
Martin Lenzhofer, SiliconAustriaLabsGmbH, Austria
Diego Liberati, National Research Council of Italy, Italy
Eduard Llobet, Universitat Rovira i Virgili, Spain
Jerzy P. Lukaszewicz, Nicoulaus Copernicus University, Torun, Poland
Joaquim Miguel Maia, Federal University of Technology - Paraná (UTFPR), Brazil
Oleksandr Makeyev, School of STEM | Diné College, USA
Piero Malcovati, University of Pavia, Italy
Jorge Marcos Acevedo, University of Vigo, Spain
Stefano Mariani, Politecnico di Milano, Italy

Copyright Information

Data-driven Detection and Identification of Undesirable Events in Subsea Oil Wells

Chrisander Brønstad
Dept. of Science and Industry Systems,
University of South-Eastern Norway
Kongsberg, Norway
email: c.bronstad94@gmail.com

Sergio L. Netto
Dept. of Electrical Engineering Program,
Federal University of Rio de Janeiro
Rio de Janeiro, Brazil
email: sergioln@smt.ufrj.br

Antonio L. L. Ramos
Dept. of Science and Industry Systems,
University of South-Eastern Norway
Kongsberg, Norway
email: antonior@usn.no

***Abstract*—Condition-Based Monitoring (CBM) systems have grown in popularity in recent years owing to innovations in areas, such as sensor-technology, communication systems, and computing. That has fostered the development of more efficient systems to monitor, analyze, and identify failures in industrial plants, production lines, and machinery. Gas and oil industries lose billions of dollars yearly related to abnormal events and systems failures. Thus, Abnormal Event Management (AEM), which aims at early detection and identification of these events, has become their number one priority so that preventive actions can be taken timely. This work addresses the issue of detection and classification of faults in offshore oil wells. The aim is to create a CBM system based on the random forest classifier to support decision-making. The events used in this work are part of the 3W database developed by Petrobras, Brazil, one of the world's largest oil producer. Seven events categorized as faulty events are considered, as well as several instances labeled as normal operation. We conducted two experiments related to two different classification scenarios. The proposed systems achieved an overall accuracy of 90%, indicating that the system is not only able to detect faulty events but can also anticipate incoming failures successfully.**

Keywords - condition-based monitoring; machine learning; data-driven detection and classification; random forest classifier.

I. INTRODUCTION

Recent advances in sensor technologies, communication systems for data acquisition, storage, and computational capability gave birth to an era of massive automatic data gathering, storage, and processing. This has resulted in a paradigm shift bringing new opportunities for developing innovative solutions and systems for a wide range of applications. As an example of that, Germany launched recently a project known as "Industry 4.0" to revitalize the industry based on such systems, commonly referred to as smart technology. Today, Condition-Based Monitoring (CBM) applies state-of-art technology and is often related to solutions such as Cyber-Physical Systems (CPS) and Internet of Things (IoT) [1], [2].

Systems for CBM are being widely adopted to monitor and evaluate the condition of processes, machinery, and components of interest. The goal is to anticipate and detect incoming failures so that preventive actions can be taken minimize downtime and guarantee a stable production. Such solutions often involve data-driven analysis, where acoustic and vibration signatures, current, and temperature are examples of features that are monitored to evaluate the condition of bearings, motors, and other machinery [3]. In the oil and gas industry, keeping a stable production is particularly important. This is because undesirable abnormal events can cause production losses for days and even weeks, not to mention potential disasters with catastrophic consequences for the environment. It is estimated that the oil and gas industries lose 20 billion dollars every year due to abnormal events. Thus, they have rated abnormal event management (AEM) as their number one problem that needs to be addressed. Similarly to CBM systems, AEM addresses fault detection and diagnosis, and has as main objective timely detection, diagnose, and correction of abnormal conditions or faults in a process [4].

Researchers and engineers have been studying and proposing the application of detection and classification algorithms in the oil and gas industry at the different stages, from as early as drilling and construction stages to production and operation phases of the oil well and its subsystems. An example is the work of Ahmadi et al. [5] that investigates the issue of early detection of flow influx during drilling. The authors present an approach to determining underlying reservoir models from noisy pressure data with the use of Random Forest (RF), Support Vector Machine (SVM), Linear Regression (LR), and Probabilistic Neural Networks (PNN) as classifiers for well-testing model classification. Another example is the work of Tang and S. Zhang, F. Zhang, and Venugopal [6], that presents a method of applying statistical features on real-time drilling data to automatically detect flow influx during drilling. The authors report a reliable performance and claim to be able to predict undesirable flow influx trends on average 10 minutes before detection.

Other examples of detection algorithms in later stages include the work of Liu et al. [7] which discusses an approach for semi-supervised classification to detect failures in artificial lift systems. Artificial lift systems are techniques to enhance oil production by increasing the pressure within the reservoir, which directly lifts fluids to the surface. The authors present a framework that combines features with Decision Trees (DT), SVM, and Bayes Net to enable learning and separation of failures from normal patterns based on noisy and poorly labeled multivariate time series. In addition, Liu, Li, and Xu [8] present an integrated model for the detection and location of leakages in pipelines. The authors investigate two modules:

one that can detect larger leakages and another one for micro-leakages. In [9], the authors present an approach to predict valve failures in gas compressors from oil fields, with the use of sensor data from multiple sensors. The authors' approach consisted of the use of feature extraction and selection, combined with DT. In [10], the authors present data-driven models to predict failure rates and their influencing factors of equipment based on data from six Norwegian oil and gas facilities.

This work presents a proper CBM system using random forest classifier to identify and detect undesirable events in subsea oil wells. The aim is to create a CBM system based on the random forest classifier to support decision-making. Specifically, we propose two classification scenarios that have shown promising results under testing. The rest of this paper is organized as follows. Section II introduces background knowledge about sub-sea oil wells and the eight different types of faults characterized as undesirable abnormal events in oil wells. Section III presents the test results related to model performance. Section IV and Section V provide an in-depth analysis, summarize the achieved results of the system and propose ideas for future work.

II. Data Analysis

This section provides an overview of offshore oil wells, followed by relevant details regarding the sensors used in this work to detect undesirable events during oil production and a description of the 3W dataset collected for the purpose of this study. It also gives a general description of the eight fault types contemplated in the 3W dataset.

A. *Offshore Oil Wells*

An oil well is a boring in the Earth, inshore or offshore, build using traditional drilling, and designed with the finality of extracting petroleum oil hydrocarbons from underground reservoirs. Usually, associated petroleum gas is also released in the process. The term "oil well" usually refers to a complex system consisting of several subsystems: a production tubing, which is the main path for the well fluid; a wellhead to ensure structural safety during drilling and production; and a "Christmas tree" installed on the top of the wellhead giving access to the production tubing. The 'Christmas tree" controls the production with several valves and sensors that can be accessed from the surface. Figure 1 illustrates a typical offshore oil well set-up.

The communication link between the surface and the oil well on the seabed is referred to as an "umbilical". An "umbilical" is an electro-hydraulic unit responsible for transmission of electrical signals and hydraulic power. It is connected to the Christmas tree and to the surface control system, i.e., a nearby production platform [12].

B. *3W Dataset*

The 3W dataset is a public dataset released by Petrobras, the Brazilian state oil company [11]. The dataset consists of real, simulated, and hand-drawn data of oil wells sensor data

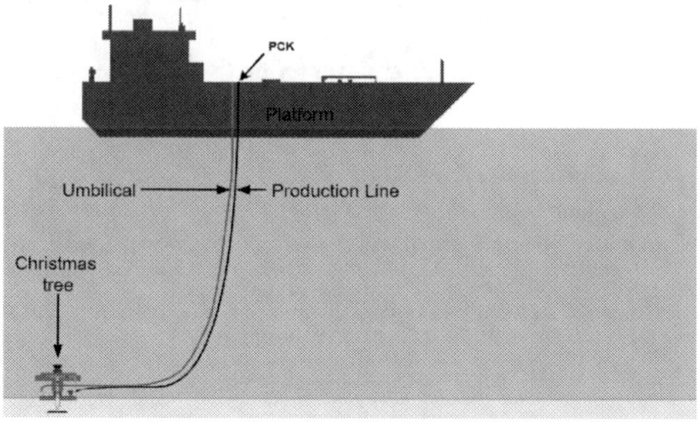

Fig. 1: Simplified schematic of a typical offshore naturally flowing well based on [11].

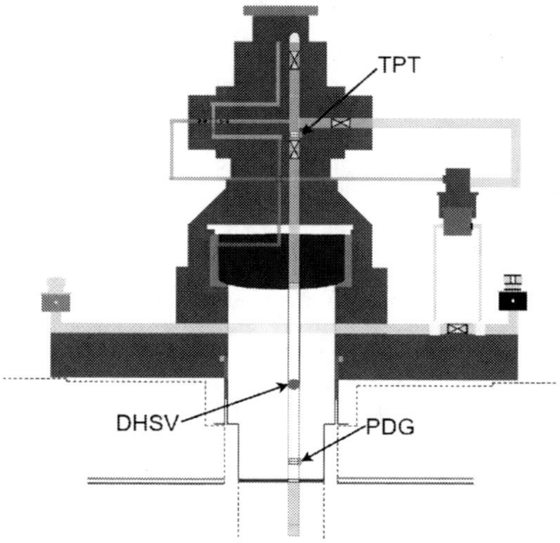

Fig. 2: Simplified schematic of a typical subsea Christmas tree based on [11].

gathered during operation. The data is acquired during oil well normal operation and featuring occurrences of undesired or abnormal events in the oil. This is shown through the closure mechanism of the Downhole Safety Valve (DHSV) and sensor readings extracted from five monitored variables: Pressure at the Permanent Downhole Gauge (PDG); Pressure at the Temperature and Pressure Transducer (TPT); Temperature at the TPT; Pressure upstream of the Production Choke Valve (PCK); and the Temperature downstream of the PCK. The PCK and DHSV and their impact are explained further on. Figure 1 illustrates Simplified schematic of a typical offshore oil well, whereas Figure 2 shows a simplified schematic of a typical subsea Christmastree [11].

The 3W dataset was build targeting eight types of undesirable events in oil wells. Factor such as Water, sediment, natural gas, and flow rate are found to be correlated to the undesirable events under consideration. As mentioned earlier, there are real, simulated, and hand-drawn undesirable events in the dataset, where all real instances have been extracted from the plant information system of Petrobras. Every undesirable event in the dataset is a sequence of observations with three states, namely *normal*, *faulty transient*, and *faulty steady state*. A normal state is characterized by the absence of any evidence of abnormal behavior, whereas in the faulty transient state the dynamics caused by undesirable events are ongoing. When these dynamics cease, the faulty steady state period begins. These states are defined to allow early detection of a given failure event. Properties considered when dining the events are pressure in Pascal [Pa], volume flow in standard cubic meters per second [sm^3/s], and temperature in degree Celsius [°C].

C. Fault Description

The reference in [11] defines eight types of fault as follows:

Class 1 - Abrupt Increase of Basic Sediment & Water: Basic Sediment and Water (BSW) is defined as the ratio between the water and sediment flow rate and the liquid flow rate, both measured under Normal Temperature and Pressure (NTP). During the life cycle of a well, its BSW is expected to increase due to increased water production. However, a sudden increase of BSW can lead to several problems related to flow assurance, lower oil production, and incrustation.

Class 2 - Spurious Closure of DHSV: The Downhole Safety Valve (DHSV) is placed in the production tubing, where its purpose is to ensure the closing of the oil well. It provides safety by shutting off the well in situations in which the production unit and well are physically disconnected or in the event of an emergency or catastrophic failure of surface equipment. However, the closing mechanism will eventually fail in a spurious manner. This kind of failure is problematic because there are often no indications of the failure on the surface, which causes production losses and additional cost.

Class 3 - Severe Slugging: This type of undesirable event occurs frequently at irregular intervals, on mature oil fields. Severe slugging takes place when "slugs" of liquid separate bubbles of gas through the pipeline. In the 3W dataset, it is considered a critical type of instability and can result in stress or even damage to equipment in the well and/or the industrial plant.

Class 4 - Flow Instability: During flow instability, there is a periodical change of pressure but with acceptable amplitudes. Flow instability is not necessarily equal to slugging, what separates those two anomalies is the lack of periodicity. Though flow instability can result in slugging. As instability can progress to severe slugging, its prognosis avoids all the negative aspects associated with this more severe anomaly.

Class 5 - Rapid Productivity Loss: There are several factors that can change the productivity of a naturally flowing well, the factors consist of the diameter of the production line, percentage between water and basic sediment, static pressure of the reservoir, and the viscosity of the produced fluid. When any of these factors are changed to the extent that the system's energy is not sufficient enough to overcome the losses, the flow of the well will slow down or even stop, which causes productivity loss.

Class 6 - Quick Restriction in PCK: Production Choke (PCK) is a control valve located at the beginning of the production unit. It is responsible for well control and can restrict, control, and regulate the flow. The choke can be controlled from the surface and when operated manually problems may occur.

Class 7 - Scaling in PCK: Inorganic deposits will occur during production. Therefore, it is important to monitor the Production Choke since it significantly reduces oil and gas production. If detected, losses of oil and gas production can be avoided. Thus, detecting it a early stage is favorable, so actions can be taken.

Class 8 - Hydrate in Production Line: This undesirable event occurs when water and natural gas form a crystalline compound, which happens under extreme pressure and temperature conditions. This crystalline compound resembles ice and when it is formed in production lines it can stop production for days and weeks. This is one of the biggest problems in the oil industry. Thus, avoiding this is desirable.

D. Data Review and Challenges

Despite its great technical value, the 3W dataset includes many of missing and frozen variables and unlabeled observations. In this case, a 'variable' refers to the monitored operational settings and sensor readings. Furthermore, an 'instance' refers to a recorded event of one of the eight fault types in the 3W dataset, while an 'observation' is a sample from an instance, showing the true label, timestamp, operational settings, and sensor readings. These definitions are used in the following subsections, which review challenges related to the 3W dataset.

1) Unlabeled Observations: An observation is considered unlabeled when there is no label of the fault type for a given sample of an instance. A total of 5,130 (0.01% of all 50,913,215 observations of all 15,872 variables of all 1,984 instances) observations are considered unlabeled in the 3W dataset.

2) Missing and Frozen Variables: A variable is considered missing when all observations of that particular variable in an instance have a missing value. 4,947 (31.17% of all 15,872 variables of all 1,984 instances) variables are considered missing in the 3W dataset. In the case of frozen variables, they are considered frozen when all observations of that particular variable in an instance have the same constant value. 1,535 (9.67% of all 15,872 variables of all 1,984 instances). variables in the 3W dataset is considered frozen.

3) Hand-drawn Instances: A challenge of this dataset is related to hand-drawn instances because the behavior varies a lot compared to real instances. The hand-drawn instances are too artificial and are quite distinct from the real ones. Therefore, the subsequent analysis omits fault type seven (Scaling in PCK) since 10 of all 14 instances are hand-drawn.

III. Experiments and Results

This section presents a comprehensive analysis of system performance. The analysis has been conducted by approaching this as a binary classification problem under two classification scenarios. In this work, these classification scenarios are characterized as *Fault versus Normal Operation* and *Fault versus Not Fault*.

In the scenario of fault versus normal operation, each binary classifier is designed to discriminate and identify between normal operation and a single specific class, categorized as a fault event. Thus, seven individual uncorrelated classifiers are required (one for each event representing an anomaly). Furthermore, all samples from normal operation (event/class 0) are combined to a single unique class, with the samples that show normal dynamic behavior preceding the given fault class (initial normal). For the classification scenario of fault versus not fault, each binary classifier discriminates and identifies between a single specific fault against everything that does not belong to that specific fault. This is done by designing seven uncorrelated classifiers, one for each fault, and combining the remaining events into a single unique class.

The experiments above have been conducted to achieve a greater understanding of the system and to acquire more information about each fault class. Besides, this continues and contributes to the work of Marins et al. [13], which have shown that a CBM system can be used to classify the faults, with binary and multiclass classifiers. This work introduces a new classification scenario (fault versus not fault). The samples that belong to the faulty transient and faulty steady states for each fault are combined to one unique class in the two classification scenarios described above. In this work, the model performance is assessed in detail: firstly, by measuring the overall model performance; secondly, by measuring the capability to discriminate between normal operation and each transitional state; and lastly, by individually measuring the simulated and real instances of the latter two metrics.

A. Experiment 1: Fault versus Normal Operation

This section reviews the experiment characterized as *fault versus normal operation*. In this experiment, each classifier is fit on data from normal operation (class 0) and their respective fault. The only change in any hyperparameter relates to the subsampling factor. In this case, fault events with less than 20 real instances apply a subsampling factor of 1 for real instances. This is with the intent to balance the distribution ratio, between simulated and real instances. Moreover, the window sizes related to the feature extraction of each classifier consist of 900, 400, 1200 samples for classes 1, 2, and 8, respectively; and, 300 samples for the remaining classes. These specific window sizes represent the best performance for their given classifier.

The test results of the 3W dataset for the transitional states and overall accuracy can be seen in Table I. In this table, 'Transitional ACC' denotes the overall accuracy for the transitional states, i.e., initial normal (normal operation preceding an anomaly event), faulty transient state, and faulty steady-state. Additionally, 'Overall ACC' represents the accuracy for all transitional states combined with samples from class 0. The reason for showing the overall and transitional accuracy separately is because approximately 30% of all instances from the complete 3W dataset belongs to Class 0. Thus, the overall accuracy is not sufficient alone and may misrepresent the performance of the classifier. More details can be seen in Table II, which shows real and simulated test results for class 0 and each transitional state.

TABLE I: TEST RESULTS OF CLASSIFICATION SCENARIO FAULT VERSUS NORMAL OPERATION.

Fault	Window Size	Type	Transitional ACC	Overall ACC
Class 1	900	Real	0.214	0.989
		Simulated	0.999	0.999
Class 2	400	Real	0.986	0.999
		Simulated	0.996	0.996
Class 3	300	Real	0.998	0.999
		Simulated	0.998	0.998
Class 4	300	Real	0.967	0.986
		Simulated	-	-
Class 5	300	Real	0.888	0.992
		Simulated	0.993	0.993
Class 6	300	Real	0.972	0.999
		Simulated	0.951	0.951
Class 8	1200	Real	0.892	0.999
		Simulated	0.956	0.956

TABLE II: TEST RESULTS OF CLASSIFICATION SCENARIO FAULT VERSUS NORMAL OPERATION.

Fault	Window Size	Type	Normal (Class 0)	Initial Normal	Transient State	Steady State
Class 1	900	Real	1.000	0.779	0.098	0.011
		Simulated	-	0.999	0.999	0.999
Class 2	400	Real	0.999	0.952	0.996	1.000
		Simulated	-	1.000	0.970	1.000
Class 3	300	Real	0.999	-	-	0.998
		Simulated	-	-	-	0.998
Class 4	300	Real	0.990	-	-	0.967
		Simulated	-	-	-	-
Class 5	300	Real	0.999	0.514	0.904	-
		Simulated	-	0.134	0.999	1.000
Class 6	300	Real	0.999	0.981	0.882	1.000
		Simulated	-	0.876	0.955	0.956
Class 8	1200	Real	0.999	0.000	1.000	1.000
		Simulated	-	0.258	0.996	0.999

The imbalance of 3W dataset reflects on the performance of each classifier. This is evident in the case of classes 1 and 8, where both classifiers seem to struggle with real data. These two classes have less than 10 real instances combined, in contrast to classes 2, 3, and 4, which have 22, 34, and 344 instances, respectively. One can also observe that class 5 has difficulties correctly classifying samples of the initial state. This applies to the case of both real and simulated instances. On the other hand, the classifier achieves satisfactory accuracy in correctly classifying samples belonging to normal operation and the transient state. In this case, the results show an accuracy of over 90% for the latter two events.

1) System Efficiency and Reliability Evaluation: This section reviews the system in a real-world scenario as a CBM system. To be a reliable CBM system, the system must have the capability to detect any event as soon as possible. To assess how reliable and efficient the system is to anticipate incoming failures, three time-intervals have been applied. These time intervals (in seconds) are defined as following: how fast each classifier is to detect the transient state (time of detection); how many consecutive correct predictions are made after the time of detection; and how long time there is to take action before the incoming failure occurs, respectively denoted as t_1, t_2, and t_3. Table III shows the average values of the time-intervals t_1, t_2, and t_3 for each classifier and their respective faults, where each number designated in parenthesis is the percentage of the corresponding time-interval concerning the transient state. Classes 0, 3, and 4 are not included as their transient phase is absent in the 3W dataset.

TABLE III: EFFICIENCY AND RELIABILITY ANALYSIS OF FAULT VERSUS NORMAL OPERATION.

Fault	Type	t1 [s]	t2 [s]	t3 [s]
Class 1	Real	2463.0 (11.73%)	2710.0 (12.90%)	18530.0 (88.26%)
Class 2	Real	15.5 (0.33%)	4700.1 (99.67%)	4700.1 (99.67%)
Class 5	Real	564.2 (1.06%)	41879.0 (78.87%)	52533.7 (98.93%)
Class 6	Real	73.5 (11.87%)	546.0 (88.20%)	546.0 (88.20%)
Class 8	Real	1.0 (0.00%)	20078.0 (100%)	20078.0 (100%)

B. Experiment 2: Fault versus Not Fault

In the the classification scenario fault versus not fault, each classifier is fit on data from all classes. The same settings from the latter classification scenario apply in this case, with regards to hyperparameter selection and training routine. As for the training routine, the subsampling factor had to be increased, since each classifier is fit on data from every class. Each classifier under training applied a subsampling factor of 100 for instances that did not belong to their given class (Not Fault). Also, real instances belonging to their given class were not subsampled, but simulated instances applied a subsampling factor of 10.

The test results of this classification scenario of the 3W dataset can be seen in Tables IV and V, where empty entries indicate the absence of data for that given fault type. The classification method shows satisfactory results with the classifiers of classes 2, 3, and 4. These classes are correctly classified with an average accuracy of over 90% of Class 0 and all transitional states when it comes to real instances. Simulated instances of these classes indicate to be harder to predict, where the accuracy drops as low as 80% for the transient state and 93% for the steady-state for classes 2 and 3, respectively.

1) System Efficiency and Reliability Evaluation: The assessment of each classifier based on the time-intervals t_1, t_2, and t_3 can be seen in Table VI, where the time-intervals are given in seconds and the designated numbers in parenthesis are the percentage of the corresponding time-interval concerning the total transient state. Besides Class 5, the system shows similar results when compared to Experiment 1. In particular, Class 5 performs poorly in the transitional states t_1 and t_2 due to the appearance of inconsistent classification behavior.

IV. Discussion

The results achieved from Experiment 1 and Experiment 2 show that the system is capable of correctly classifying

TABLE IV: TEST RESULTS OF CLASSIFICATION SCENARIO FAULT VERSUS NOT FAULT.

Fault	Window Size	Type	Transitional ACC	Overall ACC
Class 1	900	Real	0.213	0.992
		Simulated	0.999	0.999
Class 2	400	Real	0.991	0.999
		Simulated	0.862	0.997
Class 3	300	Real	0.995	0.980
		Simulated	0.936	0.990
Class 4	300	Real	0.977	0.985
		Simulated	-	1.000
Class 5	300	Real	0.373	0.966
		Simulated	0.993	0.996
Class 6	300	Real	0.868	0.999
		Simulated	0.925	0.987
Class 8	1200	Real	0.892	0.999
		Simulated	0.972	0.982

TABLE V: TEST RESULTS OF CLASSIFICATION SCENARIO FAULT VERSUS NOT FAULT.

Fault	Window Size	Type	Not Fault (Class 0)	Initial Normal	Transient State	Steady State
Class 1	900	Real	1.000	0.779	0.098	0.001
		Simulated	0.999	0.999	0.999	0.999
Class 2	400	Real	0.999	0.970	0.998	1.000
		Simulated	0.999	1.000	0.821	0.848
Class 3	300	Real	0.979	-	-	0.995
		Simulated	0.998	-	-	0.936
Class 4	300	Real	0.987	-	-	0.977
		Simulated	1.000	-	-	-
Class 5	300	Real	0.999	0.396	0.372	-
		Simulated	0.997	0.103	0.999	0.999
Class 6	300	Real	1.000	0.997	0.384	0.150
		Simulated	0.999	0.813	0.936	0.930
Class 8	1200	Real	0.999	0.000	1.000	1.000
		Simulated	0.983	0.939	0.961	0.999

faults but also capable of predicting incoming faults from their transient state. These incoming faults are often predicted in an early stage, such that it is possible to take necessary preventive action. The amount of data at disposal for each class tends to reflect the system performance for the given classifier. This applies to both classification methods, and in particular, to real instances of classes 1 and 8. Neither of the two classification methods can correctly classify any sample related to the initial normal state of Class 8. Classes 2, 3, and 4 achieves great accuracy for their respective transitional states and Class 0, for both classification scenarios. On the other hand, the fault versus normal classification scenario accomplishes better results for classes 5 and 6 compared to its counterpart, fault versus not fault.

Comparing these results with the work of Marins et al. [13], it is noticeable that their binary classification method achieved better results when classifying the initial normal state for each class on real instances. However, when comparing their multiclass classification method, the method proposed in this work for each class exhibits higher accuracy in average on real instances over all transitional states for most classes. This can be seen in the results of the classification scenario 'fault versus normal'.

TABLE VI: EFFICIENCY AND RELIABILITY ANALYSIS OF FAULT VERSUS NOT FAULT.

Fault	Type	t1 [s]	t2 [s]	t3 [s]
Class 1	Real	2463.0 (11.73%)	2707.0 (12.90%)	18530.0 (88.26%)
Class 2	Real	9.3 (0.19%)	4706.4 (99.81%)	4706.4 (99.81%)
Class 5	Real	1.0 (0.00%)	822.3 (1.55%)	53097.3 (99.9%)
Class 6	Real	318.5 (51.5%)	237.5 (38.4%)	300.5(48.54%)
Class 8	Real	1.0 (0.00%)	20078.0 (100%)	20078.0 (100%)

A. Inconsistency

A limitations of this system is tied to the observed fluctuations in the classifications of Classes 4 and 5. To mitigate that, we suggest the use of a simple filter to smoothen these fluctuations that occur during inconsistent classifications, referred to as "time-consistency filter". The filter strides over the system classifications using a window and removes the class with the fewest output classifications in that window. Figure 3 shows an example of a real instance of Class 4, along with the system classifications and the outputs of the time-consistency filter. Here, the purple marker shows the output of the filter. In this case, the window size of the time-consistency filter is 120 samples. The filter is unable to prevent all classification oscillations, but it does smoothen out the majority of them. The filtering process may be more efficient if the window size is increased, but this also increases the delay, which is undesirable.

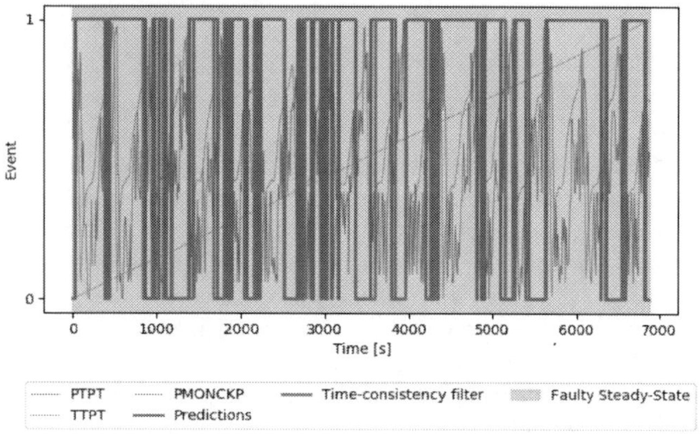

Fig. 3: Example of a real instance of Class 4 along with the inconsistent system classifications and with the time-consistency filter. Event values '1' and '0' denote normal and faulty states.

V. Conclusion and Future Work

This work develops a CBM system to detect and identify real abnormal events in offshore oil wells. The CBM system is tested in two different classification scenarios. Either case includes preprocessing of raw-sensor data, feature extraction, dimensionality reduction, and classification using the random forest algorithm. However, analysis of the results indicates that inconsistent classifications may occur for Classes 4 and 5. These inconsistent classifications occur predominantly during faulty states. That means that the system would still be able to detect the fault, which is a positive feature.

As future work, we would suggest further investigation of additional features, e.g, other second-order features that have not been considered at this stage of this work. It is also interesting to explore other promising machine learning classification algorithms such as the XGBoost algorithm, which attempts to exploit the advantages of Random Forest and gradient boosting, and the Light Gradient Boosting Machine (LGBM), which has a similar architecture to the Random Forest and the XGBoosts algorithms.

Acknowledgment

This study was financed in part by the Norwegian Agency for International Cooperation and Quality Enhancement in Higher Education (Diku), project number UTF-2018-CAPES-Diku/10002, and in part by the Coordenação de Aperfeiçoamento de Pessoal de Nível Superior—Brasil (CAPES), finance code n° 23038.018065/2018-17.

References

[1] H. Lasi, P. Fettke, H.-G. Kemper, T. Feld, and M. Hoffmann, "Industry 4.0," *Business & Information Systems Engineering*, vol. 6, pp. 239–242, 08 2014.

[2] J. Lee, B. Bagheri, and H.-A. Kao, "A cyber-physical systems architecture for industry 4.0-based manufacturing systems," *SME Manufacturing Letters*, vol. 3, 12 2014.

[3] K. K. Agrawal, G. N. Pandey, and K. Chandrasekaran, "Analysis of the condition based monitoring system for heavy industrial machineries," in *2013 IEEE International Conference on Computational Intelligence and Computing Research*, 2013, pp. 1–4.

[4] V. Venkatasubramanian, R. Rengaswamy, K. Yin, and S. N. Kavuri, "A review of process fault detection and diagnosis: Part i: Quantitative model-based methods," *Computers & Chemical Engineering*, vol. 27, no. 3, pp. 293 – 311, 2003.

[5] R. Ahmadi, B. Aminshahidy, and J. Shahrabi, "Well-testing model identification using time-series shapelets," *Journal of Petroleum Science and Engineering*, vol. 149, pp. 292–305, 2017.

[6] H. Tang, S. Zhang, F. Zhang, and S. Venugopal, "Time series data analysis for automatic flow influx detection during drilling," *Journal of Petroleum Science and Engineering*, vol. 172, pp. 1103 – 1111, 2019.

[7] Y. Liu, K. Yao, S. Liu, C. S. Raghavendra, O. Balogun, and L. Olabinjo, "Semi-supervised failure prediction for oil production wells," in *2011 IEEE 11th International Conference on Data Mining Workshops*, 2011, pp. 434–441.

[8] C. Liu, Y. Li, and M. Xu, "An integrated detection and location model for leakages in liquid pipelines," *Journal of Petroleum Science and Engineering*, vol. 175, pp. 852 – 867, 2019.

[9] O. P. Patri, R. Nabor, A. Panangadan, and V. Prasanna, "Predicting compressor valve failures from multi-sensor data," ser. SPE Western Regional Meeting, vol. All Days, 04 2015, sPE-174044-MS.

[10] L. Xie, S. Håbrekke, Y. Liu, and M. A. Lundteigen, "Operational data-driven prediction for failure rates of equipment in safety instrumented systems: A case study from the oil and gas industry," *Journal of Loss Prevention in the Process Industries*, vol. 60, pp. 96 – 105, 2019.

[11] R. E. V. Vargas, C. J. Munaro, P. M. Ciarelli, A. G. Medeiros, B. G. do Amaral, D. C. Barrionuevo, J. C. D. de Araújo, J. L. Ribeiro, and L. P. Magalhães, "A realistic and public dataset with rare undesirable real events in oil wells," *Journal of Petroleum Science and Engineering*, vol. 181, p. 106223, 2019.

[12] S. Laik, *Offshore Petroleum Drilling and Production*. Boca Raton: CRC Press, 2018.

[13] M. A. Marins, B. D. Barros, I. H. Santos, D. C. Barrionuevo, R. E. Vargas, T. de M. Prego, A. A. de Lima, M. L. de Campos, E. A. da Silva, and S. L. Netto, "Fault detection and classification in oil wells and production/service lines using random forest," *Journal of Petroleum Science and Engineering*, p. 107879, 2020.

Small Scale Unmanned Aircraft System and Photogrammetry Applied for 3D Modeling of Historical Buildings

Alexandre dos Santos Boente
Military Institute of Engineering
Rio de Janeiro, Brazil
E-mail: alexandreboente@ime.eb.br

Thiago J. M. Baldivieso
Military Institute of Engineering
Rio de Janeiro, Brazil
e-mail: thiagojmb@ime.eb.br

Paulo F. F. Rosa
Military Institute of Engineering
Rio de Janeiro, Brazil
e-mail: rpaulo@ime.eb.br

Thiago Eustaquio A. de Oliveira
Department of Computer Science
Lakehead University
Thunderbay, ON, Canada
e-mail: talvesd@lakeheadu.ca

Vinicius Prado da Fonseca
Department of Computer Science
Memorial University
St. John's, Canada
e-mail: vpradodafons@mun.ca

***Abstract*—Heritage preservation is the active conservation of cultural assets, historic structures and buildings of a specific cultural group. This paper presents a methodology for the 3D reconstruction of large-scale cultural assets, such as buildings using photogrammetry, which is a way to get measurements of objects from a set of photographs. The present study uses images from small scale unmanned aircraft systems (UAS) for the 3D reconstruction of the "Palacete da Babilônia". The study case presented here is a historical building from 1866, located in the Military School of Rio de Janeiro whose complex also includes a historical museum.The experimental setup used three mini drones in addition to flight mission planning and execution application evaluation.The final reconstruction used off-the-shelf software to generate the 3D model reconstruction, model adjustments finishing with the 3D printing of the model generated for the preservation of this historic construction.**

Keywords-Heritage Preservation; UAS; 3D Reconstruction; Photogrammetry.

I. INTRODUCTION

The conservation of historical buildings is crucial for the cultural preservation of a community, nation or social group. Therefore, access to a three-dimensional description of such assets is valuable and possibly crucial for the process of reconstruction and restoration. The three-dimensional (3D) representation of an object of interest can be achieved using 3D mapping techniques with photogrammetry [1]. In addition to the popularization of small-scale unmanned aircraft systems (UAS)[4], collecting and processing information can be automated using mission planning and off-the-shelf 3D surface applications[6]. The present paper focuses on evaluating the use of UAS for the large-scale model reconstruction of buildings in Rio de Janeiro, a 456-year-old city with hundreds of historical and cultural assets. Specifically, the present work focuses on the study case of 3D reconstruction of the "Palacete da Babilônia," a historic building part of the Military School complex in Rio de Janeiro.

Even though UASs have become popular, the present paper uses, and processes images generated by a UAS, which comprises the aircraft, control system guidance, and mission planning. Experiments used and compared three models of DJI rotary-wing drones of small size and low-price range, which allowed the generation of 3D models of the target building. Commercial aircraft usually have more straightforward flight control, reduced size and excellent portability and stability. Moreover, the efficiency of take-off and landing makes this kind of device optimized for solo control. The use of external applications and embedded technologies, such as inertial sensors, Global Positioning System (GPS) and good embedded cameras, with flight automation ability, makes this system perfect for a small-scale 3D reconstruction of historical buildings.

Weather, rain and wind, short battery life, reduced range, and small payload limit the use of small-scale drones. However, selected brands have compatible automated flight planning apps that enable easier mission planning in many devices such as smartphones. Furthermore, the evolution of the technology embedded in small-scale drones, along with the wide availability of software for the dense cloud of points, in addition to modern tools for model generation and correction, makes it the perfect tool to get a full-scale 3D model exported in a short time interval with a reduced staff.

Figure 1. "Palacete da Babilônia" Mavic Air2 aerial photo

The application of easy-to-use, off-the-shelf components means that the flight mission would require less staff, usually a single person. Training the survey personnel, they could later perform post-processing for generating and adjusting the 3D models.

The following sections present the methodology, followed by the materials and methods used in this work. Section III presents the final model 3D printed in PLA, followed by a discussion in section IV with Conclusions in section V.

II. METHODOLOGY

The present work has a general objective to present how photogrammetry [2] with small-scale UAS can contribute to the 3D reconstruction of historical buildings. In addition, technological tools allow cultural preservation by archiving 3D models that could be used as a reference for future restorations. This section will present the methodology used for the study case in the 3D model reconstruction of the "Palacete Babilônia," using drone photogrammetry.

The initial evaluation of drone images used three models, with the Mavic Air 2 performing more missions. In addition, a single external collaborator operator was able to perform several missions. Finally, some missions used a Spark and the Mavic Air 2 drones. Figure 2 shows a comparison of the camera's sensor size. An increased sensor size means better quality concerning the amount of noise in the image.

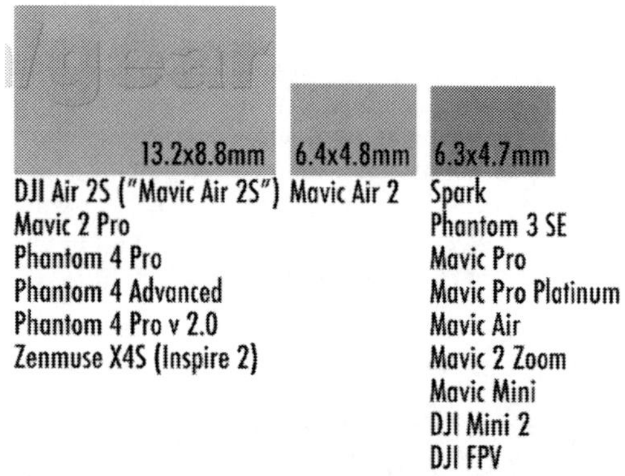

Figure 2. Sensor size comparison [7]

A. Mission Planning and Tools

First, the mission requires evaluation of weather conditions, a limiting aspect of small-scale drone use. Figure 3 shows a screenshot of UAVForecast.com that provides adequate information for the flight.

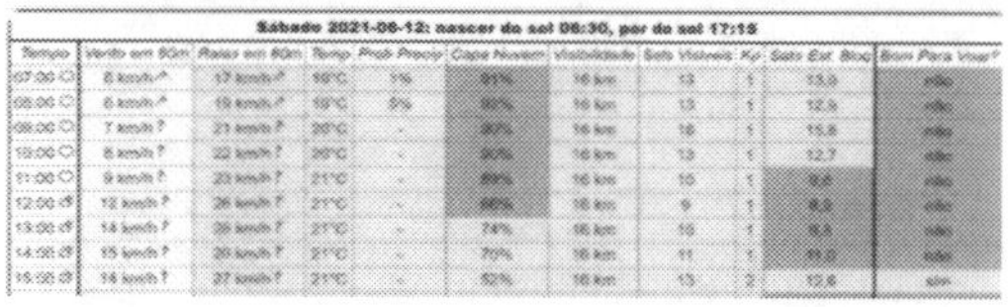

Figure 3. UAVForecast.com information for the flight

The best time for this mission is around noon when shadows have a minor influence on the images. A cloudy day may also provide favorable image conditions if good flight conditions are also available. However, we must consider that the reduced light could affect the camera's shooting speed and image quality. It is essential to highlight that the choice of a micro-SD card is an essential factor. A low recording capacity card can interfere with the recording quality of the set of obtained images. Considering that the sequence of photos should have a good overlap, we use 80% in the front overlay and 75% in the lateral overlay.

Height is also a primary factor in the relationship of pixel size with the exact measure of the object. The number of pixels in a sensor is constant, and the Ground Sample Distance (GSD) is variable with height. The GSD is a sample of the terrain in the image. Figure 4 describes the camera parameter for the drone model we used. In the present paper, this issue is favorable because we fly at a low height very close to the historical construction.

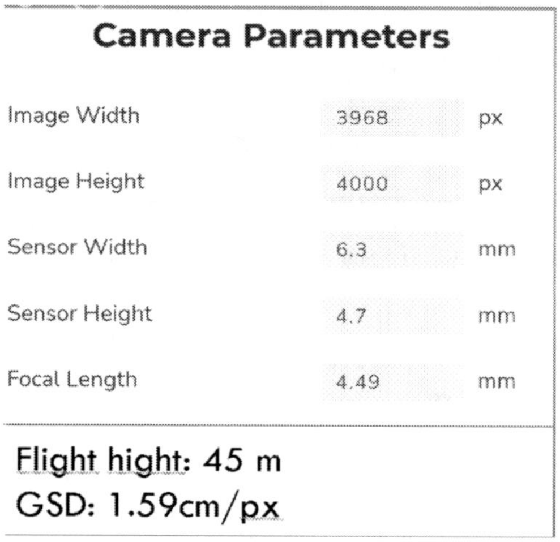

Figure 4. GSD Calculation Spark [8]

Flight automation applications are essential. Therefore, it is crucial to investigate the drone model's compatibility with the application. The present paper used three drone flight apps: Copterus, Litchi and Dronelink. The Mavic Pro drone is compatible with most off-the-shelf applications, such as PIX4D and Dronedeploy. The Spark drone also works with pix4d but has restricted automated flight modes, which requires manual mode flights. The Mavic Air 2 drone works with Dronelink and Copterus, which runs on Apple smartphone models only.

The missions planned for this study case used three main types of flights: orbiting, waypoints and grid, Figures 5, 6 and 7 respectively. First, the operator builds the polygon, line or circle centered on the construction, adjusts the height predicting safety, and checks with the desired GSD to get as much detail as possible from the construction.

Second, there is the confirmation of mission time and the drone's battery time. The possibility of dividing the mission into parts was unnecessary, considering the dimensions of the target construction. Consequently, one battery was enough for a mission. Finally, the most battery autonomy drone is the Mavic Air 2, closely followed by the Mavic Pro.

The Litchi app allows plane flights in orbit and following waypoints such as shown in Figure 5. Mission planning works well, requiring more work for the path assembly.

Unfortunately, it did not work with Mavic Air 2, considering the flight date of the drones in this work. The orbital flight requires angular velocity adjustments, radius measurement, circle height and image-taking interval.

Figure 5. Flight in orbit mode in the Litchi app.

Figure 5 shows the Litchi application. It is possible to create a point of interest (POI), referencing the gimbal to direct the drone's camera. Determining the height of this point will influence the angle of the gimbal. For example, Figure 5 shows the POI near the center of the rectangle with the building's top view, with a height of negative 6 meters. Figure 6 shows the waypoints mode, where it is possible to determine an action for each point in the chosen trajectory.

Figure 6. Flight planning waypoints in the Litchi app.

Dronelink presented a more significant number of automated flight patterns. The operator has the possibility of using a computer to plan the mission. Figure 7 shows the grid pattern, which is one of the quite comprehensive flight pattern alternatives.

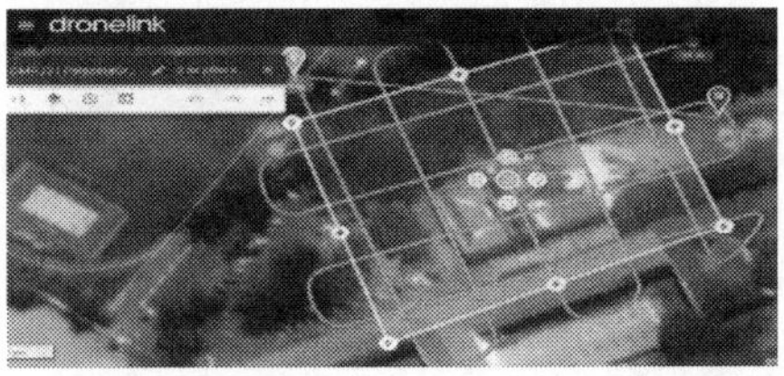

Figure 7. Grid Flight Planning in the Dronelink software.

The chosen application must automatically provide all the essential information for the model reconstruction with the drone's camera data. Manual flights were also required to circumvent another construction to the left side of the target building and near trees on the back and right side.

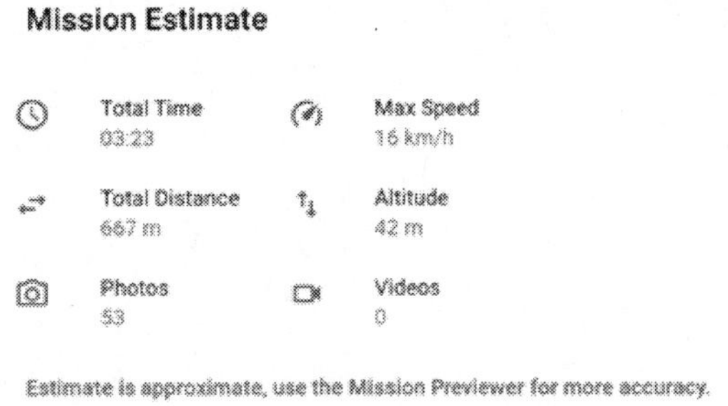

Figure 8. Mission measurements in the Dronelink app.

The solution used in this study case does not require previous camera calibration. Besides, the actual geographic coordinates of the terrain were support points taken from Google Earth images. In this way, misaligned sets of sparse dots could be fixed when they visibly did not align with the app's maps. In addition, this procedure fixed an issue while constructing points in the Agisoft Metashape software, allowing the operator to use it to perform automatic post-calibration of the cameras of the drones used. The spatial intersection was the main georeferencing used. We can align the position and orientation of two-by-two images, according to the principle of stereography. Dronelink works by allowing us to simulate missions in advance, helping to evaluate various data such as flight times, map trajectories, speeds, heights, photo shots and more. Facilitating flight execution.

Copterus was the last app tested, which works out of a smartphone. It also has several other similar functionalities to previous applications. The 4:3 photo setting was ideal because using 16:9, there is pixel loss, compromising images' overlay. Some Mavic Air 2's features, such as smart photo and the 48 Megapixel, which help reduce the noise of photos, are not available on the Mavic Pro drone. The digital negative photo (DNG) feature was also not available. Those features are also unavailable options on the Spark drone.

Briefly, the mathematics involved is in the relationship between drone translations and rotations on the three X, Y and Z axes that occur with drone movements and the fixed target building. The focal length, the number of camera sensor pixels, and the sensor dimensions are also fixed and associated with the fiducial system. Therefore, using the information above is possible to construct a projection of the camera perspective center (CP) to the points of the actual object.

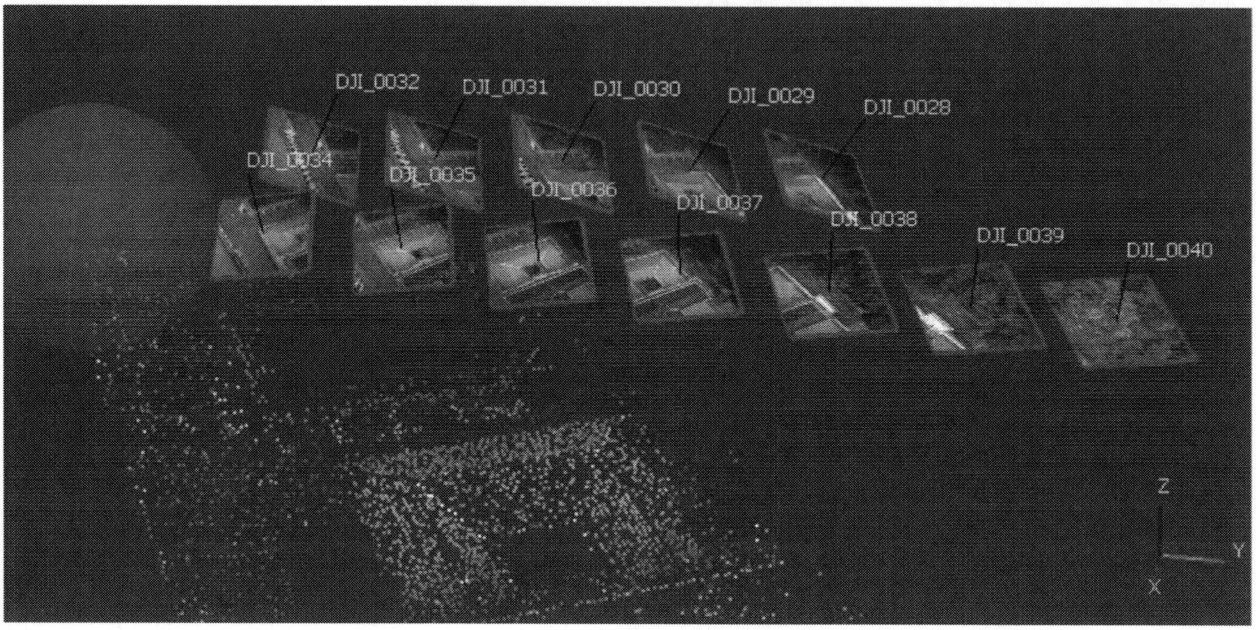

Figure 9. Drone's image shots position in relation to the object.

The drones used have an essential feature of storing the coordinates obtained by the GPS and the height in each image, facilitating the photos' alignment by the 3D reconstruction programs.

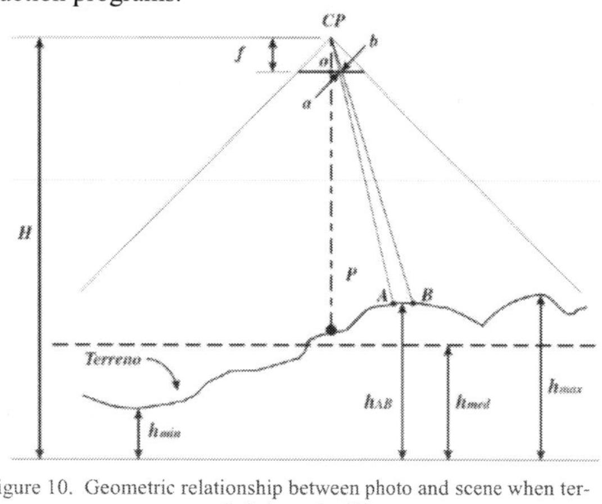

Figure 10. Geometric relationship between photo and scene when terrain is irregular [3]

The similarity of triangles can calculate the relationship for the irregularity of the heights found in the construction. Figure 10 shows this approach which can be arranged in the following equation [3]:

$$\frac{f}{H - h_{AB}} = \frac{ab}{AB}$$

Epipolar geometry [5] and stereo vision concepts of stereo vision are used here to reconstruct a 3D model such the one described in Figure 11. Then, taking the homologous points in 2D images, it is possible to describe the 3D view of the object by two cameras in different locations and the points projected in space.

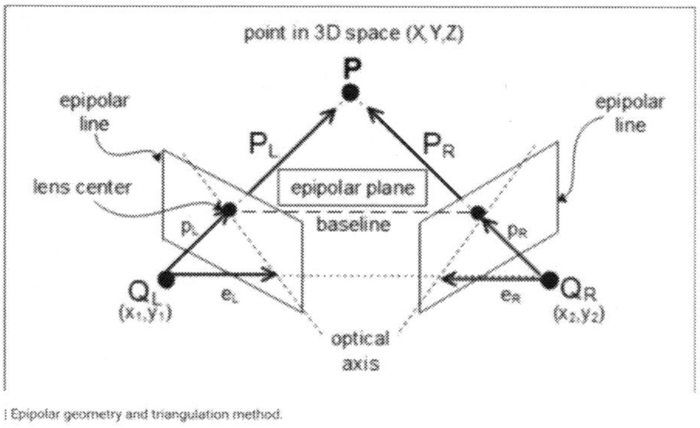

Figure11. Epipolar Geometry [9]

With the knowledge of the dimensions of the pixels, we can transform this system and the fiducial equation below:

$$\begin{bmatrix} x' \\ y' \end{bmatrix} = \begin{bmatrix} Sx & 0 \\ 0 & -Sy \end{bmatrix} \cdot \begin{bmatrix} x - \frac{W-1}{2} \\ y - \frac{(H-1)}{2} \end{bmatrix}$$

Where: x´ and y´ the coordinates of the fiducial system. Sx and Sy are pixel dimensions, and X and y are the coordinates in the screen system as described in Figure 15.

B. 3D Reconstruction Tools

This study case used three 3D reconstruction software named Meshroom, Open Drone Map and Agisoft Metashape, with the latter presenting satisfactory results.

texture. Finally, the Metashape algorithm does a very elaborate job analyzing homologous points, which leads to good results.

Figure 12. Mavic Pro 249 images in 16:9 format

Figure 13. Mavic Air 2 697 images in 4:3 format

Figure 14. Mavic Air 2 with 526 images, separated by groups of object faces.

Metashape provides an easy workflow. The operator starts by adding the drone photos. After that, it is possible to use the software photo evaluation and select only images above 70% quality. Next, it is necessary to check the geographic coordinate system.

The software workflows proceed with alignment, where the sparse cloud is generated. After that, the workflow includes a dense cloud of dots, mesh construction and

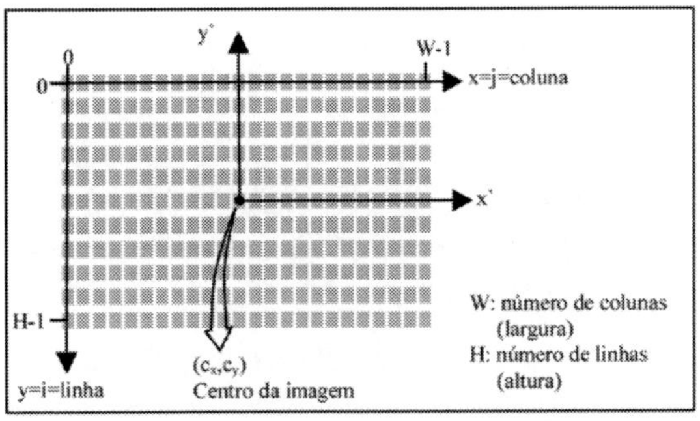

Figure15. Screen Coordinate System [1]

There was a problem using the images from the Spark drone obtained by the standard application. Even using the additional manual photos covering the lack of images on the side and background of the building, there was noticeable truncation. Marking common points concerning geographic coordinates and height obtained in Google Earth in the images manually could fix this problem, generating a considerable increase in manual work. The Spark drone also has an older sensor that only has jpeg images, generating more unsatisfactory results.

The Meshroom software presented the most automated operation. After adding the images, the operator follows a pipeline. However, this was the most time-consuming processing, making it difficult to perform many variations in the tests. Moreover, the result presented was not superior to that of the other tools. However, it is free software that, together with Meshlab, provides many possibilities for generating and correcting the 3D model. It was necessary to correct the model delivered in Metashape, which does not make corrections to the delivered part. Therefore, it is an alternative to use Meshlab in the sequence of generating the model for printing.

It is also noticeable comparing Figures 13 and 14 that using the 4:3 (dimension 4000 x 3000) instead of 16:9 uses more pixels, providing better results. Figure 15 also shows that tagging the images with the building faces groups outputs a more efficient model generation.

The Open Drone Map (ODM) software is a free software like Meshroom processing workflow. With few commands, the algorithm starts processing and delivers the finished 3D model. ODM and Metashape provide a lot of processing information, including detailed reports. Thus, they are potent tools that can be used to construct the orthophoto of the terrain. All programs worked in Windows with the main bottleneck in RAM. It takes a long time to process, even with a machine with 16 Gb.

III. Results and Discussion

The result of the three-dimensional models generated from the historic construction had to adjust their mesh to be printed on a 3D Fused Deposition Modeling (FDM) printer.

Figure 16 shows the file on the Simplify 3D software was with the appropriate firmware settings for operation with the printer. Figure 17 shows the Sethi3D S3 software also tested for the printer model.

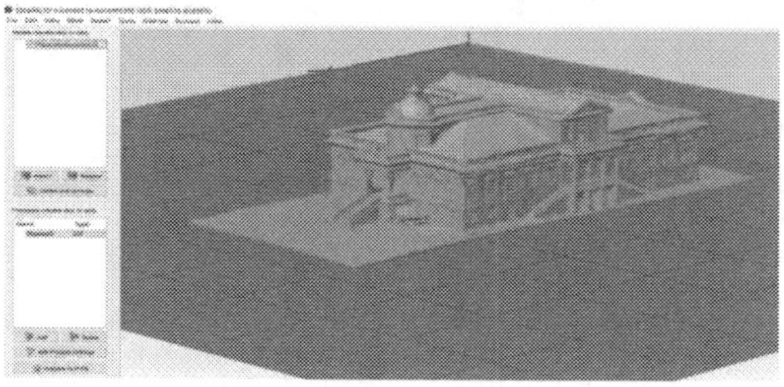

Figure 16. 3D model in Simplify 3D.

One application that worked well in automatic mode and running online was Netfabb from Autodesk. Microsoft 3D Printing works similarly but is more time-consuming and fails to process multiple STL file submissions. The Ultimaker Cura print program allows the installation of a Mesh Tools plugin that solves some problems of the generated part. The Slic3r program fixes some problems automatically. The Meshmixer program analyzes and fixes some parts automatically and allows for more advanced adjustments. MeshLab works similarly. Blender is also a free tool that allows more complex adjustments to the part.

We verified that the quality of the 3D reconstruction is directly proportional to the image quality. We must consider the quality of the camera, quality of light available at the time of taking the photos. It is important to adapt the speed of the UAS with its speed of taking images and their archiving processing.

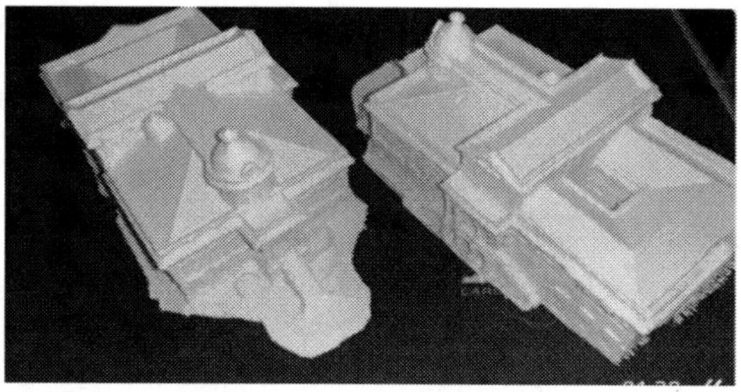

Figure 17. Full-scale printed model on Sethi3D S3.

IV. CONCLUSION

The study case of the 3D modelling of the "Palacete Babilônia" allowed an analysis based on the generation of 3D models of the historic building. The present paper presented a study on the benefits of using photogrammetry with small drones and the challenges encountered when working on the generation of the 3D model. The result includes 3D printing of the building for later preservation. In addition, the present work shows different applications and software that is constantly updated. Finally, it evaluates how each of them delivers the final model. The methods presented here make it possible to archive three-dimensional models to preserve cultural heritage with a small budget and a reduced crew.

Acknowledgement

This study was financed in part by the Cooerdenação de Aperfeiçoamento de Pessoal de Nível Superior -Brasil (CAPES) – Finance Code 001.

REFERENCES

[1] J.K.Hasegawa, Photogrammetric Restitution (Analytical and Digital): Theory of Guidelines - Introduction. 2004. 25p. Typed.

[2] E.M.Lima, T.A.M.Thomas, T.C.Severo, Digital Aerial Photogrammetric Mapping Using Medium Format Photographs. Porto Alegre, 2010. (Course Completion Work). Federal University of Rio Grande do Sul

[3] M.L.L.Reiss, Photogrammetry I. 2009. Lesson Notes

[4] E.Trucco, A.Verri, Introductory Techniques for 3-D Computer Vision. United Kingdom: Prentice Hall, 1998.

[5] "Epipolar geometry", 7 March 2021, at 21:46, Accessed on: 7 March 2021, at 21:46. [online]. Available: https://en.wikipedia.org/wiki/Epipolar_geometry

[6] P. J.Zarco-Tejada, , R.Diaz-Varela, V.Angileri, , P. Loudjani, Tree height quantification using very high resolution imagery acquired from an unmanned aerial vehicle (UAV) and automatic 3D photo-reconstruction methods. European Journal of Agronomy, v. 55, p. 89–99, 2014.

[7] "Sensor size comparison", 3 March 2021, at 21:00, Accessed on: 3 March 2021, at 21:00. [online]. https://djzphoto.com/gear

[8] "Ground Sample Distance", 3 March 2021, at 20:35, Accessed on: 3 March 2021, at 20:35. [online]. Available: https://www.propelleraero.com/gsd-calculator/

[9] "Epipolar geometry", 7 March 2021, at 21:16, Accessed on: 7 March 2021, at 21:16. [online]. Available: https://www.researchgate.net/figure/Epipolar-geometry-and-triangulation-method_fig1_334066559

Drone Operations and Communications in an Urban Environment

Sandeep Shivakoti, Aurelie Aurilla Arntzen Bechina,
Serkan Güldal
Department of Science and Industry Systems
University of South-Eastern of Norway
Kongsberg, Norway
e-mail: aurillaa@usn.no

Esther Nistal Cabañas
Transport and ICT Directorate
Ingeniería de Sistemas para la Defensa de España, S.A.,
S.M.E., M.P.
Madrid, Spain
e-mail: enistal@isdefe.es

Abstract—The last few years have seen a growing interest in Remote piloted aircraft systems (RPAS), also known as Unmanned Aerial vehicles (UAV) or drones. Domains of application The Unmanned Traffic Management (UTM), adopted in Europe as U-Space by the Warsaw Declaration, have triggered numerous research and development projects on securing drones flights in an urban area. The EU project USEPE funded by the Single European Sky ATM Research Joint Undertaking (SESAR) focuses on ensuring a safe separation of flying drones in an urban setting. There are many technical and societal challenges to tackle to ensure that drones are safely and securely integrated into European airspace (U-space). For instance, real time communication between millions of drones and Air Traffic Control (ATC) rises concerns for the implementation, especially dense aerial activities in urban areas. Therefore, the implementation of highly populated drone systems requires a reliable communication network to maintain a real time information exchange. This paper investigates a model of reliable communication of multiple drones with the web-based ATC. Based on simulations of different use cases of multiple drones flying in an urban setting, we demonstrated that the Message Queuing Telemetry Transport (MQTT) is a promising protocol for the communication of multiple drones within a network. In our simulations, four drones communicated over a single network with the limited hardware namely RaspberryPi combined with the ThingsBoard.

Keywords-Drones; network; communication; IoT; MQTT; RaspberryPi

I. INTRODUCTION

Unmanned Aerial Vehicles (UAVs) have been around before they become popular. UAVs trace their modern origin back to the development of aerial torpedoes almost 95 years ago [1]. The UAVs were first designed for surveillance by the USA military. Nowadays, a drone can be equipped with any kind of sensors, therefore drone systems flying at low altitudes open up for a different kind of domain application such as delivery [2], photography [3-5], agriculture [6, 7], disaster management [8]. The shift in initial focus of surveillance can be traced back to advancements in other sectors, including battery technologies, improvement in motor power and size ratio, communication advancements, Global Navigation Satellite Systems (GNSS) for positioning accuracy and metallurgy, which help design low-weight chassis and improve other different factors affecting drone flight. Significant improvements in technology have greatly revolutionized different sectors of the market. Therefore, advances in drone technology initiated a chain reaction revolutionizing other sectors along with it.

Increasing air traffic density is leading to issues related to security and safety. To address these problems, the European Union has launched several initiatives and regulations under the "European Drones Regulation" for European airspace use [9]. Other countries like the USA and Japan have their UTM program as NASA UTM [10, 11] and Japan as JUTM [12]. By the end of 2016, The European Commission adopted the UTM concept in Europe and called it U-Space [10]. Since then, many research activities started at the European level, with funding of the European Commission through the Single European Sky Air Traffic Management Research Joint Undertaking (SESAR JU) [9].

Several EU projects focus on various technical challenges of separation or collision avoidance in order to ensure safe integration of drones in the European airspace. Our project, USEPE focuses on drone separation methods in

high demanding environments such as cities, by exploring the use of machine learning algorithms to automate the deconfliction of drones. They are many aspects to consider and one of them, for the simulation purpose, is the investigation of a suitable protocol of real time reliable communication between drones and eventually the air traffic management (ATM) systems. Several promising Internet of Things (IoT) communication protocols could provide reliable and scalable communications for drone to drone or drone to ATM. For example, "Bluetooth is a short-range, low-power IEEE open standard for implementing wireless personal area networks", but it cannot provide drone to ATM communication [13]. IEEE 802.15.4 committee started low data rate ZigBee technology and joined forces with ZigBee Alliance to further development [14]. A typical LoRaWAN network consists of end-devices commonly known as motes, gateways, and servers. Constrained Application Protocol (CoAP) was made a full Internet Engineering Task Force (IETF) Internet standard in 2014 officially [15]. "CoAP is a specialized web transfer protocol Analogous to Hyper-Text Transfer Protocol (HTTP) designed for use with constrained nodes and networks in the IoT (Internet of Things). The protocol design is extremely (Machine to Machine) M2M application-oriented to deliver low data packets [16]. Finally, MQTT is a lightweight publish subscribe messaging protocol designed and developed by Andy Stanford-Clark (IBM) and Arlen Nipper in 1999 for M2M [17].

The listed protocols are effective in their specified context. However, there are generic issues that should be considered in the implementation phase such as:

1. Short Communication range
2. Communication Only within Visual Line of Sight (VLOS)
3. Large bandwidth requirement.
4. Higher power consumption
5. No data filter specification
6. Critical data security concern
7. Pairing and system compatibility

These advantages and disadvantages have been evaluated based on the drone's type, environment, and mission assigned to the UAVs. We considered two parameters such as flight dynamics and positioning for the selection of the proper IoT protocol. Preliminary investigations of available IoT protocols resulted that MQTT might be the most suitable one ensuring real time, reliable and scalable communications for a drone in an urban area. Section 2 outlines the adopted methodology and provides some implementation descriptions. The results of the experiments are discussed in Section 3.

II. Methodology and Implementation

One of the aims of the USEPE project is to delineate a concept of the operation of drones flying in an urban environment. A basic concept of the operation of drones is depicted in Figure 1. Due to the structural environment such as buildings, we define a zone for flying as a corridor or highway to foresee that drones could move within specific corridors or highways and in respect of flying rules. A communication system could be easily integrated.

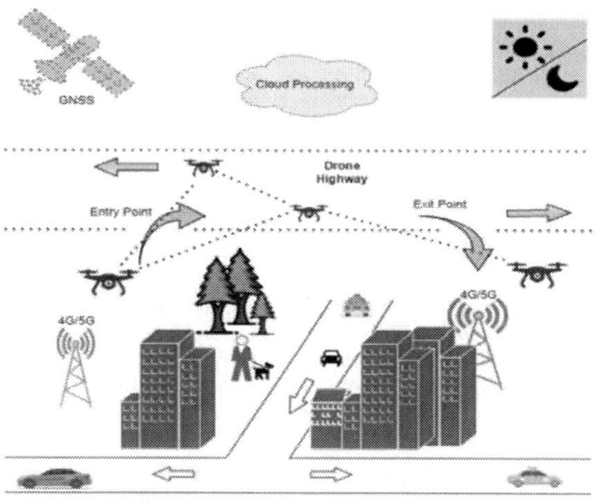

Figure 1. Concept of Operations of a drone mission.

A. MQTT Network Topology

MQTT is a lightweight publish/subscribe protocol designed around a central broker. Hence MQTT follows a simple start network topology, as shown in Figure 2. The broker acts as the centralized hub.

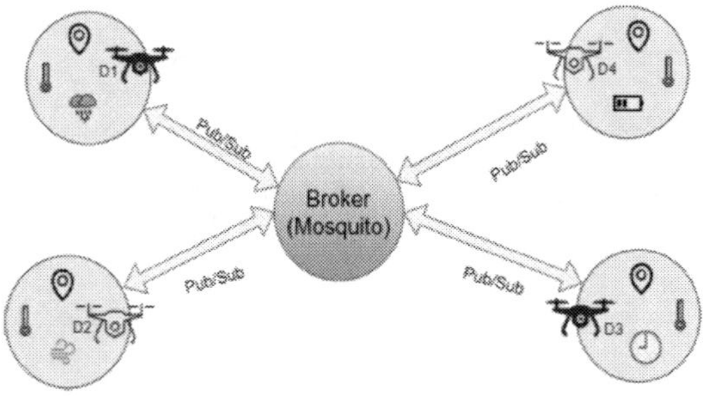

Figure 2. MQTT Star network topology.

The heart of implementing an Internet of Things (IoT) service is reliable network connectivity. Therefore, the 5G cellular network is used for reliable connectivity within urban airspace [18-21]. The generalized hardware structure is shown in Figure 3.

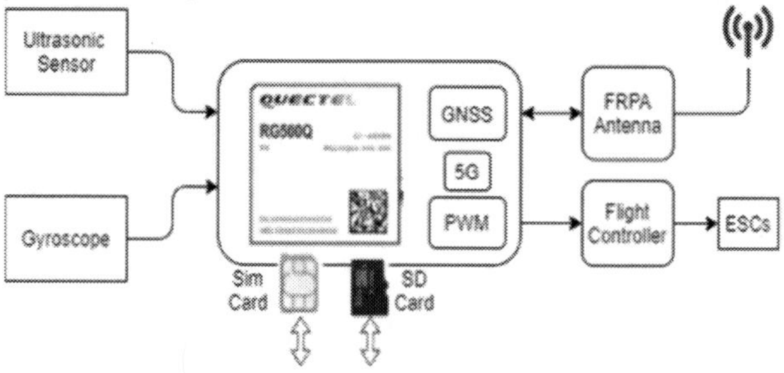

Figure 3. Interface Block Diagram.

1. Ultrasonic sensors

An ultrasonic sensor detects any nearby objects within the range. The scan distance depends on the specification of the sensor. Sensor-ranging detection capability from 1cm to 20m are commonly available types [22]. The sensor emits and detects a sonic pulse reflected by the object. HRLV-MaxSonar-EZ, an ultrasonic sensor product from MaxBotix with a range of 5m, is implemented in the practical. Any object within a range of 30 cm accounts for 30 cm. Since the sensor has a narrow beam angle of ~8°, the sensor is placed in the servo to scan 360°. The graphical representation is presented in Figure 4. The sonic pulse, time of flight between the emitter and the object, and back to the receiver is measured using the formula 1.

$$\text{Distance} = \frac{\text{Speed of sound} \times \text{Sonic time of flight}}{2} \quad (1)$$

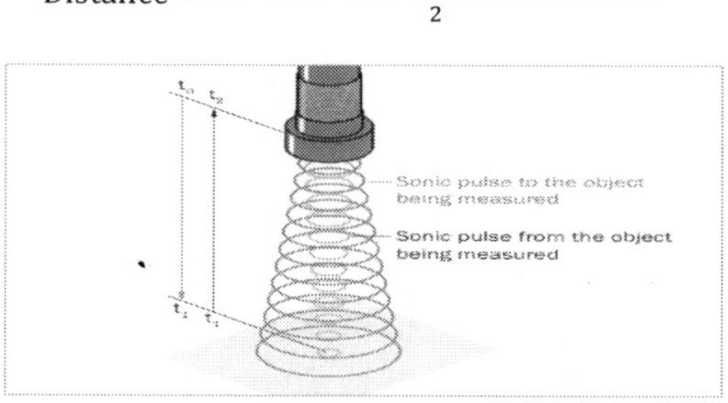

Figure 4. Time-of-flight measurement.

2. Gyroscope

A gyro sensor detects any angular tilt in the vertical and horizontal orientation of the drone. It generates an event-based trigger each time the device angle changes (See Figure 5). Some advanced gyro sensors have a programmable average window and a programmable average threshold.

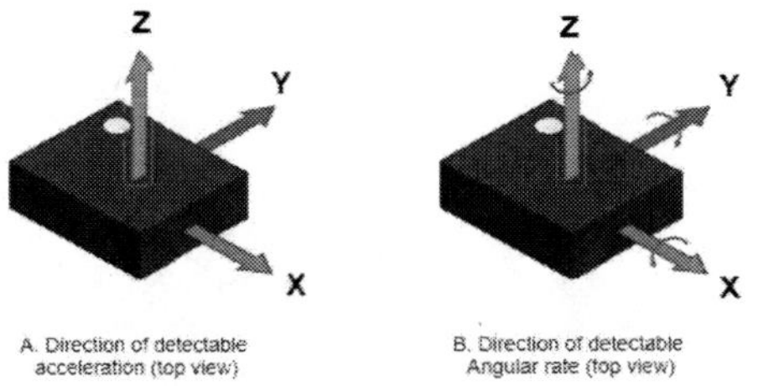

Figure 5. Lateral/Angular tilt Detection [23].

3. Raspberry Pi

The simulation of the drone communication is carried out using Raspberry pi 3b+. Features [24] of raspberry pi, 5V TTL logic level, Wi-Fi, GPIO's, and high processing power, make it ideal for simulation usage. Each raspberry pi is treated as a removed drone connected to the server. Sensors onboard to the raspberry pi continuously read the ambient data and continuously push the reading to the ThingsBoard. The data can be visualized in the ThingsBoard dashboard. The raspberry pi acts as a bridge linking the sensor data to the ThingsBoard. Therefore, it requires software that supports sensing the data from it to the server.

a) Paho MQTT

Paho is an Eclipse foundation project which helps to create an MQTT client. The client can both subscribe and publish data on any particular topic. Therefore, Paho MQTT client library is used for procuring the data to and from the ThingsBoard server.

4. ThingsBoard

"ThingsBoard [25] is an open-source IoT platform for data collection and processing, visualization, and device management". It enables connectivity via industry standard IoT protocols - MQTT, Constrained Application Protocol (CoAP), and HTTP facilitating both cloud and local deployments. ThingsBoard leverages device scalability, data visualization, cloud data processing, ensuring data protection. Features of ThingsBoard can be referred to [25].

B. Simulation Process

1. Take off approval

Only the authenticated drones must be allowed to fly and enter the flying corridors. Safety should be ensured by not only drone identification but also by monitoring how many drones are flying and where they are positioned. An approval system is therefore required.

Each drone connected to the ThingsBoard has a unique access token and device id. On creating a device, the access token and device id are autogenerated. Connection to ThingsBoard requires an access token, if not, the drone connection to ThingsBoard and the authentication will fail.

For any reason, like port number, incorrect URL, the compiler throws an error with error code 111. The error represents the socket connection error. The drone tries to reconnect to the server repeatedly with failed attempts until a valid access token is provided.

When the access token is authenticated, with connection session 0, the drone is granted permission to take off. The drone then follows the path instructed by the path planning algorithm. Static GPS coordinates are fed to the system in advance. The drone follows the static coordinates. The drones, on approved take-off, attain a vertical height of 250m which is considered default before any forward motion (See Figure 7). During the flight, all drones' states are monitored continuously as shown in Figure 6.

Drone

Drone name ↑	status	speed	battery
Drone 1	on route	89	100
Drone 2	arrived	0	100
Drone 3	climbing	40	20.0
Drone 4	decending	101.5	100

Figure 6. Drone Status.

2. Routing

The routing of a drone is divided into three different components.

a) Ascending

Once the drone is authenticated and approved for take-off, the drone firstly attains a default height of 250m, considering its initial position as the reference, as shown in Figure 7. Once the default height is attained, the drone makes any further moves.

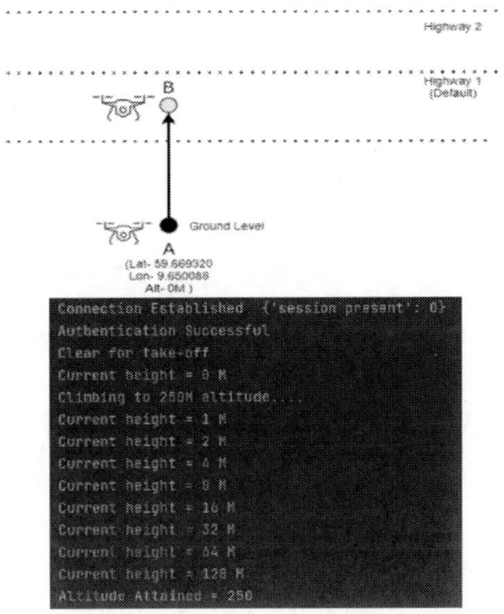

Figure 7. Drone Ascending.

Position of the drone with changing time is shown in Figure 8 during the ascending phase of the flight.

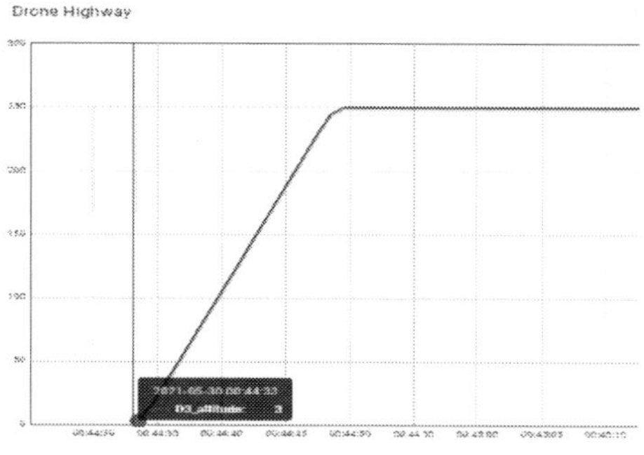

Figure 8. Drone Ascending Graph.

Once the take-off is clear, the current altitude of the drone is considered 0m. It is an assumed altitude; the initial height of the drone varies based on its area/region of operation. GPS sensor is read before in industrial practice. The drone slowly gains altitude with reference to its initial position coordinates. It follows initial reference coordinates until the drone attains the default height of 250 m. From 0m altitude to 250m, the whole process is considered as ascending of a drone.

b) On route

When the drone attains the default height of 250m, the drone then starts its forward journey towards its destination. The route from the end of ascending to the start of descending is defined as on route. In this stage, the drone makes an onward journey to the destination, continuously following the route as instructed by the routing algorithm. The GPS continuously reads the current position of the drone and continuously updates the server for any drift in position and correction of the same. Figure 9 represents the current drone status, drone 1 status as on route.

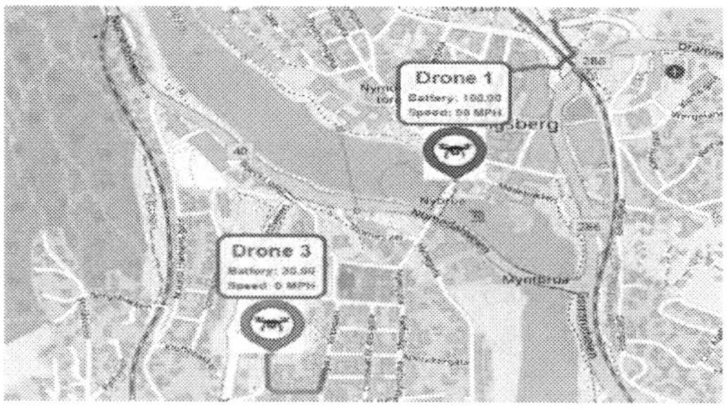

Figure 9. Drone on the route.

c) Descending

Descending is analogous to ascending, where the drone gradually climbs down the altitude from the current highway to the ground level. When the drone reaches its final GPS coordinate, the status of the drone is updated to "descending.". It then slowly climbs down, following the Euclidian path until it reaches ground level. In Figure 10, drone 1 represents the descending status of the drone. While the drone descends, the drone's speed is maintained to stop properly at the last 5m since its descending height for the safety of the drone and the payload it carries.

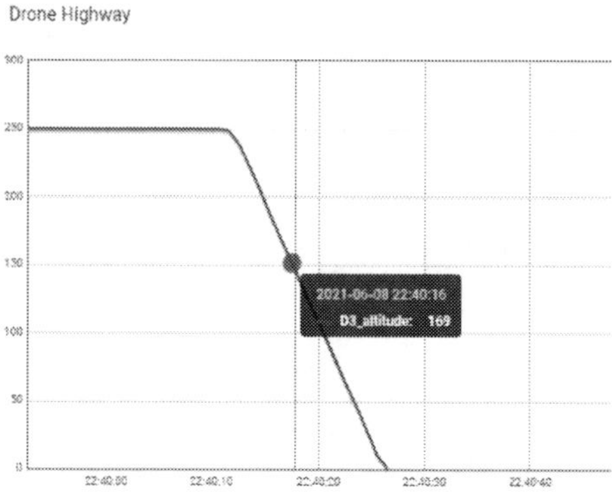

Figure 10. Altitude graph of landing drone.

3. Hovering

Hovering is a state where a drone maintains its current coordinates in the air, maintaining the same altitude. Hovering conditions, in general, can be programmed or autogenerated to prevent a collision. During the hovering state, the algorithm gets a chance to route/manage the traffic avoiding collisions or long flight time.

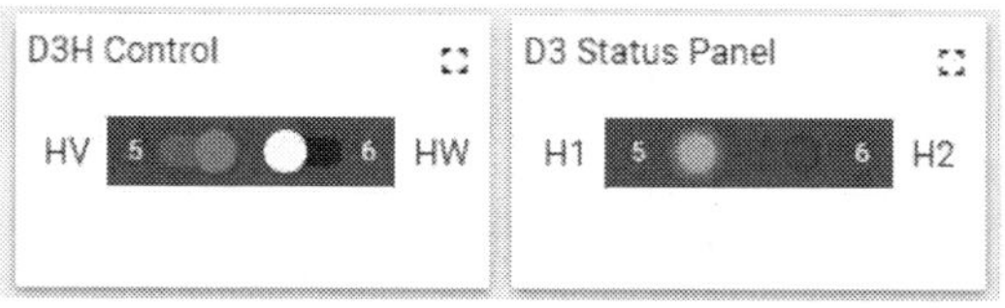

Figure 11. Hovering command and status panel.

Figure 11 shows that the hovering command is sent (HV), and the same is reflected as the drone's acknowledgment. This is the server-side command for hovering. However, an automated system is also incorporated into the project. The ultrasonic sensor onboard the drone senses the surrounding distance and objects' presence. If an object is closer than 5m, the drone updates its current status to hovering. When the other drone safely passes the shared route, the status of the hovering drone is changed back to "on the route," and the drone heads its further journey.

4. Object detection

HRLV-MaxSonar-EZ from MaxBotix is successfully implemented to detect any object in the drone trajectory. Two experimental cases were carried out in [26]. Figure 12 [26] is the trajectory of the drone. The blue line is the actual drone trajectory, while the line represents the ideal drone trajectory, and the red block is the object in the trajectory of the drone. The sensor continuously scans for any object in its vicinity.

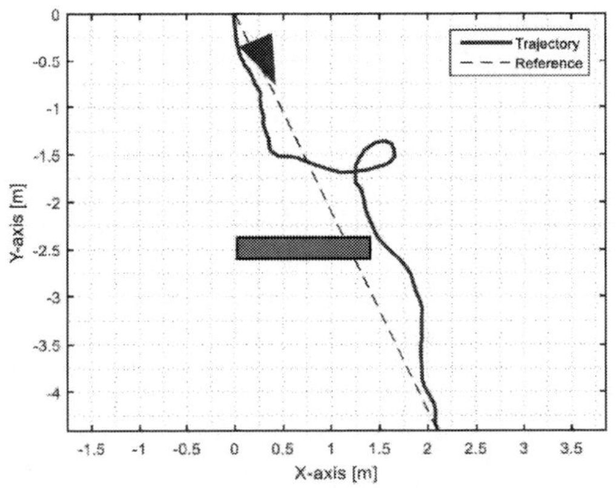

Figure 12. Drone trajectory [26].

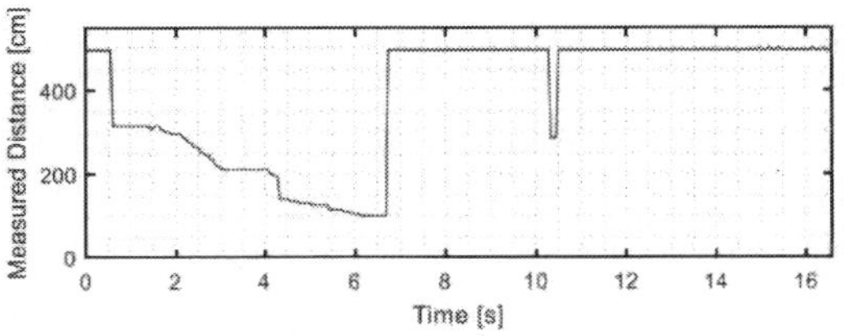

Figure 13. Distance vs Time [26].

Figure 13 [26] indicates that the drone reads the object in its trajectory and pushes itself back in ~6.4s. It then slightly changes its trajectory and avoids the object in its flight plan.

Therefore, real-time tracking of drones Beyond Visual Line of sight (BVLOS), enables dynamic routing, handle high traffic density. The monitoring and authentication of drones are efficiently completed.

III. RESULTS AND DISCUSSION

Operating them beyond a certain meter to a few kilometers is a recurrent challenge that is addressed today by the concept of Beyond Visual Line of Sight (BVLOS) as opposite to VLOS flights, which are operated within the pilot's line of sight. In order to achieve the issue, real time communication and information exchange should be tackled since drones are controlled by on-board instruments. Information should be related for instance to the altitude position, speed, etc. In this paper, we describe an experiment based on MQTT protocol for multi UAVs' communication. MQTT provides a promising service in connecting multiple devices to a central hub.

Number of Devices: Theoretically, a single MQTT broker can handle millions of devices over a single network. As seen from the implementation results, on ThingsBoard, a web-based Internet of Things (IoT) platform efficiently handles four drones in a single network.

Data Delivery: A highly flexible data delivery and acknowledgment feature of MQTT proves to be very beneficial for different applications. Three MQTT QOS provides high flexibility, unlike any other protocol.

Visual Confirmation: A large number of widgets in the ThingsBoard provide visual confirmation. Therefore, ThingsBoard proves to be very user-friendly with an attractive dashboard.

Object Detection: Object detection by Ultrasonic limits to a short range with limited information of the type, structure, and property of their object detected.

The implementation of Multi UAV communication over the Internet of Things (IoT) using MQTT has been explored. MQTT uses a basic time-based routing algorithm to send data from a drone to the IoT platform. The conducted simulations served as one of the investigations to ensure a safe separation within the EU which is one of the objectives of the USEPE project. However, we have also identified some other challenges that need to be considered before integrating MQTT or adopting it in the framework of the flying drones platform simulator that is currently being developed by the project USEPE. Some of these challenges are listed below:

- Capacity management of the U-space will impact the communication models
- Minimal considerations regarding connection failure. A better security and emergency landing system, in case of connection failure, could highly improve the overall safety.
- An emergency delivery route needs a special focus based on priority requirement
- An optimum and efficient message routing algorithm using MQTT can optimize payload.
- Extrinsic factors like wind and atmospheric pressure are not considered in our experiment
- Exploring the use of LIDAR. Ultrasonic sensors can only detect the presence of an object that has a limited range of detection of ~20m, while LIDAR can sense other properties of objects such as shape, size and have a range of detection of 75–660m [27].

IV. CONCLUSION

Autonomous aerial vehicles are gaining high interest not only from the research community but also from the business community. Drone operations in an urban environment will become a reality, but several technical challenges should be tackled for ensuring a safe separation by preventing and eliminating risks of drone collision. The USEPE U-Space is exploring techniques to solve the crucial issue of separation management for a safe integration of drones in the urban space. However, issues such as investigating the best protocol for communication and information exchange should be investigated. This paper describes an experiment conducted on the use of the MQTT protocol for communications. The conducted simulation and the outlining results show that MQTT is a promising protocol for real time and scalable communication for drones that could be integrated with the USEPE simulation drone platform for ensuring a safe flight in urban areas.

ACKNOWLEDGMENT

The USEPE U-Space project has received funding from the SESAR Joint Undertaking under the European Union's

Horizon 2020 research and innovation programme under grant agreement No 890378

The authors appreciate Srinivas Yemula because of proofreading and improving the work.

REFERENCES

[1] J. F. Keane and S. S. Carr, "A brief history of early unmanned aircraft," *Johns Hopkins APL Technical Digest,* vol. 32, no. 3, pp. 558-571, 2013.

[2] S. R. R. Singireddy and T. U. Daim, "Technology Roadmap: Drone Delivery–Amazon Prime Air," in *Infrastructure and Technology Management*: Springer, 2018, pp. 387-412.

[3] S. Hamilton and J. Stephenson, "Testing UAV (drone) aerial photography and photogrammetry for archaeology," *Lakehead University, Tech. Rep.,* 2016.

[4] S. Hamilton, "Drone mapping and photogrammetry at Brandon House 4," *Historical archaeology,* vol. 51, no. 4, pp. 563-575, 2017.

[5] B. Prodanov, I. Kotsev, T. Lambev, L. Dimitrov, R. Bekova, and D. Dechev, "Drone-based geomorphological and landscape mapping of Bolata Cove, Bulgarian coast," *Proc. of IMAM,* pp. 592-598, 2019.

[6] S. Ahirwar, R. Swarnkar, S. Bhukya, and G. Namwade, "Application of drone in agriculture," *International Journal of Current Microbiology and Applied Sciences,* vol. 8, no. 01, pp. 2500-2505, 2019.

[7] D. Murugan, A. Garg, and D. Singh, "Development of an adaptive approach for precision agriculture monitoring with drone and satellite data," *IEEE Journal of Selected Topics in Applied Earth Observations and Remote Sensing,* vol. 10, no. 12, pp. 5322-5328, 2017.

[8] K. M. Hasan, S. S. Newaz, and M. S. Ahsan, "Design and development of an aircraft type portable drone for surveillance and disaster management," *International Journal of Intelligent Unmanned Systems,* 2018.

[9] E. Bassi, "European drones regulation: Today's legal challenges," in *2019 International Conference on Unmanned Aircraft Systems (ICUAS)*, 2019: IEEE, pp. 443-450.

[10] P. Kopardekar, J. Rios, T. Prevot, M. Johnson, J. Jung, and J. E. Robinson, "Unmanned aircraft system traffic management (UTM) concept of operations," in *AIAA aviation forum*, 2016.

[11] A. S. Aweiss, B. D. Owens, J. Rios, J. R. Homola, and C. P. Mohlenbrink, "Unmanned Aircraft Systems (UAS) Traffic Management (UTM) National Campaign II," in *2018 AIAA Information Systems-AIAA Infotech@ Aerospace*, 2018, p. 1727.

[12] H. Nakamura, K. Harada, and Y. Oura, "UTM concept demonstrations in Fukushima; overview of demonstration and lesson learnt for operation of multiple UAS in the same airspace," in *2018 International Conference on Unmanned Aircraft Systems (ICUAS)*, 2018: IEEE, pp. 222-228.

[13] P. McDermott-Wells, "What is Bluetooth?," 20 December 2004, Dec. 2004-Jan. 2005.

[14] S. C. Ergen, "ZigBee/IEEE 802.15. 4 Summary," *UC Berkeley, September,* vol. 10, no. 17, p. 11, 2004.

[15] L. Coetzee, D. Oosthuizen, and B. Mkhize, "An analysis of CoAP as transport in an Internet of Things environment," in *2018 IST-Africa Week Conference (IST-Africa)*, 2018: IEEE, pp. Page 1 of 7-Page 7 of 7.

[16] C. Bormann. "CoAP, RFC 7252 Constrained Application Protocol." Coap Technology. https://coap.technology/ (accessed 2021).

[17] M. Collina, G. E. Corazza, and A. Vanelli-Coralli, "Introducing the QEST broker: Scaling the IoT by bridging MQTT and REST," in *2012 IEEE 23rd International Symposium on Personal, Indoor and Mobile Radio Communications-(PIMRC)*, 2012: IEEE, pp. 36-41.

[18] V. Petrov *et al.*, "Achieving end-to-end reliability of mission-critical traffic in softwarized 5G networks," *IEEE Journal on Selected Areas in Communications,* vol. 36, no. 3, pp. 485-501, 2018.

[19] P. Popovski, "Ultra-reliable communication in 5G wireless systems," in *1st International Conference on 5G for Ubiquitous Connectivity*, 2014: IEEE, pp. 146-151.

[20] Q. Zhang and F. H. Fitzek, "Mission critical IoT communication in 5G," in *Future Access Enablers of Ubiquitous and Intelligent Infrastructures*, 2015: Springer, pp. 35-41.

[21] P. Skarin, W. Tärneberg, K.-E. Årzen, and M. Kihl, "Towards mission-critical control at the edge and over 5G," in *2018 IEEE international conference on edge computing (EDGE)*, 2018: IEEE, pp. 50-57.

[22] S. S. Intelligance, "Ultrasonic Sensors: Ultimate Ultrasonic Sensor Solution from Sick," Online, 2019-10-15 2019.

[23] G. Allegato, C. Valzasina, and L. Zanotti, "Gyroscopes," in *Handbook of Silicon Based MEMS Materials and Technologies*: Elsevier, 2020, pp. 899-914.

[24] R. P. Foundation. (2019). Raspberry Pi Compute Module 3+ / Raspberry Pi Compute Module 3+ Lite.

[25] "Thingsboard Devices." https://thingsboard.io (accessed 13/06/2021).

[26] M. F. Rahman and R. A. Sasongko, "Obstacle avoidance for Quadcopter using Ultrasonic sensor," in *Journal of Physics: Conference Series*, 2018, vol. 1005, no. 1: IOP Publishing, p. 012037.

[27] C. Edson and M. G. Wing, "Airborne light detection and ranging (LiDAR) for individual tree stem location, height, and biomass measurements," *Remote Sensing,* vol. 3, no. 11, pp. 2494-2528, 2011.

Tracking Suspicious Entities Using UAVs in Critical Urban Areas: A R-CNN Approach

Mathias A. G. de Menezes
Computer and Systems
Graduate Program
Military Institute of Engineering
Rio de Janeiro, Brazil
E-mail: mathiasdemenezes@ime.eb.br

Paulo F. F. Rosa (PhD)
Computer and Systems
Graduate Program
Military Institute of Engineering
Rio de Janeiro, Brazil
E-mail: rpaulo@ime.eb.br

Erick Menezes Moreira (Dr Eng)
Computer and Systems
Graduate Program
Military Institute of Engineering
Rio de Janeiro, Brazil
E-mail: emenezes@ime.eb.br

***Abstract*—This paper proposes a tracking application that integrates object detection with a Region-based Convolutional Neural Network as the object detector and the Discriminative Correlation Filter with Channel and Spatial Reliability as the tracking algorithm for the tracking method. Our approach has the objective and motivation of assisting the operational actions of the security forces in Rio de Janeiro, especially the Military Police, in deflagrated regions. The results of the generated model showed an average accuracy of 86% for the object detector and an average of 74% for the object tracker when applied to the video sequences of our dataset.**

***Keywords*—object detection; object tracking; r-cnn; surveillance.**

Figure 1. Military Police helicopter, shot down by criminals during an operation in 2009. In the fall, three police officers died and five were injured.

I. INTRODUCTION

Unmanned Aerial Vehicles (UAVs) are commonly used in police and military operations [1], [2], especially for monitoring and tracking suspicious mobile entities in risky urban areas such as slums, war zones and terrorist-controlled regions. This approach enables learning and understanding the opponents tactics, providing actionable intelligence to anticipate and act on insurgent activities relating vehicles, places, and routes of locomotion [3], [4]. Monitoring and tracking are particularly challenging in low visibility enviroments where objects are ocluded [5].

In the city of Rio de Janeiro, police forces find it difficult and resisting to operate incursions into slums dominated by criminal groups. Police actions are usually accompanied by helicopters that support ground troops. However, this action reveals the intents of the police in those regions, putting an end to the surprise factor, as criminals manage to contain the advance of the police forces, as shown in Figure 1. As a consequence, the Military Police of Rio de Janeiro (PMERJ) has a high casualty rate, with 198 agents being killed in action against criminal gangs only in 2020. To reduce these casualties, the operation of UAVs in these scenarios is convenient. UAVs have reduced size, and models can no longer be seen at a height of 100 meters, which prevents them from being targeted by firearms and destroyed [6].

In 2012, the Military Institute of Engineering (IME), with support from other institutes to overcome these deficiencies, built six UAVs to be used in missions by the Rio de Janeiro security forces. The UAVs were used for surveillance, security and remote sensing and in security in stadiums and at major events, such as the 2014 Soccer World Cup and the 2016 Olympics.

The PMERJ also use other UAVs to monitor slums regions and assist in planning operations against drug trafficking. In one of the most violent slums in the city, images captured by the UAV shown in Figure 2 led police to discover two camps used by drug dealers hidden in a place of difficult access [6]. Without aerial imagery, it would be difficult to progress within these locations. The equipment shown in Figure 2 is operated by two people, one responsible for moving the UAV and the other for operating two attached cameras. However, none of the equipments operated by the military police has an autonomous application for detection and tracking of targets on board. With the motivation to contribute to solving this problem, we propose a method for detection and tracking suspicious entities, we use a Region Based Convolutional Neural Network (R-CNN) and the CSRT tracker, a python implementation of the Discriminative Correlation Filter with Channel and Spatial Reliability (DCF-CSR).

The rest of the paper is organized as follows. The Related Work is described in Section II, the problem formulation is described in Section III and our proposed tracking method is described in Section IV. The valuation of the proposed approach is carried out in Section V, and we conclude the paper in Section VI.

Figure 2. The multirotor has a camera with an infrared viewfinder attached for night monitoring, and a transmission link to enable real-time monitoring of images.

II. Related Work

Persistent tracking of targets in urban environments using UAVs is a difficult task due to the limited field of view, obstructed visibility of obstacles and uncertain target movement. The vehicle must be properly positioned, allowing visibility to the target to be maximized. In [7], an approach to target pursuit is presented, which constitutes a deep reinforcement learning technique based on Deep Q-Networks, with a curriculum training framework for the UAV to persistently track the target in the presence of obstacles and movement uncertainty. The results show that the UAV persistently tracks the target in diverse environments, avoiding obstacles in trained environments as well as in visible environments.

Another big challenge is tracking the object under occlusion conditions. The TensorFlow object detection API was used in [8] to detect moving objects. The location of the detected object is passed to a new CNN-based that was used for robust object detection. The approach proposed by [8] is able to detect the object in different illuminations and occlusions, reaching great accuracy in self-generated image sequences.

Occlusions and interactions between different objects are expected and common due to the rugged nature of these urban areas. In [9], a tracking framework employing classification label information from a deep learning detection approach was used to associate the different objects in addition to the objects positions and appearances. The results showed that object labels improve tracking performance, but that the output of object detectors is not always reliable.

In a persistent surveillance task, UAVs sometimes cannot independently complete the task and need to be supported by ground equipment. Thus, [10] presents a system of UAVs and UGVs to perform surveillance tasks, and the goal is to generate circular paths for UAVs and UGVs, respectively, to increase the operating time to complete the coverage of the environment. Keeping a circular flight in an area helps to circumvent the object's occlusion. In their approach, [10] integrates a distribution estimation algorithm (DEA) and a genetic algorithm (GA) to solve the problem. The advantages of DEA and GA in global and local search fully consider the demands in the different phases of the iterative process. This way, one can scan and determine the ideal sequence of passage of the open points. Then, an online site adjustment strategy is also applied to deal with changing land area coverage requirements. Simulation results demonstrate that UAV and UGV systems can increase surveillance efficiency.

The detection and tracking problem for reconnaissance and surveillance of UAVs requires that they fully cover an area of interest along their trajectories. Thus, [11] presents a two-phase strategy to solve this UAV recognition problem with a specified altitude. First, an easily implementable estimation algorithm is developed at a given altitude, and the minimum and how to targeted number of cameras is determined to provide complete coverage of the target area. The second phase deals with the distribution of achievements in one or more UAVs and creates the paths for them to recognize a corresponding area of interest. The results reported support the feasibility of their proposed solution.

Another work [12], proposed an approach to detect moving objects in wide area motion imagery, in which the objects are small and well separated. The approach was based on background subtraction as an efficient and unsupervised method capable of producing object shapes. To reliably detect small, low-contrast objects, they set up background subtraction to extract foreground regions that might be objects of interest. Although this dramatically increases the number of false alarms, the CNN, considering spatial and temporal information, is then trained to reject false alarms. In high-traffic areas, background subtraction produces mixed detections. To reduce the complexity required of tracking multiple targets, they trained another CNN to predict the positions of multiple moving objects in an area.

III. Problem Formulation

We emphasize that the motorcycle is the vehicle used by criminal organizations in the slums of Rio de Janeiro. Generally, they work in groups or pairs and mingle with citizens who travel through the alleys of the environment. Therefore, it is difficult to identify a suspicious vehicle, either by a large aircraft such as a helicopter, or by a small UAV without an embedded computer application. Thus, it is necessary to create the model of the target to be tracked, preserving its aspects in order to classify it.

An ideal approach to solve this problem is the use of Region-based Convolutional Neural Networks (R-CNN). These networks use as input data regions cut out of the image to detect whether a number of objects of a certain category are present, as well as detecting where each object is located in the image. This type of network is very robust and can discern several clustered objects simultaneously, regardless of the occlusion of parts of the target object.

The UAV that PMERJ uses is a multirotor with an integrated infrared camera and a radio link for communication. Two human operators manage the drone during the mission: where one operates the camera and the other moves the aircraft. Basically, the application we propose will help the camera

Figure 3. Men armed with rifles (a) move on a street in a slum (b).

operator to detect and track suspicious entities and monitor them within the camera's field-of-view, as shown in Figure 3.

IV. Proposed Tracking Method

Our proposed object tracking method contains two parts: the trained object classifier and the generation of the object detection model from the training result. The selective search algorithm that takes the regions and delivers them to the object detection model to predict the object location and classify it as a object class. The detection output predictions feed the tracking algorithm to track the predicted box of the object class. Any other circumstance of the object prediction change tracker will trigger the object classifier and restart the process from the beginning.

The tracker, known as Discriminative Correlation Filter with Channel and Spatial Reliability (DCF-CSR), uses spatial reliability to define the filters support for a portion of the selected area of the frame for tracking. This expands and locates the selected zone and tracks non-rectangular areas or objects. This tracker practices two standard features, HoGs and Colornames. Furthermore, it works at frames below 25 fps [13].

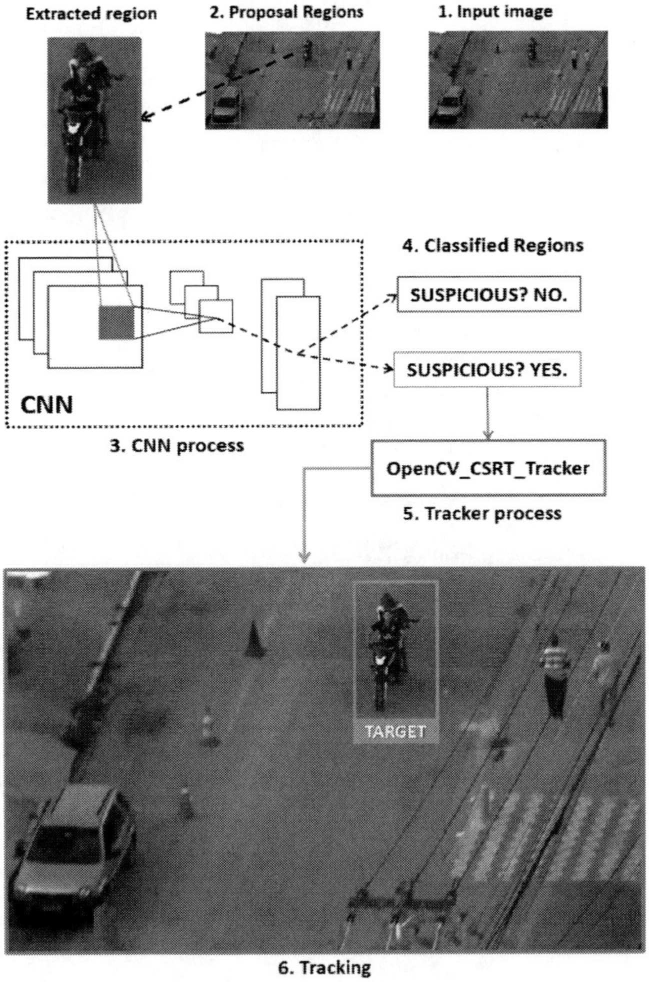

Figure 4. Proposed Tracking Method

A. R-CNN for Object Detection

The R-CNN method in [14], is a machine learning model that performs segmentation based on the results of object detection. The R-CNN initially uses the selective search algorithm to extract a large amount of proposed regions and then calculates the characteristics for each one of them through a Convolutional Neural Network (CNN). Finally, it classifies each region using a specific linear classifier, typically a Support Vector Machine (SVM). The R-CNN is capable of performing more complex tasks, such as object detection and coarse image segmentation.

B. Extracted Regions

The R-CNN initially generates around 2000 proposed regions using the Selective Search algorithm [15], which is based on simple traditional computer vision techniques. The process is as follows: first, each proposed Region of Interest (RoI) is deformed into a square image of standard size; second, the image is fed to a CNN that generates a array with 4096 dimensional features as output; and finally, a SVM classifies the feature array producing two outputs: a classification, and an indication of deviation (offset) that can be used to adjust the bounding box.

C. Processing of Convolutional Characteristics

The extracted proposed regions will feed the CNN. We used the VGG-16 CNN [16]. Basically, the CNN will receive a proposed region passing through a series of convolutional, non-linear, clustering and fully connected layers to obtain two outputs. An output is a single class that best describes the proposed region. The CNN is structured in four layers, or stages: convolution layer, grouping layer, normalization layer, and fully connected layer.

D. Object Tracking

The basis of our proposed tracking method was taken from the DCF-CSR algorithm. Furthermore, this algorithm was implemented and integrated into the OpenCV library as a Deep Neural Network (DNN) module. We propose a tracking application that integrates object detection with R-CNN as the

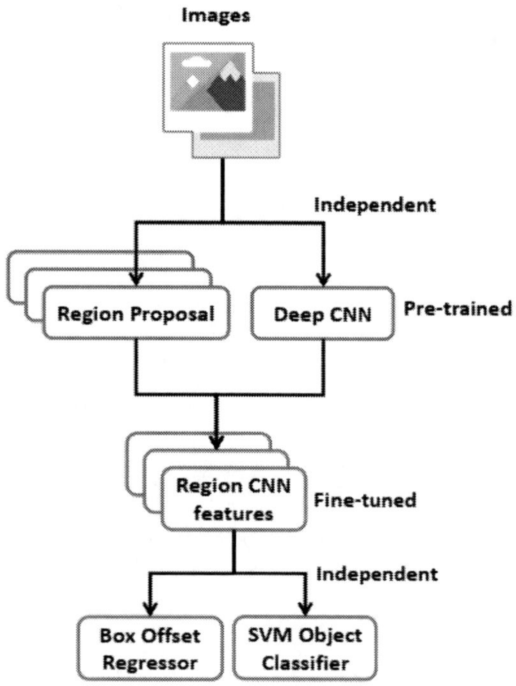

Figure 5. R-CNN Model Architecture

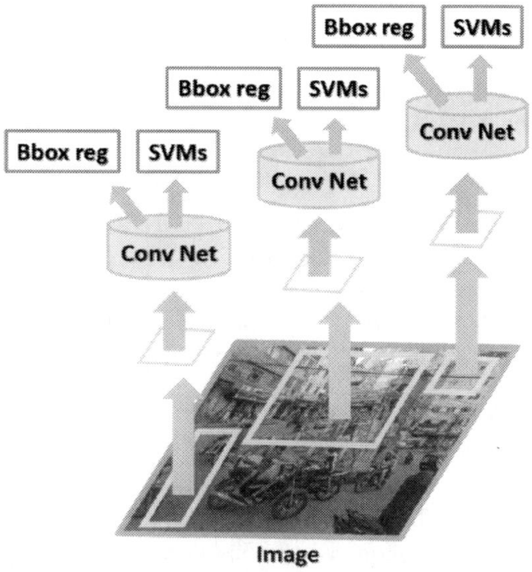

Figure 6. R-CNN architecture: Each proposed RoI is passed through the CNN to extract features then an SVM classifier

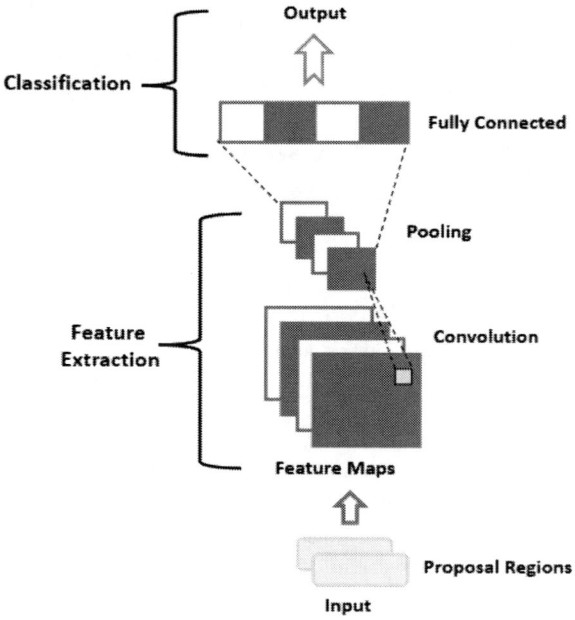

Figure 7. CNN architecture

object detector and OpenCV_CSRT_Tracker as the tracking algorithm for the tracking method.

V. Experimental Results

Our image dataset was collected from Internet resources such as blogs, reports, news portals, etc. The difference between our image collection and other image collections is that our images are taken by drone cameras, helicopter cameras and security cameras installed in local urban environment. We have collected 340 images in total, which were divided into 220 images for the training process and 120 images for the testing process. The extracted regions from images there are two categories: Suspicious Entity (SE) and Not-suspicious Entity (NE).

After finishing 5000 epoch times training with our dataset, we got our object classifier model and tested our object detection (classifier) model by applying images from different open source resources, reaching the accuracy rate of 86%, as shown in Figure 8.

We can see the remarkable results of the object detection model, where it is detecting all objects in the frame. While tracking, we may face thousands of positions, locations, shapes that means it requires more images on dataset with different positions and environments for better results, as shown in Figure 9.

We have tested our tracking method with video sequences taken by helicopter and obtained promising results. The experiments show that the R-CNN_CSRT tracker algorithm can re-detect the object once it is gone from the current frame. Figure 10 presents qualitative results for the video sequences taken by a helicopter, with frameworks below 25 fps. Even if

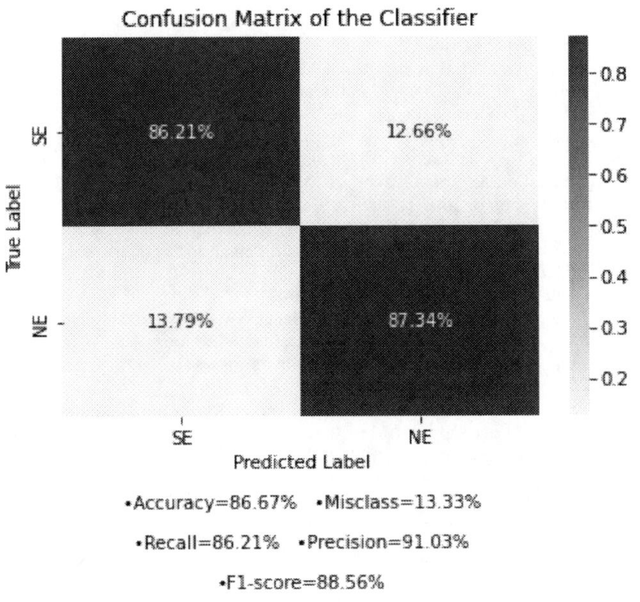

Figure 8. Statistics the trained classifier.

Figure 9. Object detection results of the trained R-CNN object classifier: images from our dataset.

the shape or appearance of the tracking object changes, the tracker can track the object properly.

In order to measure how good our object tracker is at predicting bounding boxes, we use the Intersection over Union (IoU) metric. The IoU method calculates the ratio of the overlapping area to the joint area between the predicted bounding box and the ground truth bounding box. The IoU is an evaluation metric used to measure the accuracy of an object detector/tracker against a specific dataset. This evaluation metric is often used in object detection and tracking challenges,

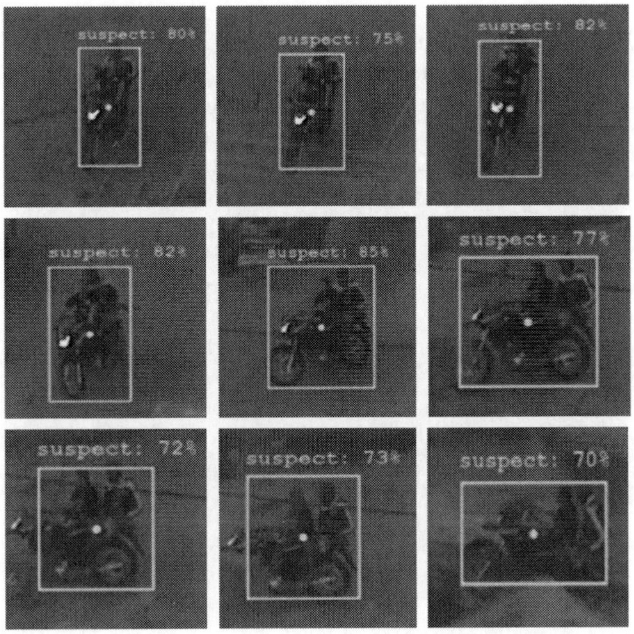

Figure 10. Qualitative results of the proposed tracking method in extracted frames.

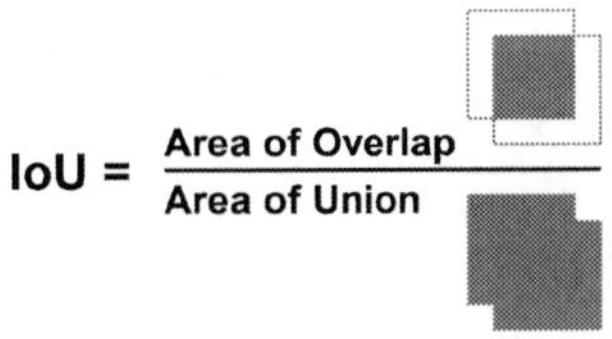

Figure 11. The calculation of the IoU is done by dividing the overlap area between the bounding boxes by the union area.

as in approaches with R-CNN, Faster R-CNN, YOLO and Deep SORT as in [17]. However, the actual algorithm used to generate the predictions does not matter. The intersection over the union is simply an evaluation metric. Any algorithm that provides predicted bounding boxes as output can be evaluated using IoU.

More formally, in order to apply the IoU to evaluate an (arbitrary) object detector/tracker, we need: (i) the ground truth bounding boxes (that is, the hand-labeled bounding boxes of the test suite that specify where the object is in the Image); and (ii) the predicted bounding boxes of the generated model as show Figure 11. The average accuracy of classification of our proposed method reached 74.83% when applied to video sequences.

VI. Conclusion

We presented a R-CNN_CSRT tracker to track suspicious entities in critical urban environments. With this method, we integrate the object classifier model based on deep learning with the OpenCV implementation version of the CSRT tracker of the DCF-CSR algorithm supported by the DNN OpenCV module. Our results showed that our trained object classifier model was accurate after 5000 epoch times training times, with only 220 images for training and 120 images for testing. However, when applied to video sequences with images captured by helicopters, the tracker performed below expectations. These images need to be in good resolution, with a greater amount of angulation, detailing the position and shape of the entities present.

In conclusion, our work had some limitations. We need a greater number of images representing the class of suspicious entities, as well as an improvement in the CNN structure, increasing its convolutional layers and the number of training cycles. In future works we will use variations of R-CNN, such as a Faster R-CNN. These changes can increase the accuracy of the proposed method, possibly making the tracker more robust and effective.

ACKNOWLEDGMENT

This study was financed by the Coordenação de Aperfeiçoamento de Pessoal de Nível Superior - Brasil (CAPES) - Finance code 001.

REFERENCES

[1] T. Samad, J. S. Bay and D. Godbole, "Network-Centric Systems for Military Operations in Urban Terrain: The Role of UAVs," in Proceedings of the IEEE, vol. 95, no. 1, pp. 92-107, Jan. 2007, doi: 10.1109/JPROC.2006.887327.

[2] E. Semsch, M. Jakob, D. Pavlicek and M. Pechoucek, "Autonomous UAV Surveillance in Complex Urban Environments," 2009 IEEE/WIC/ACM International Joint Conference on Web Intelligence and Intelligent Agent Technology, 2009, pp. 82-85, doi: 10.1109/WI-IAT.2009.132.

[3] H. Geng, J. Guan, H. Pan and H. Fu, "Multiple Vehicle Detection with Different Scales in Urban Surveillance Video," 2018 IEEE Fourth International Conference on Multimedia Big Data (BigMM), 2018, pp. 1-4, doi: 10.1109/BigMM.2018.8499095.

[4] C. Hu , G. Qu , H. S. Shin, A. Tsourdos, "Distributed synchronous cooperative tracking algorithm for ground moving target in urban by UAVs," International Journal of Systems Science, 2020. DOI: 10.1080/00207721.2020.1844340.

[5] M. Daikoku, S. Karungaru and K. Terada, "Automatic detection of suspicious objects using surveillance cameras," The SICE Annual Conference 2013, 2013, pp. 1162-1167.

[6] L. S. Alves P. Integrated Aerial Imaging Systems in Special Operations in an Urban Environment. Thesis (Masters in Defense Engineering) – Military Institute of Engineering (IME). Rio de Janeiro, p. 84. 2020.

[7] S. Bhagat and P. B. Sujit, "UAV Target Tracking in Urban Environments Using Deep Reinforcement Learning," 2020 International Conference on Unmanned Aircraft Systems (ICUAS), 2020, pp. 694-701, doi: 10.1109/ICUAS48674.2020.9213856.

[8] S. Mane and S. Mangale, "Moving Object Detection and Tracking Using Convolutional Neural Networks," 2018 Second International Conference on Intelligent Computing and Control Systems (ICICCS), 2018, pp. 1809-1813, doi: 10.1109/ICCONS.2018.8662921.

[9] H. L. Ooi, G. A. Bilodeau, N. Saunier, D. A. Beaupré, "Multiple Object Tracking in Urban Traffic Scenes with a Multiclass Object Detector," In: Bebis G. et al. (eds) Advances in Visual Computing. ISVC 2018. Lecture Notes in Computer Science, vol 11241. Springer, Cham. https://doi.org/10.1007/978-3-030-03801-4_63.

[10] Y. Wu, S. Wu and X. Hu, "Cooperative Path Planning of UAVs UGVs for a Persistent Surveillance Task in Urban Environments," in IEEE Internet of Things Journal, vol. 8, no. 6, pp. 4906-4919, 15 March15, 2021, doi: 10.1109/JIOT.2020.3030240.

[11] J. Zhang and Y. Zhang, "A Method for UAV Reconnaissance and Surveillance in Complex Environments," 2020 6th International Conference on Control, Automation and Robotics (ICCAR), 2020, pp. 482-485, doi: 10.1109/ICCAR49639.2020.9107972.

[12] Y. Zhou and S. Maskell, "Detecting and Tracking Small Moving Objects in Wide Area Motion Imagery (WAMI) Using Convolutional Neural Networks (CNNs)," 2019 22th International Conference on Information Fusion (FUSION), 2019, pp. 1-8.

[13] A. Lukežič, T. Vojíř, L. Čehovin Zajc et al., "Discriminative Correlation Filter Tracker with Channel and Spatial Reliability," Internacional Journal of Computuer Vision 126, pp. 671–688 (2018). https://doi.org/10.1007/s11263-017-1061-3.

[14] R. Girshick, J. Donahue, T. Darrell and J. Malik, "Rich Feature Hierarchies for Accurate Object Detection and Semantic Segmentation," 2014 IEEE Conference on Computer Vision and Pattern Recognition, (2014), pp. 580-587, doi: 10.1109/CVPR.2014.81.

[15] J. R. R. Uijlings, K. E. A. van de Sande, T. Gevers et al., "Selective Search for Object Recognition," Internacional Journal of Computer Vision 104, pp. 154–171 (2013). https://doi.org/10.1007/s11263-013-0620-5.

[16] k. Simonyan and A. Zisserman, "Very Deep Convolutional Networks for Large-Scale Image Recognition," 2015 The 3rd International Conference on Learning Representations, pp. 1-8 (ICLR2015). https://arxiv.org/abs/1409.1556.

[17] A. Pramanik, S. K. Pal, J. Maiti and P. Mitra, "Granulated RCNN and Multi-Class Deep SORT for Multi-Object Detection and Tracking," 2021 in IEEE Transactions on Emerging Topics in Computational Intelligence, doi: 10.1109/TETCI.2020.3041019.

A UAV-based Infrared Small Target Detection System for Search and Rescue Missions

Victor J. Hansen
Dept. of Science and Industry Systems,
University of South-Eastern Norway
Kongsberg, Norway
email: vjhansen7@gmail.com

Antonio L. L. Ramos
Dept. of Science and Industry Systems,
University of South-Eastern Norway
Kongsberg, Norway
email: antonior@usn.no

José A. Apolinário Jr.
Dept. of Electrical Engineering,
Military Institute of Engineering
Rio de Janeiro, Brazil
email: apolin@ime.eb.br

***Abstract*—Using infrared imaging cameras mounted on unmanned aerial vehicles to assist in search and rescue missions by gathering and processing images can substantially improve the chances of survival of missing people. Indeed, infrared imaging cameras are well suited to support the detection of heat signatures in dark and cloudy conditions. The critical point herein is detecting heat signatures emitted by the human body. This stresses feasibility of application of infrared small target detection for search and rescue missions in wide areas. This paper presents and discusses a deep learning and a low-rank and sparse matrix decomposition approaches for infrared small target detection. Further, a framework tailored for unmanned aerial vehicles is developed. The proposed infrared small target detection system is capable of detecting heat signatures in images with complex backgrounds. Experimental results demonstrate that an infrared small target detection method based on deep learning is a valuable supporting system in search and rescue missions.**

***Keywords*—UAV; infrared imaging; object detection; computer vision; machine learning.**

I. INTRODUCTION

In recent years, several missing people have been located by Unmanned Aerial Vehicles (UAVs) equipped with Infra-Red (IR) imaging cameras [1][2]. Indeed, autonomous UAVs are becoming very popular in applications such as surveillance and search and rescue missions. Generally, search and rescue missions are limited by time, area of coverage, costs, and availability of UAV pilots. This work considers a system suited for multi-rotor UAVs, as well as other vertical take-off and landing UAVs. In comparison to helicopters, UAVs require less traffic management, and are less expensive to operate and easy to deploy. In addition, they offer a high degree of design flexibility and can be equipped with a wide range of sensors. Moreover, UAVs can access confined spaces that helicopters cannot, including areas deemed hazardous to humans.

The use of automated object detection in search and rescue missions can reduce human errors, which are likely to occur in cases where the operator has to monitor a video stream for hours. The obvious consequence of this in the case of search and rescue missions is failure in locating the missing person. Compared to automated object detection, human operators have the advantage of understanding the context of a video and recognizing where to search based on experience. However, a challenging task for a human is to detect crucial details in a high-definition video, because the human eye could potentially be focusing only on a small section of the video frame.

The task of detecting missing victims is time-critical and particularly challenging since parts of the victim might be exceedingly small, and sometimes blend in with the surroundings. In natural disaster scenarios, using autonomous UAVs to discover any human activity can save lives. Object detection techniques and IR imaging are useful in automatizing the process of detecting humans in adverse conditions, thereby increasing the likelihood of survival. The combination of IR and color imaging can provide a relatively short search time in remote areas since IR small targets will appear as brighter than the local background and therefore distinguishable from the surroundings. IR imaging [3][4] is used in civilian and military applications owing to its ability to operate in dark and low-visibility conditions, such as cloudy and smoke-covered areas, making IR imaging suitable for detecting humans in low light situations. However, IR imaging cameras are not as effective in supporting search and rescue teams in finding missing people in warm areas because the heat from the surroundings might mask the heat signature of the target. This issue becomes exceptionally challenging when the target is covered by objects with thermal radiation shielding properties, or when multiple interfering heat sources are present.

In aerial IR images [3][5], IR targets occupy just a few pixels on the imaging plane due to the long imaging distance. An IR small target [6] can be defined as an object having a total size of less than 0.15% of an image. As a result, the target's thermal radiation is likely to appear weak. This makes the target difficult to recognize, as it lacks obvious shape, size, and texture characteristics. Mid-wave IR and long-wave IR cameras [7] are popularly known as thermal imaging cameras because they are capable of detecting radiation emitted by objects with a low surface temperature, typically around 25 °C. These cameras detect IR radiation and produce a thermal image that can be used to determine surface temperatures. Thus, there is no need for an external light source to detect an object. However, high-resolution IR imaging cameras are prohibitively expensive and not widely available to the public. Commercially available thermal imaging cameras typically generate low-resolution images, which make them inept at detecting small objects.

The field of IR small target detection has been dominated by model-driven methods. One of the highest performing [6] non-learning model-driven methods using low rank and sparse matrix decomposition is the Infrared Patch-Image (IPI) model [8]. Low-rank and sparse matrix decomposition methods [9] try to separate an image into a foreground component **S** and a background component **L**. A sparse matrix [10] has a considerable majority of elements equal to zero. Thus, the IR small targets are often the non-zero values in the sparse matrix, making them easily identifiable. Conversely, a low-rank matrix [10] has a small number of linearly independent rows and columns compared to the matrix's size. The background patch of an IR image has a low rank, and the IR small targets of **S** are sparse when compared to **L**.

Convolutional Neural Networks (CNNs), specifically Feature Pyramid Networks (FPNs) [11], outperform non-learning model-driven methods [5], indicating that learning from data can lead to high accuracy in IR small target detection. But, most CNNs learn high-level features by downsampling feature maps. As a result, the IR small targets become engulfed by the background features in the deepest layers. To ensure adequate detection results, a specialized network design is required [5][6]. Using a pre-trained network for the task of IR small target detection is not advised [3], but rather to train the CNN's weights from scratch using only IR small target images.

Meta-architectures, such as Faster R-CNN [12] and YOLO [13] only use the last layer's feature map to localize objects and make predictions. These models are ineffective at localizing small objects due to the absence of low-level features [14] at the last layer. The problem of detecting small objects can be alleviated by using a more fitting feature extractor (e.g., ResNet) [15]. According to [16], the main drawback of employing a CNN for the task of IR small target detection is that feature learning will become particularly challenging, as an IR small target generally lacks any prominent shape. Further, extracting features from low resolution images is difficult, and the IR small targets may disappear in the deep layers of a network due to their small size. Dai et al. [5] state that a high-resolution prediction map is crucial for detecting IR small targets, and thus propose the Attentional Local Contrast Network (ALCNet). ALCNet achieves better results than the completely data- and model-driven methods on the SIRST (Single-frame Infra-Red Small Target) dataset [17], indicating that when detecting IR small targets, one should prioritize combining CNNs with domain-specific knowledge, e.g., methods for measuring local contrast. To conserve small targets and extract feature maps, ALCNet employs a modified ResNet as its feature extractor. Further, Wang et al. [3] suggests restricting the number of downsampling operations in the feature extractor, thus gaining a sufficiently large feature map which conserves features of the IR small targets.

Having a deep network is desirable, as a deeper network can learn more features. However, as the network gets deeper, there may be instances where the accuracy saturates and then rapidly decreases. This is known as degradation [18]. Moreover, a deeper network leads to more parameters, which results in a more resource intensive model. As a solution to this problem, ResNet [19] introduced the residual block. The residual block takes the output $\mathcal{F}(\mathbf{x})$ of one or more layers and combines it with a shortcut connection containing the value $\mathbf{x}$ which is feeding those layers. Since the residual block prevents degradation, the network's depth can increase, and the accuracy will improve over time. Results from [19] demonstrate that the effect of the residual connections increases proportionally with the number of layers.

The remainder of this paper is organized as follows. Section II outlines the methods employed in this work and the rationale behind the selection of these methods. Further, Section II describes the evaluation metrics and outlines the testing process. Section III summarizes the test results and discusses the significance of the results. Section IV provides a discussion of the proposed system. Finally, Section V summarizes the performance results of the proposed system, and presents conclusions and future research opportunities on the topic.

II. METHODOLOGY

In this work, two different methodologies for detection of IR small targets are proposed and tested, namely a data-driven CNN-based method and a model-driven method using low-rank and sparse matrix decomposition. These are discussed next, beginning with some general considerations on the dataset.

A. IR Small Target Dataset Analysis

The Single-frame IR Small Target (SIRST) dataset [17], which contains 427 short-wave IR and mid-wave IR images, is used for training and testing of the proposed methods. The dataset sample size was augmented to improve the training of the model. The main reason is that scarcity or low variance in the training dataset will result in a model that performs poorly on new data. Certain targets are difficult for humans to discover as they require one to perform a focused and thorough search discriminate whether they are a target or just noise. Therefore, the classification task of IR small target detection is binary [6]. Moreover, as most of the targets in the images lack any definite features, they are all placed into a general class called "Target".

B. Data-driven Approach

Numerous CNN models are available, and it is difficult to differentiate between them. A model with a good trade-off between accuracy and speed (i.e., inference time for a single image) is desired. Based on suggestions from the literature review, the final choice fell on CenterNet ResNet50 V1 FPN (512×512) from the *TensorFlow 2 Detection Model Zoo* [20].

CenterNet [21] is a keypoint-based object detector, which means that it represents an object as a single point in the center of a generated bounding box. Other object properties, such as size and dimension, are obtained by moving from the center location towards the bounding box's outline. First, an input image is fed into a feature extractor (e.g., ResNet) in order to create a key-point heatmap. Peaks in the heatmap are mapped as object center points. An object's bounding box size is inferred from its center point.

1) Modified ResNet: The ResNet50 V1 FPN (512×512) is used as the object detector's feature extractor. The SIRST dataset contains images that are smaller than the original 512×512 pixels input size to the network. Thus, instead of upscaling the input images to 512×512 pixels, which would distort them, they are resized to 224×224 pixels. This is performed for the original ResNet50 as well.

We followed the general consensus reflected in most current research in the field that the downsampling operations of the feature extractor should be reduced to improve the detection of small objects. To achieve satisfactory results in terms of accuracy, the depth of the ResNet is maintained at 50 layers. The downsampling is reduced by changing the stride from 2 to 1 in the first convolutional layer of the original ResNet50. The output shape of the modified ResNet's last convolutional layer has an output shape of 14×14, whereas the output shape of the original ResNet's last convolutional layer has an output shape of 7×7.

2) Training the Data-driven Method: Training CNNs relies a great deal on matrix multiplications. GPUs (Graphics Processing Units) are well-suited for this type of computation, as their architecture allows for $100\times$ greater speed than CPUs (Central Processing Units) at this task [22].

The data-driven models are trained from scratch. The learning rate determines how fast the network learns. Goodfellow et al. [23] states that a high learning rate increases the training loss, while a low learning rate increases the risk of a slow training process, which, potentially, could become stuck at a high training loss. The original hyperparameters listed in Table I were used for training the data-driven methods, as these hyperparameters are commonly fine-tuned by the model's developers.

TABLE I: PIPELINE VALUES USED FOR TRAINING THE DATA-DRIVEN METHODS.

Pipeline values	
Warmup learning rate	2.5×10^{-4}
Base learning rate	0.001
Batch size	64 / 32
Warmup steps	5000

The batch size [23] is the number of training-samples from the dataset used in a single forward-pass. Typically, the batch size is less than the total number of training samples in the dataset. A large batch size consumes more memory. The data-driven method based on the original ResNet uses a batch size of 64. The modified ResNet uses a batch size of 32 due to the reduced downsampling which requires additional GPU memory. The training is stopped when the loss is stagnating. The training of the modified ResNet50 was stopped when the total training loss reached approximately 0.3, requiring significantly more steps than the original ResNet50, which had a training loss of approximately 0.15.

C. Model-driven Approach

The IPI model proposed by Gao et al. [8] is capable of producing accurate results even when confronted with complex scenes [9]. However, background edges, corners, or blobs infiltrate the sparse matrix, resulting in multiple discrepancies that the IPI model could treat as targets. In the IPI model, image patches from an IR image are rearranged using a sliding window to form a data matrix $\mathbf{D}$. The data matrix is then decomposed into a low-rank matrix $\mathbf{L}$ and a sparse matrix $\mathbf{S}$ using the Robust Principal Component Analysis (RPCA) algorithm in conjunction with the Principal Component Pursuit (PCP) [24]. Continuing with the IPI model, $\mathbf{D}$ can be decomposed into three components:

$$\mathbf{D} = \mathbf{L} + \mathbf{S} + \mathbf{N}, \tag{1}$$

where $\mathbf{N}$ is the noise. PCP can recover $\mathbf{L}$ and $\mathbf{S}$ from $\mathbf{D}$ by solving the following optimization problem [8]:

$$\min_{\mathbf{L},\mathbf{S}} \left(\|\mathbf{L}\|_* + \lambda \|\mathbf{S}\|_1 + \frac{1}{2\mu} \|\mathbf{D} - \mathbf{L} - \mathbf{S}\|_F^2 \right), \tag{2}$$

where μ and λ are positive-valued parameters.

The problem stated in Equation (2) can be solved through the Accelerated Proximal Gradient (APG). Solving RPCA-PCP via APG requires a significant amount of time to converge for a single IR small target image. Fortunately, however, several algorithms are available in the literature that solve the PCP. The proposed model-driven method is based on the IPI model [8] and RPCA-PCP via the Inexact Augmented Lagrangian Method (IALM) [25]. IALM is at least five times faster than APG and has a higher precision [26].

D. Evaluation Metrics

In the context of search and rescue missions, missed detection is more costly than false alarms, and this should be taken into account in the performance evaluation of the system. For the model-driven method, the sparse matrix $\mathbf{S}$ is the prediction. The center of a predicted target will be the location of pixels with a value higher than a certain threshold. The accuracy of the model-driven method is measured by checking if the center of the ground truth target intersects with the center of the predicted target. Additionally, the True Positive (TP), False Positive (FP), False Negative (FN), and True Negative (TN) outcomes are recorded after testing each method. To deem a prediction to be TP, the predicted location must be within proximity of the ground truth location. This includes situations where the predicted bounding box and the ground truth bounding box are proper subsets of one another.

An applicable evaluation metric is the F-score given by

$$F_\beta = \frac{(1+\beta^2)(PPV)(TPR)}{\beta^2 PPV + TPR}, \tag{3}$$

where PPV is the Positive Predictive Value, also known as *precision*, and TPR is the True Positive Rate, also known as *recall*. Precision is a measure of how many of the predicted targets correspond to ground truth targets, and recall is the number of ground truth targets detected. For the proposed system, it is preferable to select a $\beta = 2$ in Equation (3), as the recall is more critical for evaluating the proposed methods.

Another applicable metric is the Matthews Correlation Coefficient (MCC), which returns a value in the range $[-1, 1]$.

The modified SIRST dataset is unbalanced, as it contains 268 positive samples plus 210 negative samples. Chicco and Jurman [27] recommend using the MCC rather than $F_{\beta=1}$ when evaluating predictions from a binary classifier, as F_1 can produce inaccurate results when applied to unbalanced datasets. MCC can resolve this issue by assimilating the imbalance. The proposed methods should have a high recall, a high F_2, and a high MCC score.

E. Testing

The modified SIRST dataset was used for experimental evaluation of the model- and data-driven approaches. The dataset has 210 negative images and 214 positive images containing 268 IR small targets.

The model-driven methods MD-v1 and MD-v2 are evaluated by adjusting the parameters listed in Table II. The *tolerance* ϵ_1 is required by the stopping criterion. If the value of the stopping criterion is below ϵ_1 the solution of RPCA-PCP via IALM has converged. The *iteration* parameter is used to forcibly stop the IALM if it has not converged. Further, adjacent pixels with a value above the *threshold* produce an IR small target. A high threshold removes false positives, but it could also exclude true positive predictions.

TABLE II: MODEL-DRIVEN METHODS AND THEIR PARAMETERS.

Abbreviation	Tolerance (ϵ_1)	Iterations	Stride	Patch size	Threshold
MD-v1	0.1	500	20	80	150
MD-v2	0.01	1000	20	80	150

According to [8], a patch size of 80×80 pixels, and a sliding step or stride of 14 in the sliding window produces acceptable results. However, a stride of 20 was selected for MD-v1 and MD-v2 as this decreases the required computational time. Furthermore, if the patch size exceeds 80×80, performance degrades.

The score threshold S_{th} is adjusted when evaluating the data-driven methods. The score threshold discards predictions which have a confidence score less than S_{th}. Table III contains abbreviations used for the various data-driven methods.

TABLE III: ABBREVIATIONS FOR DATA-DRIVEN METHODS.

Abbreviation	Stride	Batch size	Score threshold (S_{th})
DD-v1-03	2	64	0.3
DD-v1-05	2	64	0.5
DD-v2-03	1	32	0.3
DD-v2-05	1	32	0.5

III. RESULTS

All results from evaluating the data-driven and model-driven methods on the modified SIRST dataset are shown in Table IV. The DD-v1 methods are clearly the fastest methods, with an average time of 0.2 seconds per image. A set of predictions performed by the proposed methods are shown in Figure 1. None of the methods are able to detect all five IR small targets in Figure 1a. However, four IR small targets were detected by MD-v2 and DD-v1-03, as shown in Figure 1c and 1e, respectively.

A. Analysis of the Model-driven Methods

As expected, and demonstrated in Table IV, the model-driven methods are inaccurate when compared to the data-driven methods. MD-v1 ($F_2 = 0.604$, $MCC = 0.224$, $PPV = 0.585$) outperforms MD-v2 ($F_2 = 0.586$, $MCC = -0.024$, $PPV = 0.345$) in terms of F_2, MCC and precision. In comparison to MD-v1, MD-v2 performs a meticulous decomposition, which may account for the low precision value, i.e., the large share of FP predictions.

MD-v2 with a reduced patch size and stride extracts excess noise from the image. In addition, a low patch size and stride results in a longer processing time.

To summarize, the MD-v1 and MD-v2 cannot compete with the data-driven methods in terms of accuracy. Also, MD-v1 and MD-v2 have an excessive computational time, requiring approximately 5 seconds per image. The lengthy computation time is primarily caused by the sliding window and singular value decomposition used for solving RPCA-PCP via IALM. The model-driven methods are, however, effective at identifying targets in complex environments.

B. Analysis of the Data-driven Methods

As illustrated in Table IV, all data-driven methods have a high precision, with the best scores going to DD-v2-05 ($PPV = 0.990$). A S_{th} of 0.3 results in a high recall, MCC and F_2. A $S_{th} < 0.3$ will introduce additional FP predictions. A S_{th} equal to 0.5 discards a portion of the false predictions, however, this also reduces the TP predictions. Further, an even higher S_{th} increases the amount of FN predictions. This is not desirable, as the system should aim at detecting all potential targets.

DD-v1-03 ($F_2 = 0.908$, $MCC = 0.817$, $TPR = 0.904$) and DD-v2-03 ($F_2 = 0.900$, $MCC = 0.842$, $TPR = 0.885$) are the most accurate methods. DD-v2-03 has a marginally lower F_2 than DD-v1-03. DD-v1-03 has the highest recall and F_2, and is the most appropriate approach for IR small target detection when considering the average time required to process a single image. DD-v1-03 processes a single image in approximately 0.2 seconds. However, this is not comparable to running object detection on a continuous video stream. The processing speed would, however, be higher if the methods were deployed on a GPU-equipped machine.

There is no statistically significant difference between the modified (stride = 1) and original (stride = 2) ResNet50 in terms of performance. This might originate from the modified ResNet50 not being downsampled sufficiently, or alternatively, the original ResNet50 already had suitable feature map sizes. Further reduction of the downsampling operations results in a slower system. As shown in Table IV, the modified ResNet models (i.e., DD-v2-03 and DD-v2-05) run slower due to the increased parameter count caused by the reduced downsampling.

The modified ResNet was trained with a batch size of 32, which is likely to be the reason why the training process is slower than the training of the original ResNet. A low batch size should result in a model that generalizes well

TABLE IV: RESULTS FROM EVALUATING THE DATA-DRIVEN AND MODEL-DRIVEN METHODS.

Metric	MD-v1	MD-v2	DD-v2-03	DD-v2-05	DD-v1-03	DD-v1-05
Recall	0.610	0.711	0.885	0.722	**0.904**	0.800
Precision	0.585	0.345	0.966	**0.990**	0.926	0.963
MCC	0.224	−0.024	**0.842**	0.720	0.817	0.760
F_2	0.604	0.586	0.900	0.763	**0.908**	0.828
Avg. time [s]	4.98	5.04	0.85	0.8	**0.2**	**0.2**

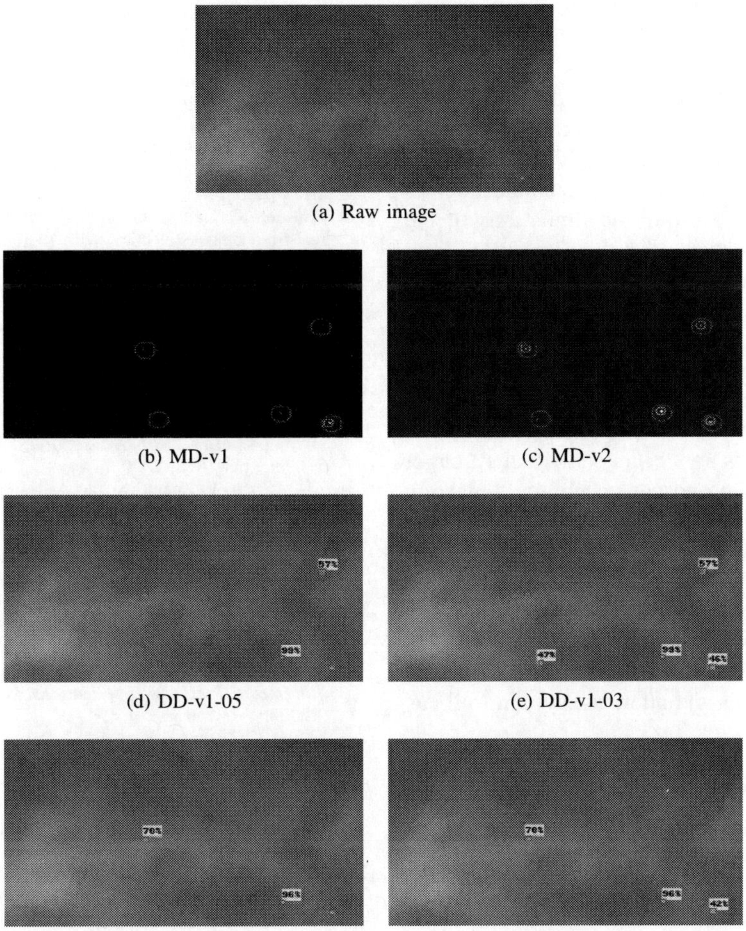

(a) Raw image

(b) MD-v1 (c) MD-v2

(d) DD-v1-05 (e) DD-v1-03

(f) DD-v2-05 (g) DD-v2-03

Figure 1: Predictions performed by proposed methods. Red boxes represent the ground truth targets. Green boxes represent predictions. (a) raw image from the dataset. (b) obtained using MD-v1. (c) obtained using MD-v2. (d) obtained using DD-v1-05. (e) obtained using DD-v1-03. (f) obtained using DD-v2-05. (g) obtained using DD-v2-03.

to previously unobserved data. Yet, there are no significant differences between using a batch size of 64 or 32 in terms of accuracy. The high accuracy of the data-driven methods could be the result of using the CenterNet meta-architecture with the ResNet feature extractor. CenterNet appears to perform well at the task of IR small target detection as it extracts peaks from keypoint heatmaps generated by ResNet.

IV. Discussion

What should the system do when a target or multiple targets are detected? Further, how can the location of a target be determined? Another challenge is to define how the system should behave in response to previously predicted targets. The system could register specific GPS positions. Moreover, the system should ignore heat signatures coming from the ground crew. Computational cost of CNNs results in slow inference on computationally constrained devices. Due to physical constraints, the system proposed in this work will have limited onboard computational power. To accelerate intensive tasks, edge computing can be used. Edge computing requires data transfer from the UAV to the *edge*, where required computations are carried out, then the results are relayed back to the UAV. This is a challenging task, and will likely result in unacceptable latency [28]. With edge computing, a collection of computing devices brings the capability to solve computationally intensive tasks closer to the UAVs, thereby reducing latency [28]. However, the computers located at the edge may be insufficient to perform real-time (e.g., more than 20 frames per second) inference due to restricted memory and processing power.

V. CONCLUSION AND FUTURE WORK

This work investigates the detection of IR small targets. The results of using autonomous UAVs, IR imaging, and object detection to assist search and rescue missions are promising. In particular, a model-driven approach based on low-rank and sparse matrix decomposition which employs RPCA-PCP via IALM, and a deep learning-based data-driven approach using CenterNet with ResNet proved to be suitable choices towards solving this problem. Despite the limitations of the dataset, experimental results indicate that the proposed system is effective at detecting IR small targets. As expected, the data-driven approach outperformed the model-driven approach. Although accurate, however, the data-driven methods are slow. Training the data-driven methods on additional IR small target samples will further improve their accuracy.

The results of this work establish unequivocally that CNN-based object detection methods are accurate at IR small target detection. Conclusively, the proposed system can make a substantial impact by assisting search and rescue missions. Several areas are worth investigating further. The IR small target detection system remains incomplete. Validation of the proposed system in real-world circumstances should be given considerable attention. Furthermore, target tracking methods should be researched as they could increase the system's ability to locate missing victims and allow the system to focus on a single target if necessary.

ACKNOWLEDGMENT

This study was financed in part by the Norwegian Agency for International Cooperation and Quality Enhancement in Higher Education (Diku), project number UTF-2018-CAPES-Diku/10002, and in part by the Coordenação de Aperfeiçoamento de Pessoal de Nível Superior—Brasil (CAPES), finance code n° 23038.018065/2018-17.

REFERENCES

[1] DJI. (2020, 12) DJI counts more than 500 people rescued by drones around the world. https://www.dji.com/newsroom/news/dji-counts-more-than-500-people-rescued-by-drones-around-the-world, retrieved: 2021.10.27.

[2] J. Frantzen. (2020, 4) Missing elderly woman found by drone pilot: Drones are saving lives in Norway (*Savnet eldre kvinne funnet av dronepilot: Nå redder droner liv i Norge*). https://www.uasnorway.no/savnet-funnet-av-dronepilot-na-redder-droner-liv-ogsa-i-norge, retrieved: 2021.10.27.

[3] K. Wang, S. Li, S. Niu, and K. Zhang, "Detection of infrared small targets using feature fusion convolutional network," *IEEE Access*, vol. 7, pp. 146 081–146 092, 2019.

[4] H. Zhang *et al.*, "A novel infrared video surveillance system using deep learning based techniques," *Multimedia tools and applications*, vol. 77, no. 20, pp. 26 657–26 676, 2018.

[5] Y. Dai, Y. Wu, F. Zhou, and K. Barnard, "Attentional local contrast networks for infrared small target detection," *CoRR*, vol. abs/2012.08573, 2020. [Online]. Available: http://arxiv.org/abs/2012.08573

[6] Y. Dai, Y. Wu, F. Zhou, and K. Barnard, "Asymmetric contextual modulation for infrared small target detection," in *IEEE Winter Conference on Applications of Computer Vision, WACV 2021*, 01 2021, pp. 949–958.

[7] M. Vollmer and K. Möllmann, *Infrared Thermal Imaging: Fundamentals, Research and Applications*. Wiley, 02 2018.

[8] C. Gao *et al.*, "Infrared patch-image model for small target detection in a single image," *Image Processing, IEEE Transactions on*, vol. 22, no. 12, pp. 4996–5009, 2013.

[9] H. Wang, M. Shi, and H. Li, "Infrared dim and small target detection based on two-stage u-skip context aggregation network with a missed-detection-and-false-alarm combination loss," *Multimedia Tools and Applications*, vol. 79, no. 47, pp. 35 383–35 404, 2020.

[10] S. L. Brunton and J. N. Kutz, *Data-Driven Science and Engineering: Machine Learning, Dynamical Systems, and Control*. Cambridge University Press, 2019.

[11] T.-Y. Lin *et al.*, "Feature pyramid networks for object detection," *CoRR*, vol. abs/1612.03144, 2017. [Online]. Available: http://arxiv.org/abs/1612.03144

[12] S. Ren, K. He, R. Girshick, and J. Sun, "Faster R-CNN: Towards real-time object detection with region proposal networks," *CoRR*, vol. abs/1506.01497, 2016. [Online]. Available: http://arxiv.org/abs/1506.01497

[13] J. Redmon, S. K. Divvala, R. B. Girshick, and A. Farhadi, "You Only Look Once: Unified, real-time object detection," *CoRR*, vol. abs/1506.02640, 2016. [Online]. Available: http://arxiv.org/abs/1506.02640

[14] G. Chen *et al.*, "A survey of the four pillars for small object detection: Multiscale representation, contextual information, super-resolution, and region proposal," *IEEE Transactions on Systems, Man, and Cybernetics: Systems*, pp. 1–18, 2020.

[15] Z.-Q. Zhao, P. Zheng, S. tao Xu, and X. Wu, "Object detection with deep learning: A review," *CoRR*, vol. abs/1807.05511, 2019. [Online]. Available: https://arxiv.org/abs/1807.05511

[16] H. Fang, M. Chen, X. Liu, and S. Yao, "Infrared small target detection with total variation and reweighted ℓ_1 regularization," *Mathematical Problems in Engineering*, vol. 2020, pp. 1–19, 1 2020.

[17] Y. Dai. (2021) Yimiandai/sirst. https://github.com/YimianDai/sirst, retrieved: 2021.10.27.

[18] Y. Xiao *et al.*, "A review of object detection based on deep learning," *Multimedia Tools and Applications*, vol. 79, no. 33, pp. 23 729–23 791, 9 2020.

[19] K. He, X. Zhang, S. Ren, and J. Sun, "Deep residual learning for image recognition," *CoRR*, vol. abs/1512.03385, 2015. [Online]. Available: https://arxiv.org/abs/1512.03385

[20] TensorFlow. (2020, 9) TensorFlow 2 Detection Model Zoo. https://github.com/tensorflow/models/blob/master/research/object_detection/g3doc/tf2_detection_zoo.md", retrieved: 2021.10.27.

[21] X. Zhou, D. Wang, and P. Krähenbühl, "Objects as points," *CoRR*, vol. abs/1904.07850, 2019. [Online]. Available: https://arxiv.org/abs/1904.07850

[22] B. Pang, E. Nijkamp, and Y. N. Wu, "Deep learning with TensorFlow: A review," *Journal of Educational and Behavioral Statistics*, vol. 45, no. 2, pp. 227–248, 2020.

[23] I. Goodfellow, Y. Bengio, and A. Courville, *Deep Learning*. MIT Press, 2016. [Online]. Available: http://www.deeplearningbook.org

[24] E. J. Candès, X. Li, Y. Ma, and J. Wright, "Robust principal component analysis?" *CoRR*, vol. abs/0912.3599, 2009. [Online]. Available: https://arxiv.org/abs/0912.3599

[25] Z. Lin, M. Chen, and Y. Ma, "The augmented Lagrange multiplier method for exact recovery of corrupted low-rank matrices," *CoRR*, vol. abs/1009.5055, 2010. [Online]. Available: https://arxiv.org/abs/1009.5055

[26] T. Bouwmans, A. Sobral, S. Javed, S. K. Jung, and E.-H. Zahzah, "Decomposition into low-rank plus additive matrices for background/-foreground separation: A review for a comparative evaluation with a large-scale dataset," *Computer Science Review*, vol. 23, p. 1–71, 2 2017.

[27] D. Chicco and G. Jurman, "The advantages of the Matthews Correlation Coefficient (MCC) over F1 score and accuracy in binary classification evaluation," *BMC Genomics*, vol. 21, no. 1, p. 6, 2020.

[28] J. Chen and X. Ran, "Deep learning with edge computing: A review," *Proceedings of the IEEE*, vol. 107, no. 8, pp. 1655–1674, 2019.

3D Reconstruction with Drone Images: Optimization by Reinforcement Learning

Thiago João Miranda Baldivieso
Department of Defense Engineering
Military Institute of Engineering
Rio de Janeiro, Brazil
e-mail: thiagojmb@ime.eb.br

Taise Grazielle da Silva Batista
Department of Defense Engineering
Military Institute of Engineering
Rio de Janeiro, Brazil
e-mail: taisegbs@ime.eb.br

Luiz Carlos Pacheco Rodrigues Velho
Department of Computer Graphics
Institute for Pure and Applied Mathematics
Rio de Janeiro, Brazil
email: lvelho@impa.br

Paulo Fernando Ferreira Rosa
Department of Defense Engineering
Military Institute of Engineering
Rio de Janeiro, Brazil
e-mail: rpaulo@ime.eb.br

***Abstract*—This paper aims to develop three-dimensional reconstructions using aerial images in different environments and using dedicated software. The subject is relevant to this conference because, due to the characteristics of photogrammetry with UAV/drone, they provide easy access, accuracy, and time-saving and mission equipment for civil and military applications. During the study, experiments were carried out with aircraft in an external and internal environment. After acquiring aerial images, the reconstruction was carried out in specific photogrammetry software, with typical commercial and open-source software, followed by a qualitative evaluation of the results. Concluding with indications for improvements and future research work related to artificial intelligence techniques using machine learning and reinforcement learning to optimize.**

Keywords*—*Dimensional Reconstruction; UAV; Aerophotogrammetry

I. INTRODUCTION

With increasing demand and actual needs, the functions and performance of Unmanned Aerial Vehicles (UAVs) are continually advancing. Technological advances mainly drive the area of microprocessors, sensing, communications, and open demands in the areas of computer vision and computer graphics in the reconstruction of objects and threedimensional environments. Furthermore, applications with autonomous and semi-autonomous UAVs, characterized with total or partial independence from human operators, provide greater visibility in the image, as it is not necessary for the operator to aim the aircraft during the entire mission. Furthermore, in the scope of applications in the civil and military sectors, it has reduced operating costs and encouraged financing initiatives in the area.

The use of unmanned aerial vehicles for three-dimensional mapping and reconstruction requires mission planning considering the object or environment from which the images will be taken and factors that can influence the process, such as weather, lighting, target geometry, camera calibration, and type of aircraft used. With the studies carried out based on reference works, it is possible to observe that some parameters are not considered, such as attitude control, calling attention to observe the parameters that influence and if not using any parameter is valid for the process as a whole.

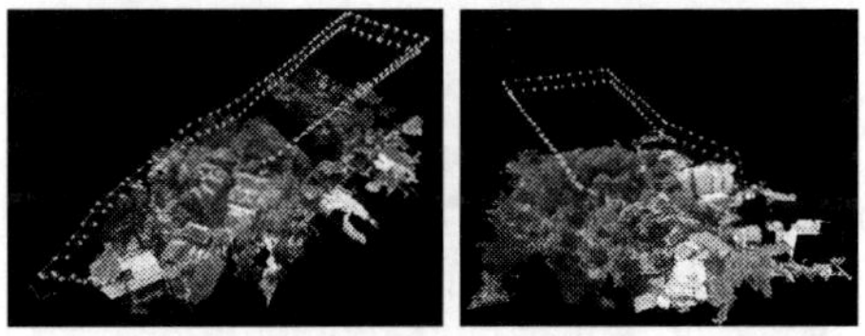

Figure 1. Mapped and reconstructed outdoor area.

Three-dimensional reconstruction is a highly researched area in computer vision and scientific visualization. Its objective is to obtain a three-dimensional geometric representation of environments or objects, making it possible to inspect details, measure properties, and reproduce them in different materials. Applications with UAVs can help in architecture, 3D cartography, robotics, augmented reality, conservation of monuments, and historical heritage [2]. There are several ways to get information related to the 3D geometry of an object, environment, or body. They can be acquired by laser scanning, photographs, sonar, tomography, and 3D sonar. On the other hand, photo-based systems make 3D reconstructions from a single photo or with several photos at different angles, using multiple photos, which after image registration, consists of transforming different sets of data into a coordinate system. After this step, visual reference points are defined, automatically generated by the reconstruction software, or entered manually. To establish typical visual landmarks in the scene to identify joint edges of the object to be processed in the photographs. From the processing of this information, three-dimensional geometry is obtained. In addition, each photograph is registered by the UAV with information about the location of the Global Positioning System (GPS) sensor and the time of capture, information that is also considered in the processing to obtain the model's georeferencing. Figure 1 presents a result of the 3D reconstruction of an external scene. The green dots are the poses of the drone's camera.

Given the above, the project in which this work is part aims to relate images captured by UAVs to develop three-dimensional reconstructions from them and the continued study for optimization with learning by reinforcement.

Section 2 of this work presents the methodology with some relevant concepts for understanding. Then, in section 3, some experiments that were carried out are described. Then, in section 4, the results were discussed, and finally, in section 5, the conclusion with the analysis of what was proposed.

II. METHODOLOGY

In recent years, aircraft used for terrain mapping in civil and military applications have been widely explored, especially unmanned aircraft and their use related to three-dimensional reconstruction.

Computer vision is defined as the science and technology of machines that see. In [3], the author develops theory and technology for the construction of artificial systems for obtaining information from images or any multidimensional data

The concepts of machine vision were initially restricted to the construction of lenses and cameras for image capture and operations. However, over the past few years, this reality has been modernized due to the growth of artificial intelligence and the application of the concept of neural networks, along with the improvement of studies on the self-progression of algorithms, known as machine learning [4]. Soon then, computer vision can be included in a sub-area of Artificial Intelligence that addresses how machines see the environment. Furthermore, a body of knowledge that seeks the artificial modeling of vision can also be defined to replicate its functions through advanced software and hardware development.

Applied 3D reconstruction software uses the Structure for Motion method [5], which uses said relative motion for the inference about the 3D geometry of the object to be reconstructed. The methodology also encompasses bundle adjustment, which initially compares the key point descriptors identified in the images to determine between two or more similar images. Then a procedure optimization is performed to infer the camera positions for the collection of images.

Structure From Motion (SfM) is a range imaging technique studied in machine vision and visual perception. The SfM methodology uses this relative motion to infer the 3D geometry of the object to be reconstructed. It takes into account the point trajectories of the object in the image plane and allows the determination of the 3D shape and movement that best reproduces most of the estimated trajectories. The process is similar to stereoscopic vision in that it is done to obtain two or more images of a scene from different points of view [6].

Consider a picture arrangement comprising of K pictures I_k, with K = 1,...,K. Leave A_k alone the 3 x 4 camera framework comparing to picture I_k. Utilizing the compared highlight focuses, the boundaries of a camera model A_k are assessed for each casing [5]. As displayed in Figure 2, for each element track a relating 3D item point not really set in stone, bringing about set of J 3D article focuses P_j, with j = 1,...,J, where:

$$p_{j,k} \simeq A_k Pj \tag{1}$$

Accordingly, the 2D component focuses $p_{j,k} = (p_x, p_y, 1)^T$ and 3D item focuses $P_j = (p_x, p_y, p_z, 1)^T$ are given inhomogeneous directions.

The camera network A can be factorized into

$$A = KR[I| - C] \tag{2}$$

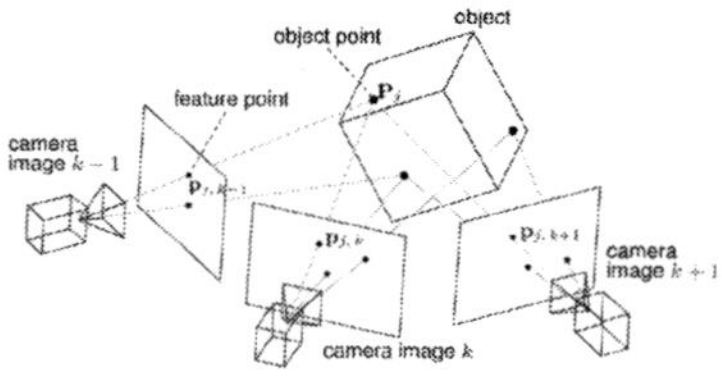

Figure 2. Result after structure-from-motion estimation. The projection of a 3D object point Pj in the camera image at time k gives the tracked 2D feature point $P_{j,k}$ [6]

The 3 x 3 adjustment lattice K contains the inherent camera boundaries (e.g., central length or chief point offset), R is the 3 x 3 turn framework addressing the camera directly in the scene, and the camera place C depicts the situation of the camera in the scene. SFM is considered state of the art in reconstruction software because it solves camera poses and lens calibration in addition to defining geometries [5].

3D reconstruction is an old problem. Ways to improve the process have become a focus of research with reconstruction forms using current AI that reinforces the use of SFM by programs. In [4] provides a comprehensive survey of recent developments in this field, works that use deep learning techniques to estimate the 3D shape of generic objects. The work provides an analysis and comparison of the performance of some critical documents, summarizing some of the open problems in this field and discussing promising directions for future research.

III. EXPERIMENTS

We performed several experiments, which can be seen in Table I, outdoor and indoor experiments, using UAVs and also ground cameras. After the images were taken, reconstructions were carried out in different software such as PIX4D, Metashape, OpenDroneMap, and Colmap using default configurations.

BOC 60 is the new campus of the Institute of Pure and Applied Mathematics (IMPA) to be built in Jardim Botanico, in the ^ south of the city of Rio de Janeiro.

In the flight test of Figure 3, it was with the help of GPS in an urban setting with different types of buildings, vegetation, and complex shapes, resulting in three-dimensional models with high processing demand when performing the image matching step. These outdoor flights were carried out in partnership with IMPA with the UAV research group of

TABLE I
GENERATED DATASETS, IMAGES AND RECONSTRUCTION SOFTWARES USED.

Dataset generated	Acquisition Device	Images	PIX4D	Meta-shape	ODM	RC
Crystal's valley	Mavic Pro	337	x	x	x	
BOC 60 - High Res.	Mavic Pro	302	x	x	x	
BOC 60 - Med. Res.	Mavic Pro	169	x	x	x	
BOC 60 - Low Res.	Mavic Pro	138	x	x	x	
LARC	Sub-250	150	x	x		
PIRF - Fan Scene	Tello	62				x
PIRF - Human Scene	Tello	50			x	x
PIRF - Bags Scene	Smartphone	217	x			
Object - Plant	Tello	35	x	x		x
Object - Robot	Smartphone	154	x			
Object - Castell	Smartphone	64	x	x	x	x

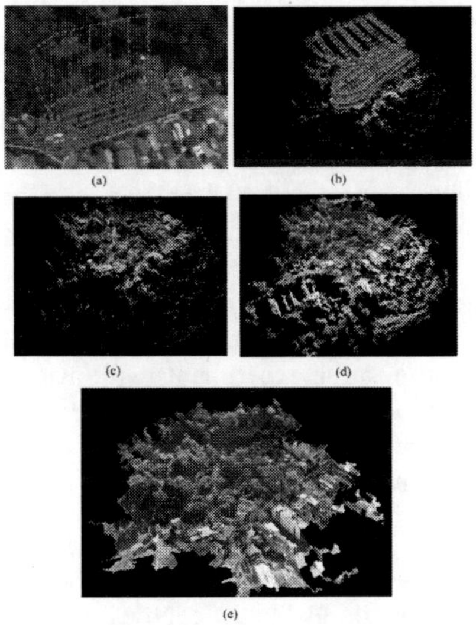

Figure 3. BOC 60 Steps to Rebuild PIX4D software; (a) Snapshot points on the map; (b) 3D image taking points; (c) Tie Points; (d) Dense cloud of points; (e) Textured 3D Model.

Figure 4. Visual comparison of three-dimensional reconstruction results.

the Laboratory of Robotics and Computational Intelligence of IME to obtain images aimed at aero photogrammetry and create a dataset. More information about it is in [7].

The outdoor experiment was divided into three missions aiming to obtain a differentiated resolution, high resolution, medium resolution, and low resolution, with the variation of height and number of photos obtained.

Next, in Figure 3, the steps for reconstruction are observed, in (a) all points of image collection by the UAV are gathered, then in (b) the camera pose is presented (position + orientation) in a three-dimensional plane; (c) shows the initial step in which the tie points are characteristic points mapped between the images; (d) are the initial points gathered clustered with neighboring points resulting in a dense cloud of points; and finally in (e) the three-dimensional object is obtained in which a mesh structure and texture connect the cloud of points is applied based on a montage of images, forming an object close to urban reality.

With the creation of the dataset of images, the next step was to reconstruct the mapped terrain. For this, three different software were used for the three-dimensional reconstruction. They are PIX4D (whose process was discussed earlier), Metashape, and OpenDroneMap. The visual comparison between results can be seen in Figure 4. Another outdoor experiment can be visualized in our generated dataset [7].

Another experiment was related to the use of a Ground Truth model of a medieval castle. First, the object was printed to obtain the physical object. The model is available from the website Thingiverse, modeled on two castles: Schloss Lichtenstein and Neuschwanstein Castle, both located in Germany. In addition, authors of the design and graphic modeling of the object make it available for download through [8]. Next, in Figure 5, you can see the file to be printed and the part that has already been printed. The model is approximately one meter high and is divided into 22 pieces, the model used in the experiment was glued by the assembly instructions, but due to deformations caused during printing, some parts need finishing and painting to be as close as possible the virtual model.

Figure 5. Medieval Castle experiment, 3D file visualization, printed parts and image of dataset.

The experiment with the medieval castle printed in 3D was carried out in order to generate a reconstructed model to later compare with a new experiment to be carried out using a UAV on an indoor scene. In this partial experiment, the acquisition of the image collection was performed using a smartphone camera. Soon after obtaining the images, processing in three-dimensional reconstruction software was performed. With these results and the following experiments, the aim is to apply reinforcement machine learning algorithms to optimize the generated three-dimensional models.

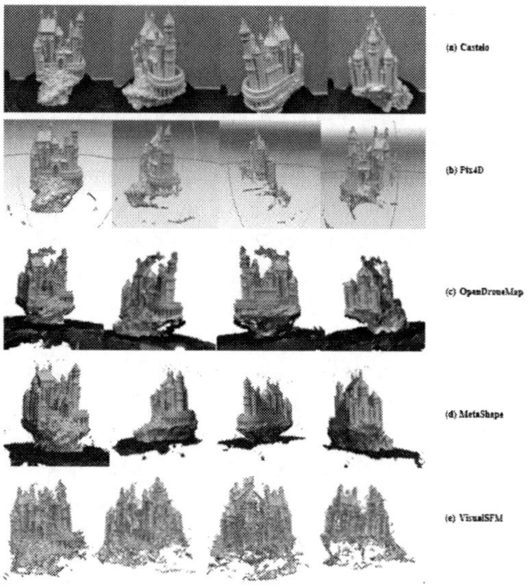

Figure 6. Medieval Castle experiment, reconstruction using different tools.

IV. Discussion

With the particularities of each tool, the clouds of generated points present their differences, and it becomes interesting to compare them for analysis of the results.

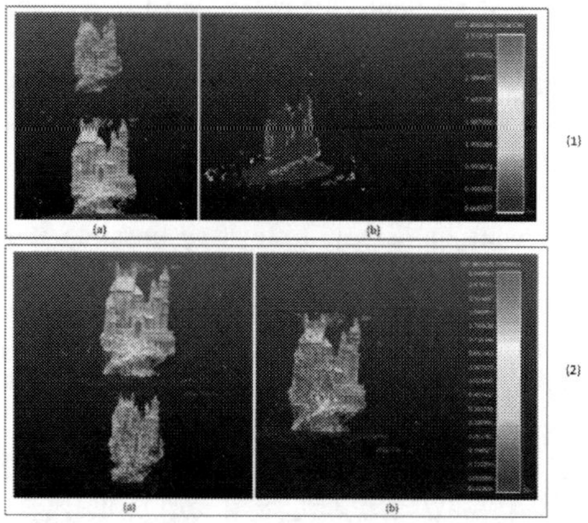

Figure 7. Comparison point cloud Metashape and OpenDroneMap. (1) Metashape reference. (2) OpenDroneMap reference. (a) Insertpoint cloud; (b) Generated heat map.

CloudCompare software was used for comparison between point clouds [9]. CloudCompare is a point cloud processing tool with multiple metrics; it is an open-source and free project with a framework that provides a set of essential tools for manually editing and rendering 3D point clouds and triangular meshes.

The initial analyses were carried out from the reconstruction of the image set of the medieval castle that obtained a good result. Since not all tools make the files available to be exported, the comparison was performed with the files generated by the Metashape and OpenDroneMap tools.

For the research, an analysis of the distance between points with heat cloud generation was performed, the clouds generated in each tool were inserted, and the analysis was performed in two stages. The first step was using the cloud generated by Metashape as a reference cloud. The second step was using the cloud generated by OpenDroneMap as a reference cloud. The result obtained is shown in Figure 7.

It is observed that the distance between the points of the clouds presents a significant difference, and the scale and orientation factors of each cloud must be treated with due care in the comparison. With the result generated, it is possible to qualitatively analyze the generated clouds and identify the software that presents better performance and the need for improvements through machine learning by reinforcement.

V. Conclusion and Future Work

The contribution made by this project includes the creation of datasets with scenes and 3D objects obtained through reconstruction and images captured by drones. These data are available to the academic community and have several capture devices, processed by exposed dedicated software in Table 1. In the continuation of the work, it is expected to use these data for optimization experiments with machine learning and reinforcement learning to improve the distortions caused during image processing and increase the visible accuracy of the three-dimensional models.

Acknowledgement

This study was financed in part by the Coordenação de Aperfeiçoamento de Pessoal de Nível Superior - Brasil (CAPES) - Finance Code 001. This work was carried out with the support of the Cooperation Program Academic in National Defense (PROCAD-DEFESA). It is also aligned with the cooperation project between BRICS institutions related to computer vision and applications of AI techniques.

References

[1] E. Casella, et al. "Mapping coral reefs using consumer-grade drones and structure from motion photogrammetry techniques". Coral Reefs, vol. 36, pp.269–275, 2017.
[2] E. Colica, et al. "Using unmanned aerial vehicle photogrammetry for digital geological surveys: case study of Selmun promontory, northern of Malta". Environ Earth Sci 80, pp. 551, 2021.
[3] I. Craig, Vision as process. Robotica, Cambridge University Press, vol. 13, n. 5, pp. 540, 1995.
[4] X. Han, H. Laga and M. Bennamoun, "Image-Based 3D Object Reconstruction: State-of-the-Art and Trends in the Deep Learning Era", IEEE Transactions on Pattern Analysis and Machine Intelligence, vol. 43, no. 05, pp. 1578-1604, 2021.
[5] S. M. Seitz, B. Curless, and J. Diebel, and D. Scharstein, and R. Szeliski, "A Comparison and Evaluation of Multi-View Stereo Reconstruction Algorithms," 2006 IEEE Computer Society Conference on Computer Vision and Pattern Recognition (CVPR'06), 2006.
[6] C. Kurz, T. Thormählen, and H. Siedel, "Visual Fixation for 3D Video Stabilization". Journal of Virtual Reality and Broadcasting, pp. 12, 2011.
[7] L. C. P. Velho, Drone Datasets. 2020. Available at: https://www.visgraf.impa.br/dds/boc60/index.html [Retrieved: November, 2021]
[8] Boldmachines, Medieval Castle, 2018. Available at: https://www.thingiverse.com/thing:862724 [Retrieved: November, 2021]
[9] CloudCompare - Open Source Project. Available at: https://www.cloudcompare.org [Retrieved: November, 2021]

Influences on the Detection Probability of Ferromagnetic Objects

Lukas Heindler
Johannes Kepler University Linz
Linz, Austria
email: lukas.heindler@jku.at

Ruben Piepgras
Johannes Kepler University Linz
Linz, Austria
email: ruben.piepgras@jku.at

Bernhard G. Zagar
Johannes Kepler University Linz
Linz, Austria
email: bernhard.zagar@jku.at

***Abstract*—The detection of small masses of ferromagnetic materials within an existing magnetic circuit can be very challenging. It is particularly difficult if the ferromagnetic material is only coupled loosely via comparably large air gaps while the rest of the circuit is ferromagnetic as well as a good electrical conductor. The problem is further aggravated by the fact that the mass can exhibit a substantial remanence of unknown strength and polarity. In principle, the influence of remanence would be suppressed using an AC excitation of the readout circuit. However, this would excite very strong eddy currents in any conductor within and in close proximity to the sensing device. Thus, even non-magnetic metallic components would cause a non-zero measurement reading. Therefore, we optimized a DC magnetic circuit that allows the detection of ferromagnetic materials. In our use case, we concentrated on cylindrical objects separated from the sensor by an air gap of up to 5 cm.**

***Index Terms*—magnetic field; Hall sensor; remanence; magnetic disturbances**

I. Introduction

Detecting ferromagnetic objects with a coil induced magnetic field over a certain distance from the sensor relies amongst other things on the size of the solenoid. It determines how far the magnetic field extends, as well as the change of reluctance caused by the object within the magnetic circuit. Ideally, this idea of the measurement works over any separation of the object from the sensor and with any disturbance, like an object's remanence. In reality, however, the finite resolution of the sensing element is limited to certain constraints. For different use cases, different sensors for magnetic fields are available which differ in price, precision, size, and sensibility. Simple Hall-effect sensors [8, page 48-18] are widely used in many areas because of reliability, size, and robustness against mechanical impacts. Typical implementations [8, page 48-1] of Hall sensors are position sensors [8, page 6-119], frequency sensors [8, page 16-10], limit position switches, current sensing meters [8, page 38-6], angular velocity and flow rate meters [8, page 6-21] to name a few. Usual sensitivities of Hall-effect sensors reach from $32.5\,\mathrm{mV/mT}$ to more than $50\,\mathrm{mV/mT}$ with a range of up to thousands of mT. In our particular use case, the sensor has a sensitivity of $100\,\mathrm{mV/mT}$ and a range of $\pm 20\,\mathrm{mT}$. In Figure 1, the schematic of our setup is shown with all relevant components. Please note that for confidentiality reasons, the ferromagnetic object of the magnetic circuit, is not indicated here. The Hall sensor is attached in close proximity to the end face of a cuboid iron core with a length of $l_C = 69\,\mathrm{mm}$ and equal sides of $w_C = 18.5\,\mathrm{mm}$ in width. Furthermore, the characterization setup consists of an xy-translation stage driven by two Oriel stepper motors, allowing micrometer displacement resolution. For the characterization of the prototype of our envisioned sensor we are targeting a measurement grid of 195 times 40 measurements, with a lateral displacement per step of $\Delta x = 250\,\mu\mathrm{m}$ and $\Delta y = 1200\,\mu\mathrm{m}$ and axially of $\Delta z = 480\,\mu\mathrm{m}$, resulting in a measurement data matrix of 7800 readings. Detection results of ferromagnetic objects using a solenoid and a Hall sensor, can greatly vary if the object has a remanent magnetic field. Therefore the impact of a remanence on the existing measurement system will be discussed in the following sections.

Furthermore, this contribution is structured in four more sections. In Section II, we detail and characterize the sensing element. The results of which are used to decide on the magnetic field sensor principle. Section III details the devised measurement system, and Section IV provides some selected measurement results, limited to simple cylindrical test objects.

II. Theory of Sensor Operation

Understanding the underlying sensor principles is necessary to follow the decision making during our work. Therefore, some theory is presented in this section.

A. Hall-Effect, Lorentz Force, and Remanence

Electric current is defined as charge per time which passes through a specified area. If a conductor is placed in a magnetic field, the Lorentz force [8] deflects charge carriers out of their paths following the locally acting electric field. The Lorentz force is given by

$$\mathbf{F}_\mathrm{L} = Q \cdot (\mathbf{v} \times \mathbf{B}) \ , \tag{1}$$

where Q is a charge, $\mathbf{v}$ its mean velocity, and $\mathbf{B}$ a magnetic field.

In Figure 2, a schematic sensor is shown. A Hall-effect sensor consists of a semi-conducting thin sheet with a thickness much smaller than its width and length. Driven by a constant control current, it allows to measure the magnetic flux density component B_y passing the sensor's surface orthogonally. The charges of the control current get deflected, resulting in the

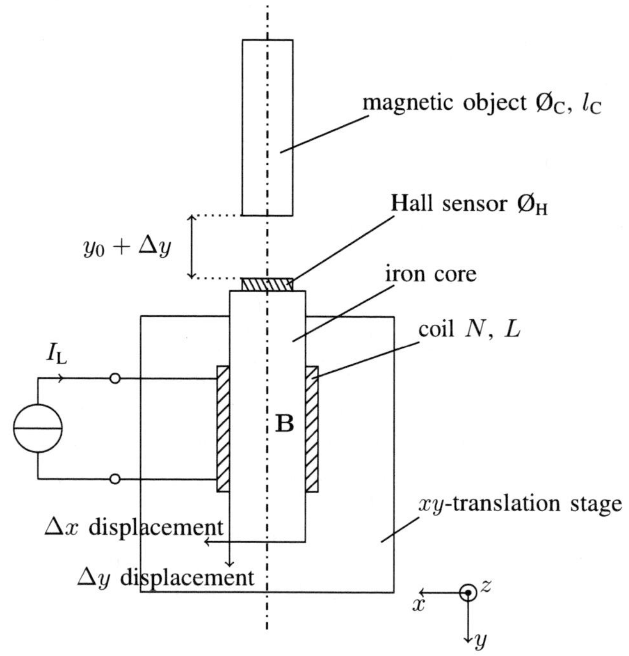

Fig. 1. The schematic of the built measure consisting of the magnetic object, Hall sensor, iron core, coil, translation stage, and the current source.

formation of an electric field strength component E_x that can be picked up. This yields a measurement proportional to the magnetic field strength. Applying the right-hand-rule a current, and a magnetic field result in a voltage between the electrodes orthogonal to both.

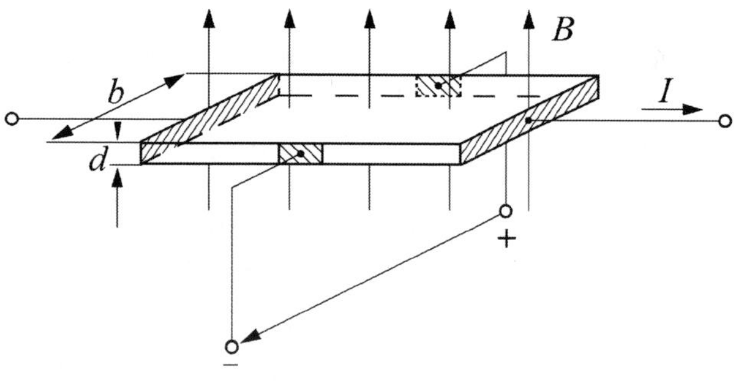

Fig. 2. The schematic of a Hall sensor [1].

magnetic fields may be caused by electric currents or magnetizations. We also analyze magnetic objects with respect to their remanent magnetizations. Remanence describes the remaining magnetic field of a body after magnetization and removal of the external magnetic field. Figure 3 shows a typical hysteresis loop for a soft magnetic iron. In the hysteresis curve remanence can be displayed on the ordinate where the external magnetic excitation H is zero [8].

Since we are interested in the detection of a ferromagnetic object in a certain distance to the sensor, any magnetic remanence is limiting the sensitivity of our setup. It is thus essential, to characterize the existing prototype with respect to its susceptibility to remanence close to the sensor.

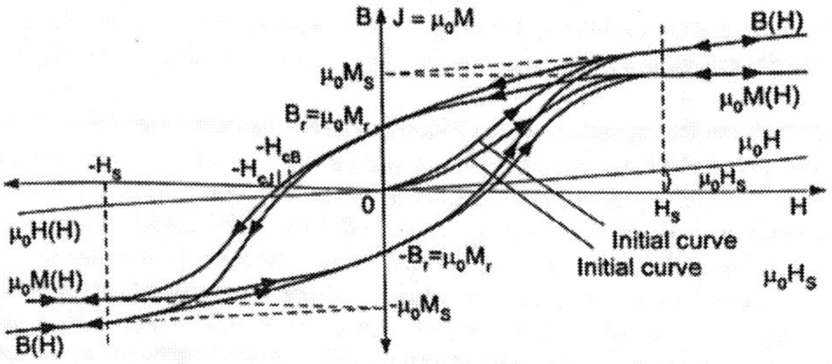

Fig. 3. Magnetic hysteresis curves including the initial curves. On the abscissa is the external magnetic field H and on the ordinate the remanent magnetic flux density B_r [2].

III. SENSOR SYSTEM

Initial analyses and experiments resulted in the choice of using a Hall-effect type sensing element. It satisfies sensitvity and temperature constraints, as well as assembly requirements.

Considerations concerning the type of magnetic excitation used, either direct current (DC) or alternating current (AC), were quickly settled for a DC-excited electromagnet. The reason is the fact that it is undetermined whether the complete system will be used and operated in close proximity to electrically conducting structural components. These would cause severe eddy currents artefacts whose secondary magnetic fields would strongly influence the detection probability.

In this section, we detail the steps to characterize the sensor system and determine its vulnerability to external magnetic fields. Whether they are caused by ferromagnetic objects located close-by or by eddy currents. Eddy currents can be caused by either a motional induction, if the sensor is moved relative to the sensed object, or transformed induction, if the sensor is at rest but exposed to a time-varying external magnetic flux.

Figure 4 shows the top view and Figure 5 shows a lateral view of the measurement setup to determine the sensor's sensitivity. The hatched areas of the photos hide, for confidentiality reasons, the typical object to be sensed.

The motor-driven xy-translation stage shifts the sensor axially and laterally relative to the fixed ferromagnetic object. The motors are controlled by an ORIEL MIKE Encoder via MATLAB. A constant current source typically feeds 100 mA into a 1000 turn solenoid. This results in a magnetic flux of $4.65\,\mathrm{mT}$, measured at the core's face-plate. To avoid motion induced eddy currents, the core consists of the non-conducting ceramic compound ferrite. A millitesla-meter from the company PHYWE [5], with a range of up to $\pm 2000\,\mathrm{mT}$, is used as the Hall sensor in these preliminary experiments. At each position of the sensor arrangement a mT-reading is

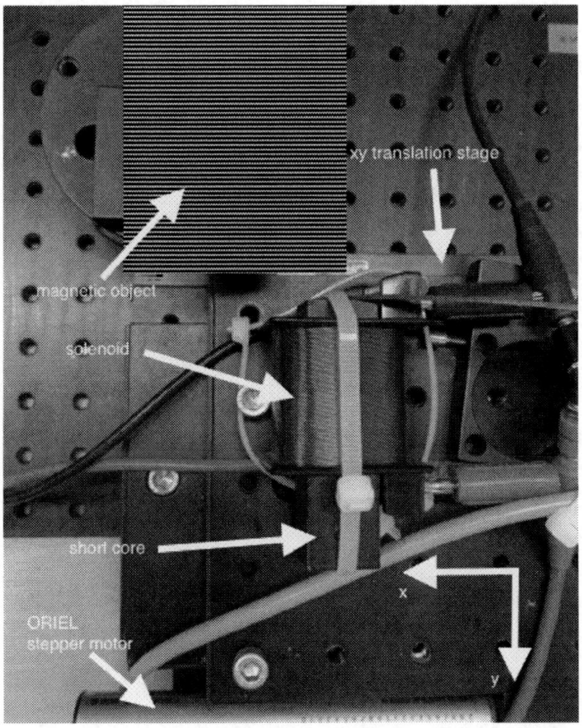

Fig. 4. An initial magnetic circuit representing the sensors parts of the measurement system consisting of a solenoid excited by a DC current to generate a magnetomotive force of a few kA. It has a ferromagnetic core and the Hall-effect sensor is located in the center of the core's face-plate. Two PC-controlled translation stages allow to traverse two-dimensional slice planes (oriented in xy and xz directions) through the three-dimensional volume around the sensor.

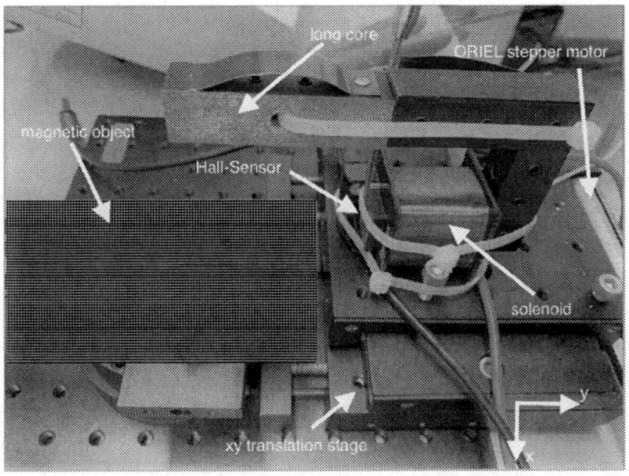

Fig. 5. Lateral view of the configuration of Figure 4 including a core that extends over and beyond the object hidden behind the hatched area.

taken. The readings from the millitesla-meter are put out as tenth of volts and measured by a HP 34401 volt-meter. The trajectory of the translation stage is a meander with step sizes in the $250\,\mu\mathrm{m}$ range. In the post processing the readings are converted to mT, saved to a matrix and plotted as shown in the following figures.

Two configurations were compared. One with a very compact excitation magnet for which the ferrite core does not extend beyond the solenoid, resulting in a particularly compact arrangement. The second configuration has a ferrite core extending beyond the solenoid by approximately $80\,\mathrm{mm}$. Thereby it guides the magnetic field lines closer to the sensed object. This results in the possibility to cover a larger air gap, increasing the sensitivity. A side effect of the protruding core is rendering the system less compact and more prone to physical damage while in operation.

IV. RESULTS

The characterization result is displayed in Figure 6 for the short core arrangement. In the top figure, one can observe that for separation distances of up to $8\,\mathrm{mm}$ between the solenoid's core and the object in y-direction, the sensitivity is good. The incurred noise floor is sufficiently low. This simple threshold discriminator circuit can reliably detect the object. If in addition to the detection also information on the relative location in x-direction were sought after, this sensor arrangement allows to estimate lateral displacements in the millimeter range. The bottom figure shows the comparably large noise floor that one has to cope with, if larger separation distances need to be covered by the system. Here, selecting a good threshold γ, is a challenging task and needs to be investigated in future work.

Figure 7 characterizes the protruding core sensor system. It is able to detect objects to a greater separation distance, exhibits a similar noise floor, but lacks the precision in locating the object in lateral direction.

We can conclude, that the detection problem can more reliably be served by the large air gap sensor. Thus further characterization is limited to this type of sensor arrangement only. As the setup is designed to tolerate a large magnetic reluctance, the resulting variation of magnetic flux density at the Hall-effect sensor is small. Its sensitivity and its detection probability [9], [10] thus are very much dependent on the incurred noise floor relative to the change in reading of the deterministic signal's mean. Referring to Figure 8 we define the signal-to-noise ratio SNR to be:

$$\mathrm{SNR} = \frac{\left[\mathbf{E}\left\{y(\mathbf{r})\,|_{\text{object present}}\right\}\right]^2}{\mathbf{Var}\left\{y(\mathbf{r})\,|_{\text{object present}}\right\}} \quad (2)$$

with $x(\mathbf{r})$ the spatially dependent (position vector $\mathbf{r}$), appropriately amplified, and band limited output signal of the Hall sensor, $y(\mathbf{r})$ the output signal of the realized matched filter (MF) (with impulse response $h(\mathbf{r}\prime)$ that is designed to maximize, at the output, the SNR, as defined in (2), $\mathbf{E}\{\cdots\}$, the expectation operator, and $\mathbf{Var}\{\cdots\}$, the variance operator.

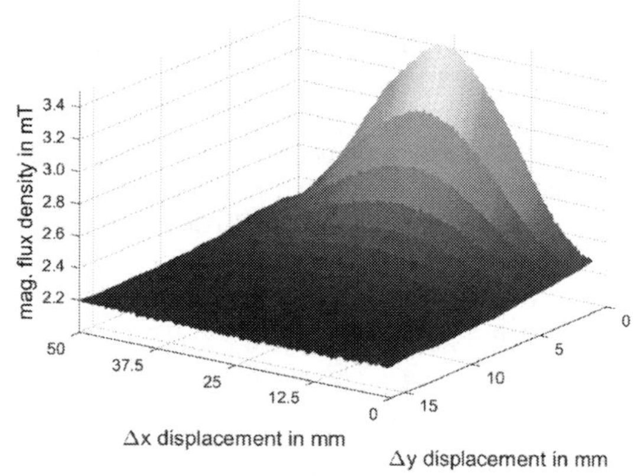

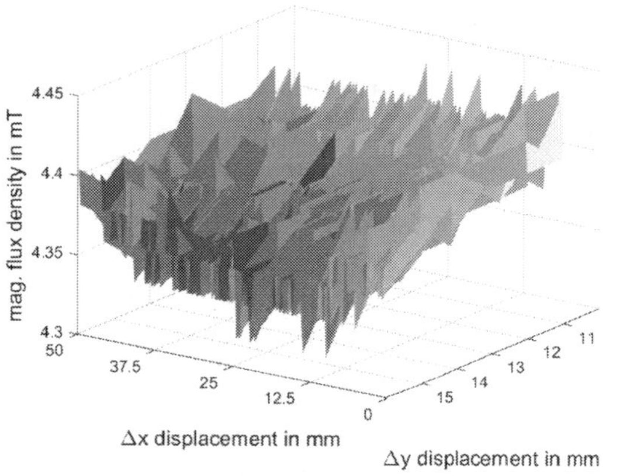

Fig. 6. Using the short core the measurement results lead to a bell-shaped dependency which declines with distance to the metallic object whose axis of symmetry is close to $\Delta x = 25\,\text{mm}$. From a Δy-displacement of $8\,\text{mm}$ on the object seems to no longer influence the sensed flux density sufficiently for a reliable detection.

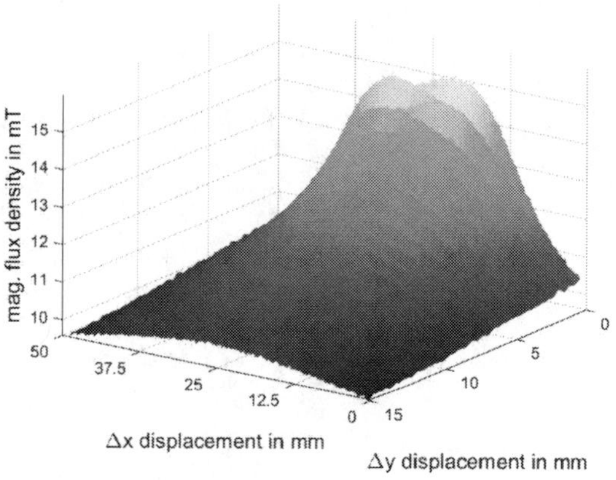

Fig. 7. As expected a longer core which reaches over the metallic object leads to greater sensibility at higher distances. Even at 15mm Δy displacement a slight difference of 0.8 mT can be detected.

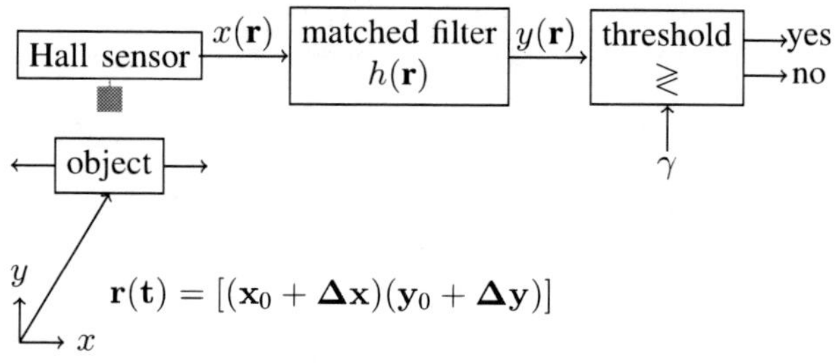

Fig. 8. Schematic of the realized signal processing scheme. The input $x(\mathbf{r})$ is the amplified and noise bandwidth-limited (we settled for a bandwidth of $2\,\text{kHz}$ in order to be able to detect at a rather high throughput of objects and their translational speed) output signal of the Hall sensor. The matched filter is maximizing the SNR as given in (2). For detection a simple threshold detector is used which computes a binary yes or no signal from the MF output $y(\mathbf{r})$.

In order to optimize the MF, a series of measurements were performed, whose results are displayed in Figures 9 and 10. Their statistical properties are listed in Table I. These characteristic parameters are used to set the threshold γ, to appropriately detect the object.

Assuming the noise being white and gaussian (WGN), the matched filter is simplified to a cross-correlator. Its signal input $x(\mathbf{r})$ can be calculated with

$$x(\mathbf{r}) = s(\mathbf{r}) + n(\mathbf{r}) \tag{3}$$

as a sum of its deterministic component $s(\mathbf{r})$, solely depending on the object's magnetic properties, and the spatially dependent noise term $n(\mathbf{r})$. The filter's reference signal $h(\mathbf{r}')$ can easily be obtained from a measurement. The object's velocity in passing the sensor, v, determines the mapping from a time-dependent noise $n(t)$ to the required spatially dependent noise in (3).

For an SNR larger than five, the chance of a false negative as well as a false positive, placed at the maximum design sensor-to-object separation, assuming a gaussian probability density function of the superposed noise, is less than 10^{-4}.

Figure 9 represents measurement results, that were obtained to simulate a remanence in the opposite direction. Therefore, we reversed the current through the coil and changed the sign of the outcome. This case is particularly interesting, because the remanence can cause constructive or destructive superposition of magnetic fields. Hence increasing or decreasing the measured value. This can cause lower peaks which cannot be detected without an adaptive threshold γ.

Figure 10 displays short core measurement results from moving the sensor over the magnetic object. This setup allows for the detection of the optimal spot to place the sensor element, relative to the magnetic object. One can observe, that measurements at a distance of $48\,\text{mm}$ are possible. However, a considerable noise floor aggravates reliable detection.

The deterministic values of Figures 9 and 10 show that the detection is possible. The stochastic properties of these measurements let us conclude, that the noise model is indeed

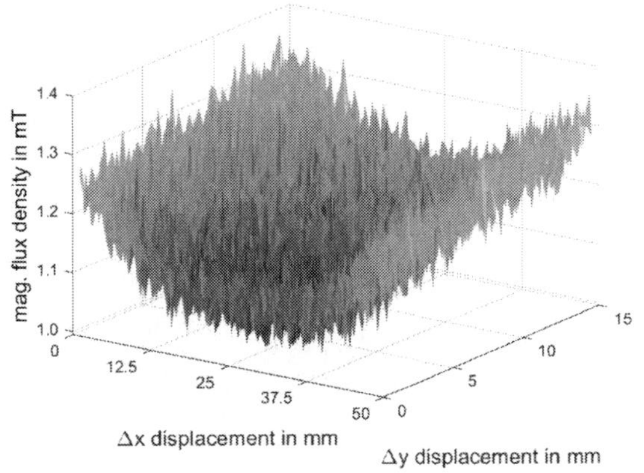

Fig. 9. Switching the field direction of the coil yields even smaller differences in magnetic flux but allows detection at higher distances.

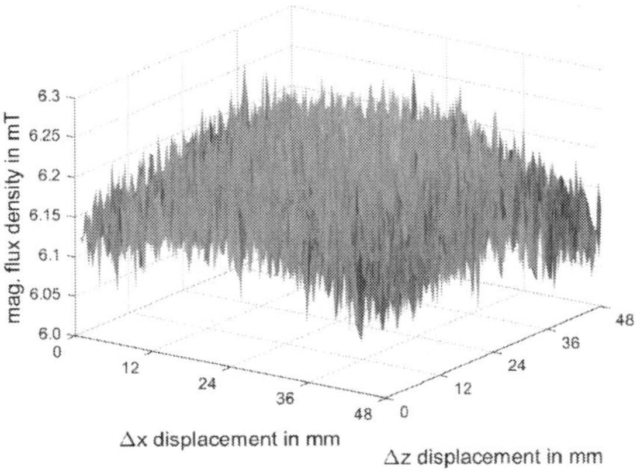

Fig. 10. Moving the sensor 48 mm over the xz-plane enables to determine the maximum magnetic flux density normal to the coil. This enables to optimize the coil coordinates for improved sensibility. The results show that directly over the magnetic object (located at $\Delta x = 24\,\text{mm}, \Delta z = 28\,\text{mm}$), the magnetic field is strongest.

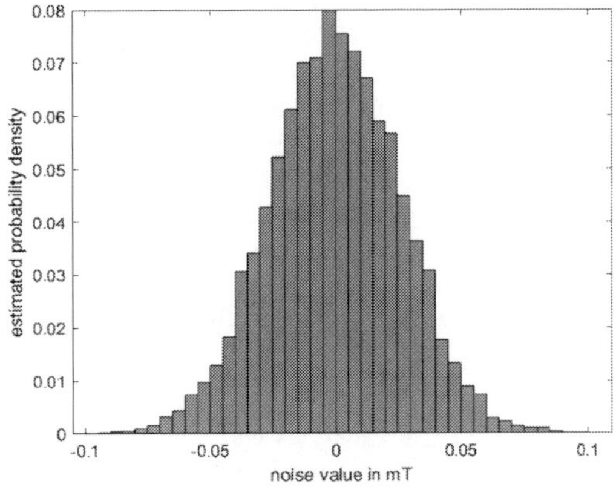

Fig. 11. Separation of the stochastic from the deterministic properties of the xy-plane measurements yields noise information which directly proofs prior noise assumptions.

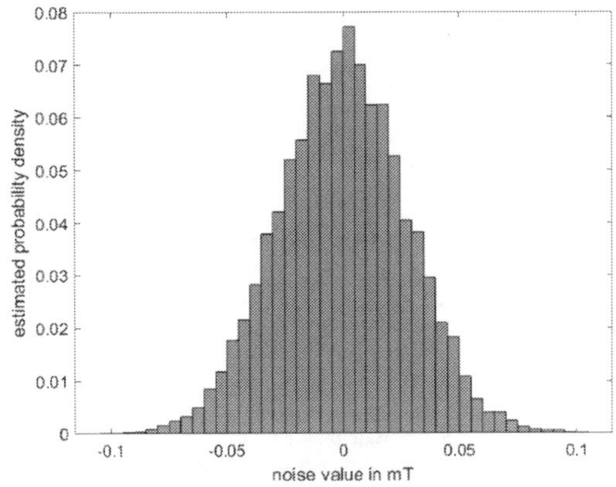

Fig. 12. Using the stochastic qualities of the measurement values of the xz-plane allows proofing prior assumptions concerning the noise model.

valid. As shown in Figures 11 and 12, both histograms of the noise floors of the xy-plane and the xz-plane, respectively, seem gaussian, which validate our assumptions. These data allow to determine the expected values and variances of both measurements. In Table I the calculated values are listed to obtain a starting point for the adaptive threshold value γ. With variances in these orders of magnitude, reliable measurements can be carried out.

V. Conclusion and Future Work

We reported on preliminary results obtained in the design and optimization process of a magnetic circuit used in a proximity detector for identifying ferromagnetic objects. The design goal of reliably detecting objects over distances up to $50\,\text{mm}$ can be shown to be attained for the experimental prototype analysed. it turns out, that the difference between measurement results using a long core contrary to the short

TABLE I
MEAN AND VARIANCE ESTIMATES OBTAINED FROM xy AND xz SLICES OF THE SPATIALLY RESOLVED MAGNETIC FIELD READINGS USED TO OPTIMIZE THE SIGNAL TO NOISE RATIO SNR OF THE DETECTION SCHEME.

Slice	Δx in mm	Δy in mm	E$\{\cdots\}$ in mT	Var$\{\cdots\}$ in (mT)^2
xy-plane	0.25	1.2	1.15	$8.89 \cdot 10^{-9}$
xz-plane	0.48	0.48	6.16	$23.93 \cdot 10^{-6}$

core arrangement is considerable. Hence, the magnetic circuit should be optimized to feature the optimal arrangement of the core relative to the ferromagnetic object.

Moreover, reversing the direction of the remanent magnetic field of the ferromagnetic object can add up destructively to the field induced by the coil. However, the peak of the outgoing signal of the Hall sensor can be lowered. If the remanence is high enough, the peak could be beneath the threshold. Thus further measures have to be taken into consideration.

Furthermore, the measured noise can be approximated by a white noise model. This simplification allows implementing basic signal processing algorithms which help to determine a suitable threshold.

The next steps will be the analysis with respect to electrical and magnetical interferences caused by the harsh environment the sensor systems are designed to reliably operate in.

REFERENCES

[1] E. Schrüfer, L. Reindl, and B. Zagar, Elektrische Messtechnik (engl. Electronic Measurement Techniques), Hanser Verlag, 2018.

[2] P. Ripka, Magnetic Sensors and Magnetometers, Artech House Inc., 2000.

[3] J. P. Bastos, Electromagnetic Modelling by Finite Element Methods, Dekker, 2003.

[4] S. Taghvaeeyan and R. Rajamani, Magnetic Sensor-Based Large Distance Position Estimation With Disturbance Compensation, IEEE Sensors Journal Vol. 15, 2015.

[5] `https://www.phywe.de/` [retrieved: Nov. 2021]

[6] R. Piepgras, S. Michlmayr, J. Egger, and B. Zagar, Potential und Einschränkungen der Messung magnetischer Mikrostrukturen mit einem Faraday-Magnetometer (engl. Potential and Constraints of Measurements of magnetic microstructures using a Faraday-Magnetometer), in tm - Technisches Messen, Vol. 86, Nr. 10, Walter de Gruyter, pp. 577–585, 2019.

[7] R. Piepgras, S. Michlmayr, and B. Zagar, Optical Analysis of Magnetic Microstructures, in SPIE: Proceedings of SPIE Volume 11144 - IMEKO Joint TC1 -TC2 International Symposium on Photonics and Education in Measurement Science 2019, Serie Proceedings of SPIE, Vol. 11144, 2019.

[8] J. G. Webster, The Measurement, Instrumentation and sensors Handbook, CRC Press LLC and Springer-Verlag, 1999.

[9] S. M. Kay, Fundamentals of Statistical Processing, Volume I: Estimation Theory, Prentice-Hall Signal Processing Series, 1993.

[10] W. A. Gardner, Introduction to Random Processes with Applications to Signals and Systems, 2nd ed. McGraw-Hill, 1990.

Environmental Monitoring in Built Environment Through Wearable Devices: a Bibliometric Review

Francesco Salamone
Construction Technologies Institute, National Research Council of Italy (ITC-CNR),
Via Lombardia, 49, San Giuliano Milanese, 20098 Milano, Italy
e-mail: salamone@itc.cnr.it

Francesco Salamone, Sergio Sibilio, Massimiliano Masullo
Department of Architecture and Industrial Design, Università degli Studi della Campania "Luigi Vanvitelli",
Via San Lorenzo, Abazia di San Lorenzo, 81031 Aversa, Italy
e-mail: francesco.salamone@unicampania.it, sergio.sibilio@unicampania.it, massimiliano.masullo@unicampania.it

***Abstract*— Wearables are mainly used for commercial purposes to enhance smartphone functionality by enabling payment for commercial items or monitoring physical activity. As emerged from a recent systematic review, many research studies focused on using wearable devices for environmental monitoring of the built environment. Those studies showed that, among the thermal, visual, acoustic, and air quality environmental factors, the last one is the most considered when using wearables, even though in combination with some others. Another relevant finding is that of the acquired studies, in only one, the authors shared their wearables as an open-source device, and it will probably be necessary to encourage researchers to consider opensource to promote scalability and proliferation of new wearables customized to cover different domains. In this case, with a bibliometric review, it was possible to complete the analysis by answering some of most statistical aspects: what are the most important authors involved in this domain of research? What are the most relevant sources? What is the geographical coverage and the collaboration among different Countries? What is the conceptual structure of the considered topic? The methodology used to answer the above questions is based on a bibliometric review using a specific package developed for R environment: bibliometrix.**

Keywords-environmental monitoring; wearable devices; wearables; bibliometric review.

I. Introduction

The term "wearable" was first used in the scientific literature in 1996 when, in [1], the author presented a personal imaging system and, in [2], where the author gave an overview of energy generation during the user's daily activities, removing the technological limitation of batteries to power wearables. A year later, in 1997, the researchers of MIT media laboratory, Picard and Healey, used the term "affective wearables" [3] to refer to a system equipped with sensors that allowed the detection of affective patterns (e.g., heart rate variability, electrodermal activity). To date, the class of wearable electronics or technologies, called "wearables" for short, has attracted increasing public interest and is generally identified as a category of devices that can be worn or tattooed on the human skin or even implanted in the human body to continuously and accurately monitor some variables (biometric in most of the cases, but also environmental in some other cases) without interrupting or restricting the user's movements [4].

Environmental Quality (EQ) can be subdivided by analysing it in terms of Indoor EQ (IEQ) or Outdoor EQ (OEQ). Both IEQ and OEQ are important to ensure the health and well-being of people.

It is well known that users spend a large part of their time indoors, so the quality of environments within buildings and the satisfaction and well-being of occupants is a hot topic today [5]. Especially in low-cost housing, where the limited indoor space may lead occupants to spend more time doing various outdoor activities, the quality of the outdoor environment is crucial [6].

Both IEQ and OEQ refer to a holistic concept that includes various environmental factors: visual, acoustic, thermal and air quality.

In all cases, monitoring all four environmental factors could be helpful to understand the complex area of interaction (cross-modal or combined) among the different environmental aspects and user perception of IEQ or OEQ.

In order to link the term wearables with the environmental aspect, some new acronyms have been introduced: Personal Environmental Monitoring System (PEMS) and Wearable Environmental Monitoring System (WEMS), to emphasise the class of wearable devices for monitoring some environmental factors [7]. This manuscript is intended to be complementary to [8], where the attention was focused primarily on the systematic analysis, defining the relevant scientific literature finding regarding environmental monitoring with wearables. The attention focused here on the bibliometric analysis, allowing to quantify the scientific production and measure its quality and impact. It is also useful to identify and analyze research's intellectual, conceptual and social structures and their evolution and dynamics.

II. Methodology

Among the different available databases (e.g., PubMed, Web of Science, Google Scholar), the Scopus search engine, developed by Elsevier, was used due to the high quality of the available resources, including the Institute for Scientific Information (ISI) and Scopus-indexed papers. It is a multidisciplinary database that allows defining Information Systems (IS) to think of the advanced search functionality available on the web platform by providing about 20% more coverage than Web of Science. Scopus focused primarily on physical sciences, health sciences, life sciences and social sciences [9], which is consistent with the aim of this research. The covered period is from 1966 to the present [9].

This aspect is consistent with our bibliometric review since, the oldest paper presenting a "wearable" device with computational capabilities was published in the 1990s. A detailed description of the reproducible methodology used to acquire the data can be found in [8].

III. Discussion

The main results of the bibliometric review are presented in the following subsections. By applying a proven methodology, results can be provided in the form of descriptive analysis, main authors involved in the topic, geographic coverage and thematic map to complement the information provided to the scientific community by the systematic review described in [8].

A. Descriptive analysis

A descriptive summary of the main bibliometric statistics is reported in Table I.

TABLE I. MAIN INFORMATION

Parameter (description)	No.
Documents (total number of documents)	68
Sources (frequency distribution of sources as journals)	55
Author's keywords -DE (frequency distribution of the authors' keywords)	237
Keywords Plus -ID (frequency distribution of keywords associated with the document by Scopus databases)	848
Period (years of publication)	2000:2021
Authors (authors' frequency distribution)	317
Authors Appearances (number of author appearances)	380
Authors of single-authored documents (number of authors of single-authors articles)	3
Authors of multi-authored documents (number of authors of multi-authored articles)	314
Authors per Article index (ratio between Authors and Documents)	4.66
Co-Authors per articles index (average number of co-authors in each document)	5.59
Average citations per Article (average number of citations in each Article)	18.78
Collaboration Index (ratio between total authors of multi-authored articles and total multi-authored articles [10] [11])	4.91

In Table I, the Co-Authors per Articles index is calculated as the average number of co-authors per Article.

In this case, the index considers the author appearances while the Authors per Article index is the ratio between the total number of articles and the total number of authors.

Consequently, even if an author has published more than one Article, it is counted only once. This is why the authors per Article index is smaller than the Co-authors per Article index [12]. Only five authors wrote each Article on average with a Collaboration Index equal to 4.91.

As the analysis period of Table 1 covers the last 20 years, only with Figure 1 it is possible to point out that the most significant increase in production was recorded only since 2012 with an Annual Growth Rate of 9.89%.

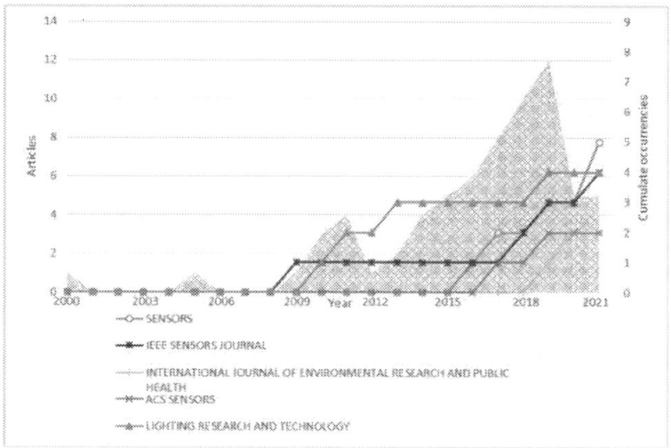

Figure 1. Annual Scientific production and Source Dynamics - Scopus, 2021

Among the 68 analysed peer-reviewed scientific articles, no preferred journal where articles on this topic were concentrated was found. However, the authors' interest in journals that deals with the all-encompassing theme of sensors is increasing in the last years, as highlighted by the distribution frequency of articles published on the "Sensors" and "IEEE Sensors Journal" as displayed in Figure 1.

B. Top 15 authors and related research studies

Figure 2 identifies the most important authors, considering the selected topic, ranked in descending order of importance as a function of the number of published articles.

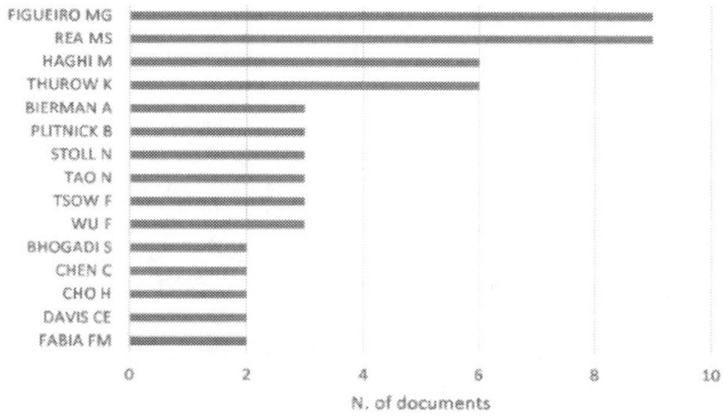

Figure 2. Top 15 authors ranked by number of articles - Scopus, 2021

A brief description of related studies identified by the Top 15 authors is reported below. While a detailed description of all the studies, subdivided by the environmental factor (i.e., visual, acoustic, thermal and air quality), can be found in [8].

The author Figueiro M.G. was actively involved in using wearable devices to assess circadian-effective light and its impact on alertness in different categories of users. In particular, in [13], office workers wear a pendant-mounted Daysimeter device, developed and calibrated at the Lighting Research Center (LRC) at Rensselaer Polytechnic Institute and used in combination with a specific questionnaire to measure participant-specific Circadian Stimulus (CS), thus allowing to identify how they effectively felt significantly more vital, energetic and alert on the days with CS $\geq$ 0.3 compared to the baseline day. In [14], a field study was conducted with eighth-grade students to determine, using the Daysimeter, the impact of morning light on circadian timing, sleep duration and performance. In [15], he documented the spectral and spatial performance characteristics of two new versions of the Daysimeter. He found that wearing the Daysimeter or Actiwatch Spectrum [16] on the wrist provides accurate light measurements relative to locating a calibrated photosensor at the cornea plane. In [16], he described a case study where light exposure and rest-activity patterns in an older adult with dementia and his caregiver spouse were monitored with a wrist-worn actigraph. This device captures and records high-resolution human activity information to collect baseline data and an eye-level wavelength-sensitive light meter (Daysimeter). The same topic was considered in [17] and [18], co-authored by Rea and Plitnick, to identify the effect of light on the person with dementia and caregivers through the use of questionnaires to acquire subjective feedback and the same instruments, the Daysimeters and the actigraphs [19]. These researches allowed verifying how ambient lighting interventions designed to increase daytime circadian stimulation can be effectively used to increase sleep efficiency in persons with Alzheimer Disease and Related Dementia (ADRD) and their caregivers. It may also be effective for other populations such as healthy older adults with sleep problems, adolescents, and veterans with traumatic brain injury. In [20], he demonstrated the feasibility of using light through closed eyelids during sleep for promoting circadian alignment and sleep health. In [21], he measured both light/dark exposures with Daysimeter and salivary Dim Light Melatonin Onset (DLMO) to study the effects of chronotype, sleep schedule and light/dark pattern exposures on the circadian phase. In [22], the daysimeter was used to verify how a lighting intervention tailored to increase daytime circadian stimulation can increase sleep quality and improve behaviour in patients with ADRD. While promising for application, the present field study should be replicated using a larger sample size and longer treatment duration. Rea co-authored most of Figueiro studies [13]-[15][17][18][21][23][24]. In [25], authors emphasize how technologies are needed to provide information about the state of our circadian system to our conscious awareness so that we can take appropriate action to avoid and correct light-induced circadian disruption. Bierman co-authored three of the articles discussed above [15][23][24]. Plitnick co-authored also three paper previously discussed [14][17][21].

Bhogadi co-authored [26] and [27]. In [27], he described the results of a European Research Council funded project (CHAI) aimed at investigating the relationship between particulate air pollution from outdoor and household sources with information from GPS, wearable cameras, and continuous measurements of personal exposure to particles.

In [26], he used data from multiple sources (continuous personal and ambient PM2.5 concentrations; questionnaire, GPS, and wearable camera data; and modelled long-term exposure at residence) to identify the relative contribution of the time of the day (when?), location (where?), and individuals' activities (what?) to PM2.5 personal exposure in periurban South India.

Cho H. in [28] described how the use of a highly sensitive Multi-Stimuli Responsive (MSR) unit applied to a wearable motion/environmental monitoring chromic device could be used to evaluate some environmental stimuli (UV radiation, temperature) with thermal mapping capability. In [7], he presented a PEMS and WEMS that were developed by considering consumers' needs to detect and avoid exposure to air pollution.

Wu et al. in [29]-[31] demonstrated the practical application in different contexts of a wearable multi-sensor IoT network system for environmental monitoring.

Haghi and Thurow co-autored two papers [32] [33] where they emphasized the role of wearables in multiparameter monitoring, miniaturization, sensor integration and data fusion. Together with Stoll in [34]-[37] demonstrated the practical applicability of a multi-layer wearable devices.

Tsow, Tao et al. [38], and then also Chen with them [39][40] used practical examples to emphasize the role of a wearable sensing system for assessment of exposures to environmental volatile organic compounds (VOCs). The same aspect was covered by the studies of Davis and Fabia et al. [41][42], where they used different wearable to quantify the same aspect: the personal exposures to VOCs.

C. Corresponding Author's Country and Country publications map

Figure 3 shows the origin of the main "corresponding authors" who have carried out specific research related to the considered theme: the United States of America (USA) is at the top of the list and significantly outdistances Spain, in second place and first among European nations. To the third-place China and Italy to equal merit.

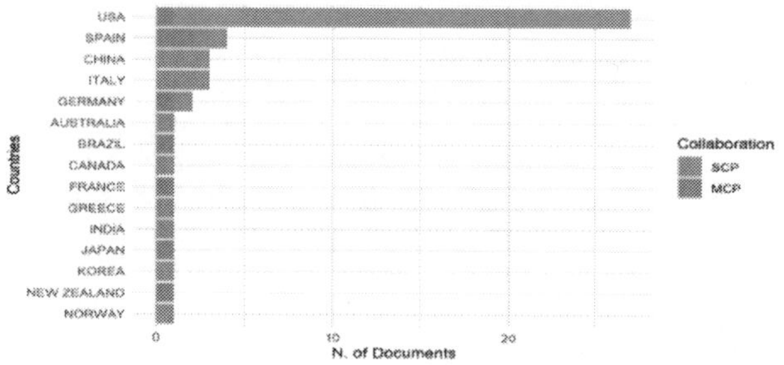

Figure 3. Corresponding Authors' Country (SCP - Single Country Publications, MCP - Multiple Country Publications)

While Figure 4 displays the geographical coverage of the Country scientific production. Each co-author of a Country, identified by the affiliation, contribute with +1 for that Country. The USA is on the top of the list of Countries with the maximum number of authors on the selected topic (200), followed by Germany (21), Italy (19), China (18), Spain (15), Australia (12), France (11), India, Romania and U.K. (10), Greece (7), Canada and Norway (6), Brazil and New Zealand (5), Belgium (4), Japan (3), Latvia and South Korea (2), Ireland and Switzerland (1).

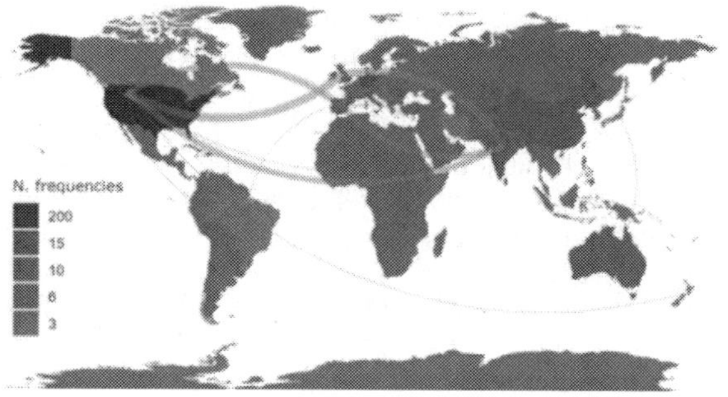

Figure 4. Co-authors Country Scientific Production and Country collaboration.

Figure 4 shows how the entire continent of Africa, Antarctica, large areas of northern Asia and the western countries of the south America, are still not involved in this scientific debate. The collaborations among the countries, highlighted by brown lines, show how USA, U.K. and India established the most active collaborations.

D. Thematic Map

The thematic mapping [43] allows delineating the conceptual structure of the topic. This latter consists of a word co-occurrence network analysis performed considering the Authors' keywords to define what science talks about in a field, main themes, and trends (see Figure 5). In Figure 5, each bubble represents a network cluster and the name attributed to each bubble is the word belonging to the cluster with the higher occurrence value. The size of each bubble is proportional to the cluster word occurrences, while the position is defined according to the cluster Callon centrality and density: the former is a measure of the importance of the selected theme in the development of the entire research domain; the latter is a measure of the theme's development [44].

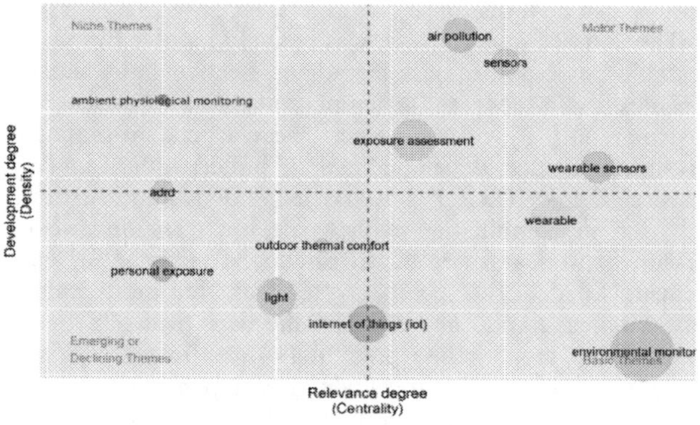

Figure 5. Thematic Map considering authors' keywords for the full period under investigation

Four different themes are shown in Figure 5. The upper-right quadrant shows the motor themes. They are characterized by both high centrality and density. Among the "motor themes" that are the more developed in the literature, the main concern is air pollution, followed by exposure assessment, which refers to studies in which exposure to air pollutants (Particulate Matter specifically) can be considered in combination with the evaluation of noise exposure.

The upper-left quadrant shows high density and low centrality themes, which are of limited importance with high development. In this case, "ambient physiological monitoring" refers to the study [32] where environmental, behavioural, and physiological domains of influencing factors in healthcare were measured simultaneously.

In the lower-left quadrant, there are the emerging or declining themes. Using the thematic evolution and different time slices it is possible to differentiate emerging and declining themes considering the direction toward the top right or the lower left, respectively [45]. Within this particular case, light measurement with wearables was an emerging theme in particular over the period 2010-2015 considering all the studies performed by Figueiro et al.

Finally, the lower-right quadrant shows the transversal themes to the different research areas of the field: wearable and environmental monitor showing the high connection between these aspects in the selected papers.

IV. CONCLUSIONS

The theme of environmental monitoring considering wearables is increasing in terms of published papers. While in [8] it was possible to emphasize the main fields covered by the scientific production, the original value of this research is the rigorous process conducted to perform the first bibliometric mapping in the field of wearables used for environmental monitoring.

For this purpose, a total of 68 different manuscripts were considered. A possible limitation in the selection of the papers could be the bias due to the authors' decision. This aspect was limited by the fact that two authors performed time-consuming screening and, in case of disagreement, reached consensus through discussion and in consultation with the third author. The analysis of selected papers could support scientific community in identifying the main domains of investigation or the main authors involved in this research. It was possible to discover how, among the different authors, Figueiro and Rea gave a great contribution in light-induced circadian disruption assessment using a wearable device.

It was also possible to discover the geographical coverage and the collaboration among different Countries.

Additionally, the thematic map, defined considering the meaning of Callon centrality and density, allows emphasizing the most occurred topic, differentiated considering motor themes, nice themes, emerging or declined themes and basic themes. In particular, considering the motor theme/s, exposure assessment was considered as the most considered and developed theme. By merging this result with that provided by [8], it was possible to emphasize how for the exposure assessment it was primary considered the aspect related to air quality assessment and visual aspects on human well-being.

The acoustic factor was minimally treated. This is probably due to the fact that some wearable instruments that measure workers' exposure at shoulder level (e.g., dosimeters SV 104A [46]), or detect environmental noise at ear level (e.g., HEAD acoustics binaural headset BHS II [47]) are already commercially available and therefore, their design, development and use for research purpose does not constitute a novelty, except in the integration with multi-parameter or 'low cost' and open-source acquisition instruments.

The same circumstance can be highlighted for thermal aspects where temperature sensors were mainly used in combination with other instruments to acquire information about the environment without properly considering a human-centric perspective. It would be useful to identify low-cost, open-source solutions that most people can use to assess, not so much the variability of environmental parameters in the indoor environment, which, when considering workers sitting at their desks, can lose its significance. But considering the variability of the environmental conditions to which the subjects may be exposed during the day, e.g., passing from the outdoors torrid or humid climates of the summer of tropical and sub-tropical areas to indoor situations that are typically more bearable or too cold due to ineffective regulation of the HVAC plants.

By linking all this information with user feedback, algorithms not based on a physical model but, instead, based on data could be effectively applied to identify the variables that most affect the individual's perception of comfort, including aspects that are difficult to take into account (e.g., transient exposure) [48].

Probably much more work can be done, in developing new hardware devices that could monitor the environment in a holistic perspective, also considering the other 3 environmental factors (visual, acoustic and thermal) in line with the studies of Haghi and Thurow (Figure 2) which emphasized the role of wearables in multiparameter monitoring, thus making it possible to take into account any combined or cross-modal aspects resulting from the potential interaction between different environmental variables.

Furthermore, by combining the results of the bibliographic review with those of the [8], even if the growth of publications has increased considerably since 2012, with a noticeable halt in the last two years (see Figure 1), it was possible, at least theoretically, to hypothesize how the sharing of open-source solutions can encourage the proliferation of application of these devices in different contexts, promoting the design and assessment of the built environment on the basis of a human-centred approach, even in those areas not yet affected by the scientific debate on this topic (figure 4).

REFERENCES

[1] S. Mann, "Wearable computing: A first step toward personal imaging, Computer" Long. Beach. Calif. vol. 30, pp. 25–32, 1997, doi:10.1109/2.566147.

[2] T. Starner, "Human-powered wearable computing" IBM Syst. J. vol. 35, pp. 618–629 1996, doi:10.1147/sj.353.0618.

[3] R. W. Picard and J. Healey, "Affective wearables" Int. Symp. Wearable Comput. Dig. Pap. pp. 90–97, 1997, doi:10.7551/mitpress/1140.003.0012.

[4] W. Gao, et al., "Fully integrated wearable sensor arrays for multiplexed in situ perspiration analysis" Nature. vol. 529, pp. 509–514, 2016, doi:10.1038/nature16521.

[5] N. E. Klepeis, et al., "The National Human Activity Pattern Survey (NHAPS): a resource for assessing exposure to environmental pollutants" J. Expo. Sci. Environ. Epidemiol, vol 11, pp. 231–252, 2001 doi:10.1038/sj.jea.7500165.

[6] M. F. Mohamed, S. N. Raman, T. M. Iman Pratama, and W. F. Mohammad Yusoff, "Outdoor Environment of Low-cost Housing: A case study of Flat Taman Desa Sentosa", E3S Web Conf. 3, 2014, doi:10.1051/e3sconf/20140301005.

[7] H. Cho, "Personal Environmental Monitoring System and network platform", Proc. Int. Conf. Sens. Technol. ICST, pp. 751–756, March 2016, doi:10.1109/ICSensT.2015.7438496.

[8] F. Salamone, M. Masullo, and S. Sibilio, "Wearable Devices for Environmental Monitoring in the Built Environment: A Systematic Review", Sensors. vol. 21, 2021, https://www.mdpi.com/1424-8220/21/14/4727 [retrieved: october, 2021].

[9] M. E. Falagas, E. I. Pitsouni, G. A. Malietzis, and G. Pappas, "Comparison of PubMed, Scopus, Web of Science, and Google Scholar: strengths and weaknesses", FASEB J. vol. 22 pp. 338–342, 2008. doi:10.1096/fj.07-9492lsf.

[10] B. Elango and P. Rajendran, "Authorship trends and collaboration pattern in the marine sciences literature: a scientometric study", Int. J. Inf. Dissem. Technol. (2012).

[11] M. A. Koseoglu, "Mapping the institutional collaboration network of strategic management research: 1980–2014, Scientometrics", vol. 109 pp. 203–226, 2016, doi:10.1007/s11192-016-1894-5.

[12] Bibliometrix R package web page. [Online]. Available from: https://www.bibliometrix.org [retrieved: october, 2021].

[13] M. G. Figueiro, M. Kalsher, B. C. Steverson, J. Heerwagen, K. Kampschroer, and M. S. Rea, "Circadian-effective light and its impact on alertness in office workers", Light. Res. Technol. vol. 51, pp. 171–183, 2019, doi:10.1177/1477153517750006.

[14] M. G. Figueiro, J. A. Brons, B. Plitnick, B. Donlan, R. P. Leslie, and M. S. Rea, "Measuring circadian light and its impact on adolescents", Light. Res. Technol. vol. 43 pp. 201–215, (2011), doi:10.1177/1477153510382853.

[15] M. G. Figueiro, R. Hamner, A. Bierman, and M. S. Rea, "Comparisons of three practical field devices used to measure

personal light exposures and activity levels", Light. Res. Technol. vol. 45 pp. 421–434, 2013, doi:10.1177/1477153512450453.

[16] P. A. Higgins, T. R. Hornick, and M. G. Figueiro, "Rest-activity and light exposure patterns in the home setting: A methodological case study", Am. J. Alzheimers. Dis. Other Demen. vol. 25, pp. 353–361, 2010 doi: 10.1177/1533317510363467

[17] M. G. Figueiro et al., "Tailored lighting intervention for persons with dementia and caregivers living at home", Sleep Heal. vol. 1, pp. 322–330, 2015, doi:10.1016/j.sleh.2015.09.003.

[18] M. G. Figueiro, et al., "Tailored lighting intervention improves measures of sleep, depression, and agitation in persons with Alzheimer's disease and related dementia living in long-term care facilities", Clin. Interv. Aging. vol. 9, pp. 1527–1537, 2014, doi:10.2147/CIA.S68557.

[19] Actigraph web page. [Online]. Available from: https://actigraphcorp.com [retrieved: october, 2021].

[20] M. G. Figueiro, "Individually tailored light intervention through closed eyelids to promote circadian alignment and sleep health", Sleep Heal. vol. 1 pp. 75–82, 2015, doi:10.1016/j.sleh.2014.12.009.

[21] M. G. Figueiro, B. Plitnick, and M. S. Rea, "The effects of chronotype, sleep schedule and light/dark pattern exposures on circadian phase", Sleep Med. vol. 15, pp. 1554–1564, 2014, doi:10.1016/j.sleep.2014.07.009.

[22] M. G. Figueiro et al., "Tailored lighting intervention improves measures of sleep, depression, and agitation in persons with Alzheimer's disease and related dementia living in long-term care facilities", Clin. Interv. Aging. vol. 9, pp. 1527–1537, 2014, doi:10.2147/CIA.S68557.

[23] A. Bierman, T. R. Klein, and M. S. Rea. "The Daysimeter: a device for measuring optical radiation as a stimulus for the human circadian system." Measurement Science and Technology, vol. 16, 2005.

[24] D. Miller, A. Bierman, M. G. Figueiro, E. S. Schernhammer, and M. S. Rea, "Ecological measurements of light exposure, activity and circadian disruption", Light. Res. Technol. vol. 42, pp. 271–284, 2010, doi:10.1177/1477153510367977.

[25] M. S. Rea, "Human health and well-being: promises for a bright future from solid-state lighting", Light. Diodes Mater. Devices, Appl. Solid State Light. XV, 2011, doi:10.1117/12.876409.

[26] C. Milà et al., "When, Where, and What? Characterizing Personal PM2.5 Exposure in Periurban India by Integrating GPS, Wearable Camera, and Ambient and Personal Monitoring Data", Environ. Sci. Technol. vol. 52, pp. 13481–13490, 2018, doi:10.1021/acs.est.8b03075.

[27] C. Tonne, et al., "Integrated assessment of exposure to PM2.5 in South India and its relation with cardiovascular risk: Design of the CHAI observational cohort study", Int. J. Hyg. Environ. Health. vol. 220, pp. 1081–1088, 2017 doi:10.1016/j.ijheh.2017.05.005.

[28] S. Zeng et al., "Multi-stimuli responsive chromism with tailorable mechanochromic sensitivity for versatile interactive sensing under ambient conditions", Mater. Horizons. vol. 7 pp. 164–172, 2020, doi:10.1039/c9mh00851a.

[29] F. Wu, C. Rüdiger, J. M. Redouté, and M. Rasit Yuce, "A wearable multi-sensor IoT network system for environmental monitoring", Internet of Things. pp. 29–38, 2019, doi:10.1007/978-3-030-02819-0_3.

[30] F. Wu, J. M. Redoute, and M. R. Yuce, "A Self-Powered Wearable Body Sensor Network System for Safety Applications", Proc. IEEE Sensors, 2018. doi:10.1109/ICSENS.2018.8589848.

[31] F. Wu, C. Rudiger, J. M. Redoute, and M. R. Yuce, "WE-Safe: A wearable IoT sensor node for safety applications via LoRa", (WF-IoT 2018) IEEE World Forum Internet Things, Jan. 2018, pp. 144–148, doi:10.1109/WF-IoT.2018.8355234.

[32] M. Haghi, S. Danyali, K. Thurow, J. M. Warnecke, J. Wang, and T. M. Deserno, "Hardware Prototype for Wrist-Worn Simultaneous Monitoring of Environmental, Behavioral, and Physiological Parameters", Appl. Sci., vol. 10, 2020, doi:10.3390/APP10165470.

[33] M. Haghi and K. Thurow, "Toward a New Approach in Wearable Devices in Safety Monitoring: Miniaturization and 3D Space Utilization", SLAS Technol. vol. 24, pp. 444–447, 2019, doi:10.1177/2472630319846873.

[34] M. Haghi, A. Geissler, H. Fleischer, N. Stoll, and K. Thurow, "Ubiqsense: A Personal Wearable in Ambient Parameters Monitoring based on IoT Platform", 2019 Int. Conf. Sens. Instrum. IoT Era, (ISSI 2019), doi:10.1109/ISSI47111.2019.9043713.

[35] M. Haghi, R. Stoll, and K. Thurow, "A Low-Cost, Standalone, and Multi-Tasking Watch for Personalized Environmental Monitoring", IEEE Trans. Biomed. Circuits Syst. vol. 12, pp. 1144–1154, 2018, doi:10.1109/TBCAS.2018.2840347.

[36] M. Haghi, K. Thurow, and N. Stoll, "Four-layer wrist worn device for sound level and hazardous gases environmental monitoring", 2017 2nd Int. Conf. Syst. Reliab. Safety (ICSRS 2017), Jan 2018, pp. 270–276, doi:10.1109/ICSRS.2017.8272833.

[37] M. Haghi, K. Thurow, and N. Stoll, "A multi-layer multi-sensor wearable device for physical and chemical environmental parameters monitoring (CO & NO2)", (IDT 2017), Int. Conf. Inf. Digit. Technol., 2017, pp. 137–141, doi:10.1109/DT.2017.8024285.

[38] F. Tsow et al., "A Wearable and Wireless Sensor System for Real-Time Monitoring of Toxic Environmental Volatile Organic Compounds", IEEE Sens. J. vol. 9, pp. 1734–1740, 2009, doi:10.1109/JSEN.2009.2030747.

[39] C. Chen, F. Tsow, X. Xian, E. Forzani, N. Tao, and R. Tsui, "A wearable sensing system for assessment of exposures to environmental volatile organic compounds", Methods Mol. Biol. vol. 1256 pp. 201–211, 2015, doi:10.1007/978-1-4939-2172-0_14.

[40] Y. Deng et al., "A novel wireless wearable volatile organic compound (VOC) monitoring device with disposable sensors", Sensors (Switzerland). vol. 16, 2016, doi:10.3390/s16122060.

[41] A. G. Fung et al., "Wearable Environmental Monitor To Quantify Personal Ambient Volatile Organic Compound Exposures", ACS Sensors. vol. 4, pp. 1358–1364, 2019, doi:10.1021/acssensors.9b00304.

[42] M. Y. Rajapakse et al., "An environmental air sampler to evaluate personal exposure to volatile organic compounds", Analyst, vol. 146, pp. 636–645, 2021, doi:10.1039/d0an01521k.

[43] M. J. Cobo, A. G. López-Herrera, E. Herrera-Viedma, and F. Herrera, "An approach for detecting, quantifying, and visualizing the evolution of a research field: A practical application to the Fuzzy Sets Theory field", J. Informetr. vol. 5, pp. 146–166, 2011, doi:10.1016/j.joi.2010.10.002.

[44] M. Callon, J. P. Courtial, and F. Laville, "Co-word analysis as a tool for describing the network of interactions between basic and technological research: The case of polymer chemsitry", Scientometrics, vol. 22, pp. 155–205, 1991, doi:10.1007/BF02019280.

[45] A. Di Cosmo, C. Pinelli, A. Scandurra, M. Aria, and B. D'aniello, "Research trends in octopus biological studies", Animals, vol. 11, 2021, doi:10.3390/ani11061808.

[46] M. Podgórski, "Methods of validation of occupational noise exposure measurement with multi aspect personal sound exposure meter", Proc. of ACOUSTICS 2016, Nov. 2016, Brisbane, Australia.

[47] M. Masullo, A. Ozcevik Bilen, R. A. Toma, and G. Akin Guler, L. Maffei, "The Restorativeness of outdoor historical sites in urban areas: physical and perceptual correlations", Sustainability, vol. 13, 2021;

[48] M. Vellei, R. de Dear, C. Inard, and O. Jay, "Dynamic thermal perception: A review and agenda for future experimental research", Build. Environ. vol. 205, 2021, doi:10.1016/j.buildenv.2021.108269.

Design, Fabrication and Characterization of a Novel Piezoresistive Pressure Sensor for Blast Waves Monitoring

K. Sanchez, B. Achour, J. Riondet, L. Anglade,
M. Carrera, A. Coustou, A. Lecestre, S. Charlot,
H. Aubert, P. Pons
CNRS-LAAS, Toulouse University
Toulouse, France
ksanchezba@laas.fr, bachour@laas.fr, jriondet@laas.fr,
laurene.anglade@outlook.fr,
miguel.carrera.iz@hotmail.com, acoustou@laas.fr,
alecestre@laas.fr, scharlot@laas.fr, haubert@laas.fr,
ppons@laas.fr

M. Lavayssière, A. Lefrançois, J. Luc
CEA-DAM
Gramat, France
maylis.lavayssiere@cea.fr, alexandre.lefrancois@cea.fr,
jerome.luc@cea.fr,

Abstract— **In several side-on configurations, the monitoring of blast wave requires sensor with very low response time (< 1 µs). The sensing area of commercial sensors are too high to fulfill this specification. New transducers are focused on miniature membrane (diameter < 100 µm), but with optical transduction which suffers from low integration capabilities for multiple transducers. In this communication, a miniature piezoresistive pressure transducer based on silicon membrane and silicon gauges is designed and fabricated. Shock tube characterizations of the sensor have shown promising dynamic behavior, with a rise time of 30 ns and a response time lower than 1 µs thanks to the membrane fundamental resonant frequency of 20 MHz. Undesirable mechanical effects leading to the response drift after 1 µs are discussed and interpreted as the result of the holder deformation.**

Keywords – shockwave ; air blast ; pressure sensor

I. INTRODUCTION

Blast waves monitoring is required for many civilian and military applications, and especially for explosives characterization. In this case, and for supersonic shock wave, the side-on over-pressure (i.e., when the transducer surface is parallel to the flow velocity) reaches quasi-instantaneously (< 10 ns) a maximum P_{max} (from several bar to several ten of bar) and then decreases rapidly (from several ten of microseconds to several hundred of microseconds).

In order to analyze the effect of supersonic shock wave on systems, the accurate estimation of P_{max} is mandatory [1]. For several setup configurations (mass of explosive, distance between source and sensor), the over-pressure decrease phase is lower than 100 µs. In these cases, sensors with response time lower than 1 µs are required.

The pressure sensors commercially available and suitable for pyrotechnic applications, use mainly piezoelectric transducers with ceramic thick disk [2][3] or polymer thin film [4]. The typical response time of such sensors is about several microseconds for side-on configuration. High response times is mainly due to the large diameter (> 900µm), of used piezoelectric layers, in order to produce enough electrical charges.

In order to reduce the response time, micro-membranes with a diameter lower than 100 µm and based on optical transduction have been reported in [5]-[8]. These sensors have good dynamic performances with frequency bandwidth often higher than 10 MHz. But the optical transduction requires complex technological steps and does not facilitate the high integration of multiple sensors.

Recently, we proposed a transducer using a miniature monocrystalline silicon membrane and silicon piezoresistive gauges [9]-[10]. The objective was to combine the advantage of miniature membrane (sensing diameter < 100 µm) and the high integration of electronic transduction. In this paper, we report the design, fabrication and characterization of this transducer, and we explore the unexpected and undesirable mechanical response observed beyond 1 µs.

The paper is organized as follows. The design of the transducer is presented in Section 2. The Section 3 is dedicated to the fabrication of the transducer. The simulated (COMSOL) static pressure response of the transducer is given in Section 4. Finally, Section 5 describes the dynamic pressure response of the sensor using a shock tube.

II. TRANSDUCER DESIGN

The topology of the transducer is displayed in Figure 1 and Figure 2.

A N-type monocrystalline 5 µm thick silicon membrane is used for the mechanical transducer. This membrane is obtained by releasing the top layer of a Silicon-On-Insulator (SOI) substrate. Its shape is rectangular with targeted width W_M = 30 µm and length L_M = 90 µm.

The electrical transducer is provided by P-type monocrystalline silicon gauges, which are inserted at the center of the N-type silicon membrane and are distributed using the Wheatstone bridge configuration. The inter-isolation of the gauges is obtained from the reverse polarization of the P/N junction. The targeted gauges width is W_J = 1 µm and length L_J = 5 µm.

The pressure is applied on the top side of the membrane and a reference cavity with vacuum is located at the bottom side of the membrane.

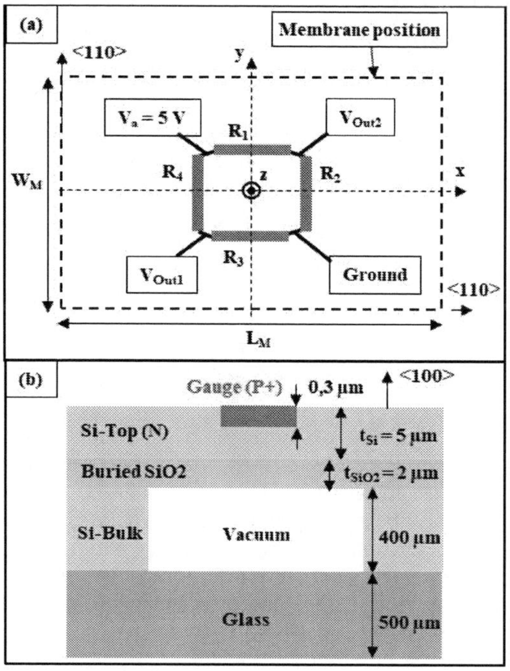

Figure 1. (a) Top view of the Wheatstone bridge reported on the membrane surface, (b) Cross sectional diagram of the transducer.

III. TRANSDUCER FABRICATION

This section describes, first of all, the different technological steps required for the fabrication of the transducer. Electrical characterization of the gauges is then discussed. The last part is dedicated to the measurement of the membrane dimensions.

A. Technological fabrication steps

The transducer fabrication uses SOI wafers, whose characteristics are given in Table 1. The transducer on its metallic holder is shown in Figure 3.

TABLE 1. SOI WAFERS CHARACTERISTICS PROVIDED BY THE SUPPLIER

Si-top	Orientation	(100)
	Type	N
	Doping level	$4.8*10^{15}$ to $1.6*10^{15}$ at/cm^3
	Thickness	(5.0 ± 0.5) µm
Buried SiO_2	Thickness	(2.0 ± 0.1) µm
Si Bulk	Orientation	(100)
	Thickness	(400 ± 15) µm

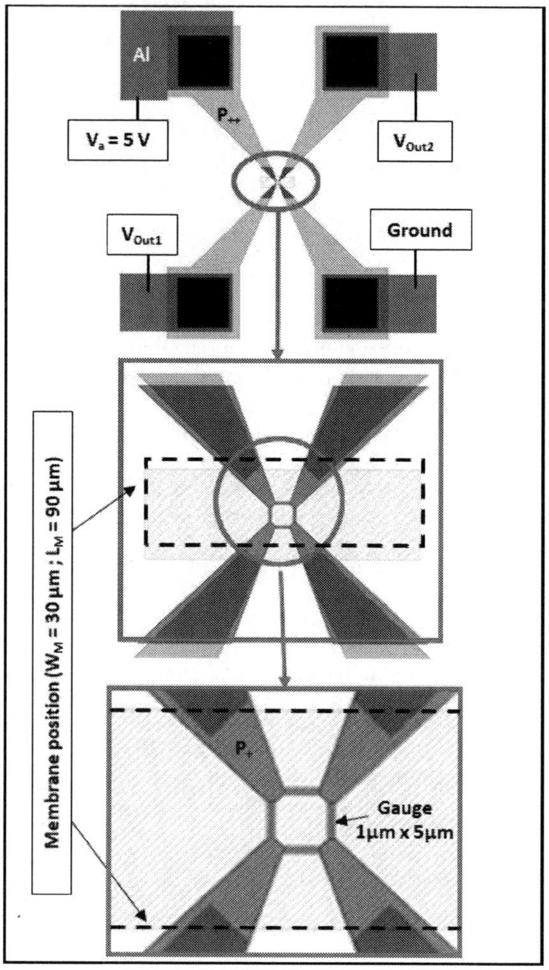

Figure 2. Top view of the mask used for the technological process

The technological process starts with the growing of a 40 nm thick thermal silicon dioxide (SiO_2) layer. Boron and phosphorus implantations are then performed respectively for the low resistivity interconnections between gauges and metallic lines and for the electrical contact on SiN-top. Both implantations are done with the same parameters (Energy = 50 keV, Dose = 10^{16} at/cm^2). The activation annealing of dopants is then performed during one hour at 1000 °C.

The next step is dedicated to the gauge's fabrication with boron implantation (Energy = 20 keV, Dose = $5*10^{14}$ at/cm^2). The activation annealing of dopants is performed with rapid thermal annealing during one minute at 1000 °C, in order to hold the dopant close to the membrane surface where the stress is maximal and then to maximize the transducer sensitivity. The surface concentration is of 3.5 10^{19} at/cm^3, which consists of a good trade-off between gauge sensitivities to strain and temperature. The junction depth is of 0.3 µm.

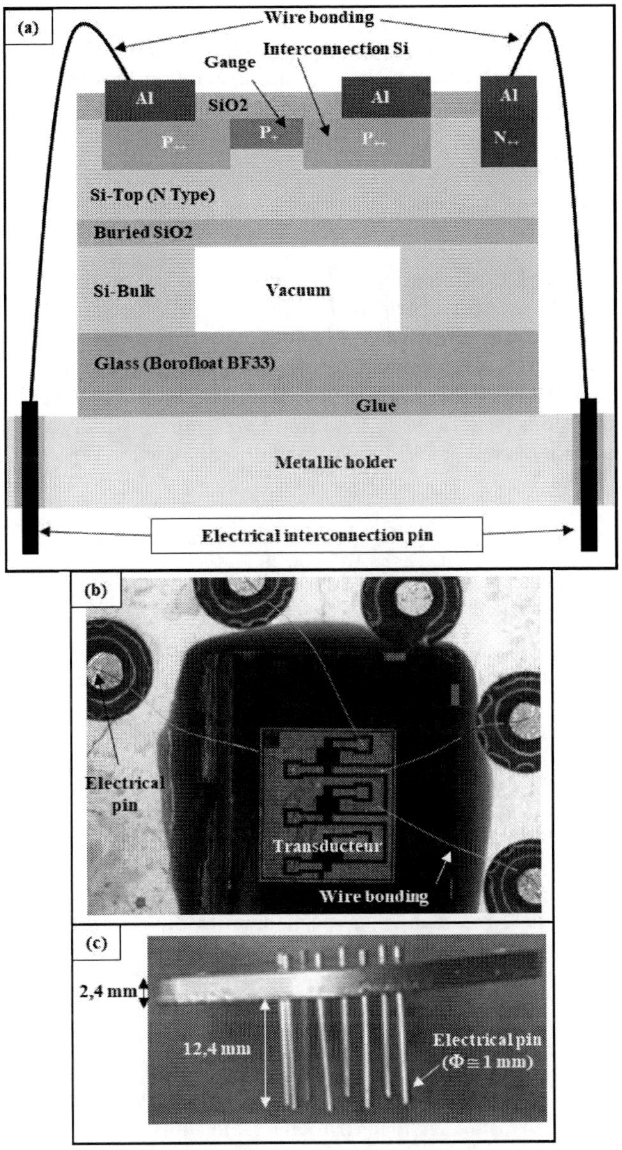

Figure 3. (a) Cross section diagram of the transducer on its metallic holder, (b) Top view of the transducer glued to the metallic holder, (c) View of TO3 metallic holder.

Next, the deposition of a 350 nm thick SiO_2 layer is performed at 300°C by Plasma Enhanced Chemical Vapor Deposition to provide enough electrical isolation between gauges and future metallic interconnections. After contact opening by liquid etching of the SiO_2 layer, a 500 nm thick aluminum layer is deposited by thermal evaporation for metallic interconnections. The silicon membrane is then released by using a Deep Reactive Ionic Etching (DRIE) of Si-bulk from back-side, up to the buried-SiO_2 etch-stop layer.

After the anodic bonding of the glass substrate on the silicon back side, the wafer is cut and the die is glued on a metallic holder. Wire bonding is finally performed between transducer pads and holder pin.

B. Electrical characteristics of the fabricated gauges

The transducer resistance R_{Transd} (between V_{out1} and V_{out2}), measured before the wafer dicing, is of (2990 ± 100) Ω. This measurement result is slightly lower than the simulated one (3650 Ω) obtained from COMSOL software, using mask dimension opening of $W_J = 1$ µm and $L_J = 5$ µm. With these dimensions, the gauge resistance R_J is of 1380 Ω. The difference with the transducer resistance R_{Transd} is due to the access resistance (mainly the P_+ interconnection between the gauges and the P_{++} interconnection).

As shown on Figure 4, the final dimensions of the fabricated gauge are impacted by the photoresist lateral under-etching d_{sur} = (110 ± 40) nm (Figure 4-a) and also by the boron diffusion d_{lat} (about 130 nm) during annealing, corresponding to a boron doping level of $1*10^{19}$ at/cm^3 (Figure 4-b). The final gauge width W_{Jf} and length L_{Jf} are respectively of 1.5 µm and 4.5 µm (equations (1) and (2)).

$$W_{Jf} = W_J + 2*d_{sur} + 2*d_{lat} \quad (1)$$

$$L_{Jf} = L_J - 2*d_{sur} - 2*d_{lat} \quad (2)$$

Using the dimensions W_{Jf} and L_{Jf} (instead of the dimension of the mask opening W_J and L_J), a very good agreement is obtained between the simulated transducer resistance R_{Transd} (3110 Ω) and the measured resistance (2990 Ω ± 100 Ω).

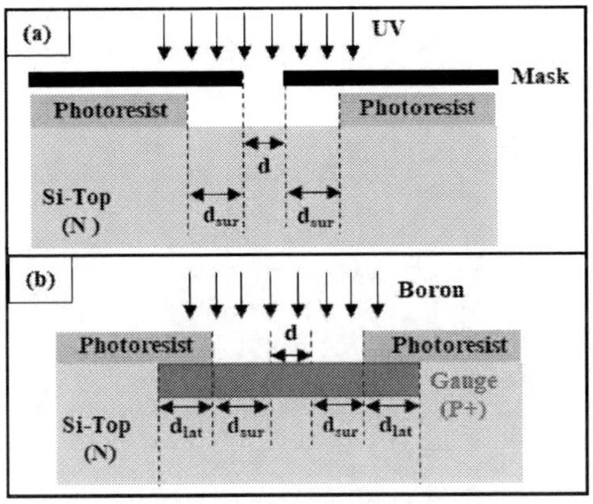

Figure 4. Cross section diagram of gauge showing lateral dimension increase due to the (a) Photoresist etching and (b) Boron diffusion.

C. Membrane dimensions

As shown in Figure 5, the membrane width is higher than the mask opening. This originates in the lateral under-etching of the 40 µm thick photoresist, the non-ideal vertical DRIE etching of silicon and finally the lateral under-etching of silicon related to the accumulation of chemical species, when the buried SiO_2 layer is reached.

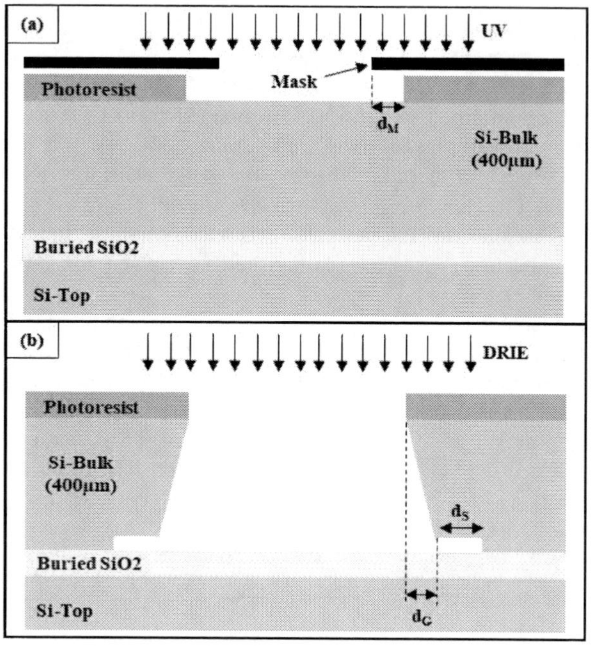

Figure 5. Cross section diagram of membrane showing lateral dimension increase due to the (a) Photoresist etching and (b) Si DRIE etching.

The dimensions of the fabricated membranes are measured on several samples using Focus Ion Beam (FIB) etching, for cross section realization, and Scanning Electron Microscopy (SEM), for dimensional measurements (Figure 6). The results obtained are given in Table 2.

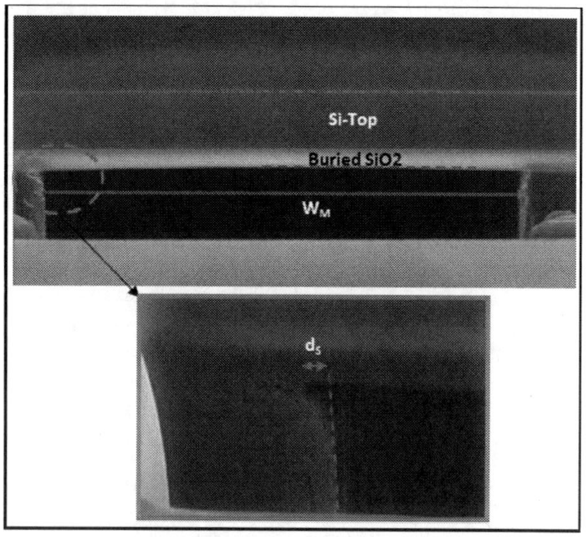

Figure 6. Cross section MEB photography after DRIE etching.

TABLE 2. MEMBRANE DIMENSIONS MEASUMED by SEM

Si-top thickness (µm)	5.0 ± 0.2 to 5.7 ± 0.2
Buried SiO_2 thickness (µm)	1.8 ±0.2 to 2.0 ±0.2
Membrane width (µm)	39.5 ± 0.2 to 42.5 ± 0.2

The Si-top and buried SiO_2 measured layers thicknesses are in good agreement with the characteristics provided by the supplier (Table 1). The average membrane width is of 41 µm, that is, 37 % larger than the mask width, with a scattering of ± 3.6 %.

IV. SIMULATED RESPONSE OF THE TRANSDUCER TO STATIC PRESSURE

COMSOL simulations were performed to predict the static transducer performances. The full design was considered (Figure 1 and Figure 2) with two membrane dimensions corresponding to the lowest and the highest mechanical stiffness given by the measured membrane dimensions (see Table 2). The static pressure sensitivity and the fundamental mechanical resonant frequency are reported in Table 3.

TABLE 3. SIMULATED (COMSOL) PERFORMANCES OF THE TRANSDUCER
Case-1: t_{Si} = 4.8 µm, t_{SiO2} = 2 µm, W_M = 43 µm, L_M = 103 µm
Case-2: t_{Si} = 5.9 µm, t_{SiO2} = 2 µm, W_M = 39 µm, L_M = 99 µm

	Case 1	Case 2
Static pressure sensitivity S_{Transd} (µV/V/bar)	209	138
Fundamental mechanical resonant frequency F_o (MHz)	25.7	34.3

The simulated static pressure sensitivity is between 138 µV/V/bar and 209 µV/V/bar. The uncertainty on the transducer sensitivity is then of ± 20.5 %.
The simulated fundamental mechanical resonant frequency of the membrane ranges from 25.7 MHz to 34.3 MHz, corresponding to an uncertainty of ± 14.3 %.

V. SHOCK TUBE CHARACTERIZATION OF THE FABRICATED SENSOR

This section describes, first of all, the setup used for the dynamic pressure characterization of the fabricated sensor. Then the sensor response, to a pressure step, is given. The last part analyses the sensor drift; that appears after 1 µs.

A. Setup description

The setup used for the dynamic pressure characterization of the sensor is illustrated on Figure 7.
A 2.7 m length and 11 cm inner-diameter metrological shock tube allows generating a pressure step with a rise time lower than 10 ns. The driver section is filled with nitrogen gas, while the driven section is at atmospheric pressure. The diaphragm, which separates the two sections, is a standard nickel rupture disc that opens fully and responds within milliseconds to the applied overpressure. Its rupture creates a shock wave that propagates along the tube until reflections by the metallic end-wall of the tube, where the pressure is measured both by our transducer and by using a commercial reference sensor (PCB Piezotronics 134A24) for comparison purpose.

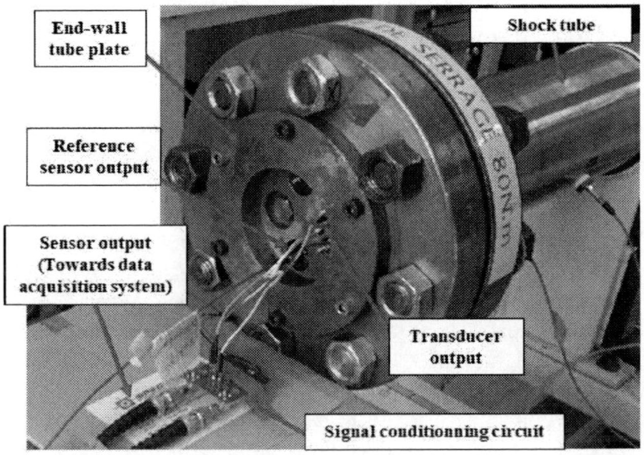

Figure 7. Experimental setup for dynamic pressure characterization

The transducer output is connected to a conditioning circuit through a length (10 cm) of shielded wires. The static gain of this circuit is of 0.9, with a cut-of frequency of 35 MHz. The sampling frequency of the data acquisition system is of 100 MHz.

B. Measured sensor response to a pressure step

The measured sensor response (at the output of the conditioning circuit) to a 10 bar pressure step is shown in Figure 8.

A typical damped oscillation is obtained in the first micro-second due to the excitation of the fundamental mechanical resonant mode of the membrane. From this measurement result, we can derive the main transducer characteristics: the rise time of 30 ns, the response time lower than 1 µs and the steady-state pressure sensitivity around 200 µV/V/bar (assuming a gain of 0.9 from the conditioning circuit). This sensitivity is then in good agreement with the simulated value.

The fundamental resonant frequency of 20.4 MHz is also in good agreement with the simulated value, as shown in Figure 9, which displays the spectral analysis of the measured sensor response. But beyond 1 µs, we observe that an unexpected drift appears. The next section is devoted to the interpretation of this drift.

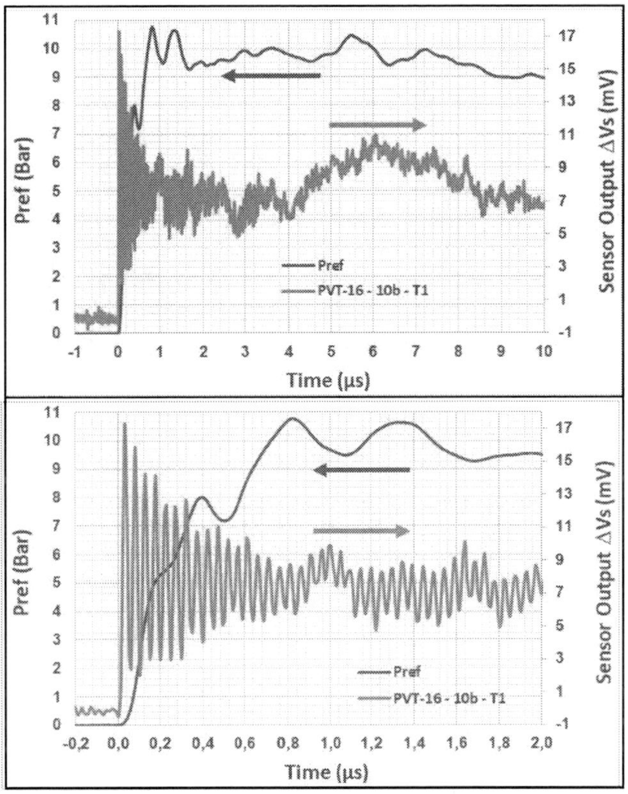

Figure 8. Measured sensor response to a 10 bar step pressure (orange line) and reference sensor (blue line)

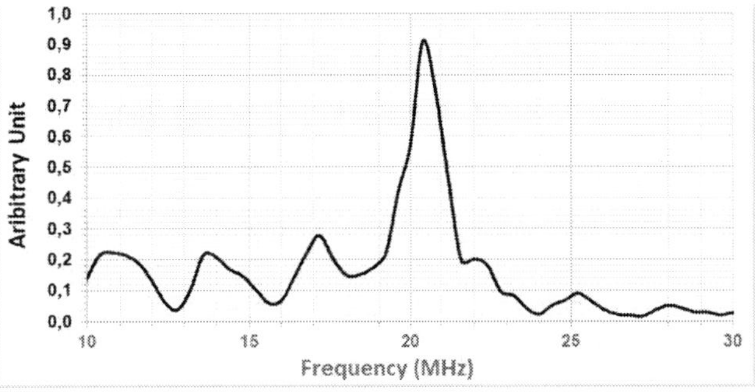

Figure 9. Spectral analysis of the sensor response derived from measurement

C. Analysis of the observed sensor drift

The sensor response to a 10 bar pressure step is shown in Figure 10 using four different measurement configurations.

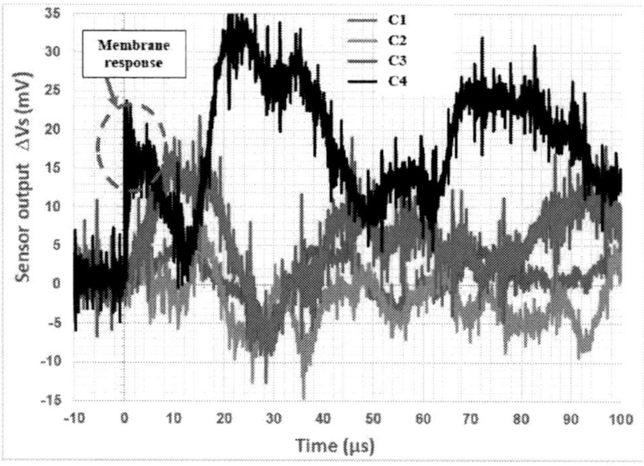

Figure 10. Sensor output with a 10 bar pressure step.
Configuration C1: Without membrane - With Cover
Configuration C2: Without membrane - Without Cover
Configuration C3: With membrane - With Cover
Configuration C4: With membrane - Without Cover

In configuration C1, the Si-Bulk is not removed below the gauges and a metallic cover is used to avoid direct shock wave effect (blue color). In this configuration, only indirect strain is applied on the gauges, without the membrane amplification. A slow variation of the sensor response is observed, with an amplitude of ± 5mV.

The same transducer is used in the configuration C2, but without the metallic cover (orange color). Compared with configuration C1, the sensor response is not significantly modified, but a higher amplitude (± 10mV) is observed due to the direct impact of the shock wave under the gauge and/or the mechanical stiffening of the metallic holder by the metallic cover.

In the configuration C3, the response of a transducer with a membrane and a metallic cover is measured (red color). The large undesirable effect observed in the response (around 3 times of one recorded in the configuration C1) can be explained by the mechanical deformations of the metallic holder, which are transmitted to the membrane and then amplified.

Finally, the same transducer used in the configuration C3 is measured in configuration C4, but without the metallic cover (black color). As expected, the membrane response is apparent in the first micro-seconds, and consequently, the drift occurs.

VI. Conclusions and Future Works

The characterization of supersonic shock wave produced by explosives requires sensor with response time lower than 1 µs in order to quantify accurately the maximum overpressure in several side-on configurations. With sensing diameter greater than 900 µm, the commercial sensors are not able to fulfill this specification. Researches are focused on miniature membranes (diameter < 100 µm), but they very often applied an optical transduction, which requires complex technological steps and are not compatible with the integration of several transducers on the same chip.

We proposed here a pressure transducer using a miniature silicon membrane and piezoresistive gauges in order to combine the advantage of miniature sensing area and microelectronic integration. A miniature piezoresistive pressure sensor was designed, fabricated and characterized within a shock tube. The proposed sensor has a very low rise time (about 30 ns) and a short response time (about 1 µs), thanks to the high fundamental mechanical resonant mode of the membrane (close to 20 MHz). Mechanical parasitic effects, that leads to large drift after few microseconds, were explored and identified. This effect was interpreted as the result of the metallic holder deformation due to the shock wave. New packaging with higher mechanical stiffness will be designed in order to reduce these undesirable effects in the pressure response of the transducer.

Acknowledgment

This work was partially funded by Occitanie Region, France, through the COCNANO project and was supported by LAAS-CNRS micro and nanotechnologies platform members of the French RENATECH network.

References

[1] L. Walter, "Air-blast and the Science of Dynamic Pressure Measurements", Sound and Vibration, Vol. 38, No 12, pp 10-17, Dec. 2004.

[2] Piezotronics PCB [https://www.pcb.com/sensors-for-test-measurement/pressure-transducers/blast-transducers].

[3] Kistler [https://www.kistler.com/?type=669&fid=85810&model=document].

[4] Muller Instrument [https://mueller-instruments.de/en/pressure-measurement/pressure-sensor-m/].

[5] N. Wu et al."An ultra-fast fiber optic pressure sensor for blast event measurements", Measurements Sciences and Technologies, Vol. 23, No 5, April 2012, doi:10.1088/0957-0233/23/5/055102.

[6] X. Zou, N. Wu, Y. Tian, C. Niezrecki, J. Chen, X. Wang, "Rapid miniature fiber optic pressure sensors for blast wave measurements", Optics and lasers in Engineering, Vol. 51, No 2, pp 134-139, Feb. 2013, doi : 10.1016/j.optlaseng.2012.09.001.

[7] Z. Wang, G. Wen, Z. Wu, J. Yang, L. Chen, W. Liu, "Fiber optic method for obtaining the peak reflected pressure of shock wave", Optic Express, Vol. 28, No 12, June 2018, doi: 10.1364/OE.26.015199.

[8] C. Chu, J. Wang, J. Qiu, "Miniature High-Frequency Response, High-Pressure-Range Dynamic Pressure Sensor Based on All-Silica Optical Fiber Fabry-Perot Cavity", IEEE Sensor Journal, Vol. 21, No 12, pp 13296-13304, June 2021, doi: 10.1109/JSEN.2021.3068456.

[9] J. Riondet et al. "Design of air blast pressure sensors based on miniature silicon membrane and piezoresistive gauges", Journal of Physics: Conference Series, Vol. 922, Aug. 2017, doi: 10.1088/1742-6596/922/1/012019.

[10] J. Veyrunes et al., "Transient response of miniaturized piezoresistive sensors for side-on pressure shockwave", Proc. Design, Test, Integration & Packaging of MEMS/MOEMS, 12-15 May 2019, Paris, France, doi: 10.1109/DTIP.2019.8752911.

HCI Preliminary Study and Implementation for a LoRa based SAR System

Christos Bouras
Computer Engineering and Informatics
University of Patras
Patras, Greece
email: bouras@ceid.upatras.gr

Apostolos Gkamas
University Ecclesiastical Academy of Vella
Ioannina, Greece
email: gkamas@aeavellas.gr

Spyridon Aniceto Katsampiris Salgado
Computer Engineering and Informatics
University of Patras
Patras, Greece
email: ksalgado@ceid.upatras.gr

***Abstract*— The subject of this paper is the study and implementation of a Long Range (LoRa) based Search and Rescue system that can help in the localization of people having a high risk of going missing. These people may suffer from dementia, attention disturbance, and distraction, or disease in the autism spectrum, and it is of great importance to be found in a specific time frame, as their life can be in danger. The system is based on LoRa network architecture that enables both long-range communication and low energy consumption. In this paper, aspects of the human-computer interaction were taken into consideration in contrast to the majority of the related papers, and the proposed system is evaluated using heuristic evaluation and questionnaires.**

Keywords—IoT; LoRa; LPWAN; UX; HCI

I. INTRODUCTION

A large percentage of individuals with dementia are at risk of wandering and go missing. These people may be injured, causing trauma to themselves and their families and caregivers, and necessitate the use of costly Search and Rescue (SAR) operations. Furthermore, according to a study, about half of children with Autism Spectrum Disorder (ASD) have attempted to elude parental control at least once and eventually go missing while walking.

In this context, the Internet of Things (IoT) can benefit vastly the SAR operations. The widespread use of fitness trackers, Global Positioning System (GPS) devices, smartwatches, and other portable IoT technology opens up new avenues for improving protection and caring for people with a high probability to go missing. The technologies are ranging from gait and behavior analysis to GPS trackers that assist in the localization of the missing. As a result, such systems have some requirements that should be met to operate effective. The core requirements are a) the communication technology and protocols, b) the localization accuracy, c) the energy consumption and d) Human-Computer Interaction (HCI).

As far as the communication technologies are concerned different wireless technologies can facilitate such systems each technology posing different advantages and disadvantages. For outdoor monitoring systems, a new class of wireless technologies has been created. This class is called Low Power Wide Area Networks (LPWAN) and the main characteristics of this class is the low energy consumption, the long-range communication, and the low cost. One of the most important technology is the Long Range (LoRa) technology. As far as the localization process is concerned the GPS technology is widely used, because it provides high localization accuracy, but this accuracy comes with a price in terms of energy consumption. Thus, a combination of LoRa use and a localization process based on LoRa instead of the GPS may enable a new potential for the SAR systems.

From a HCI standing point, such systems have a lot of parameters that affect the user experience, because there are many stakeholders, for example, the person that wears the portable device, the supervisor that uses the interactive interface through which the location is monitored. HCI is a multidisciplinary area of research that focuses on the architecture of computer technology, specifically the interaction between humans (users) and computers. HCI, which was originally concerned with computers, has since grown to include nearly all aspects of information technology architecture, and in our case IoT systems.

Many systems have been proposed for SAR systems. In [1] the authors studied a LoRa based system, and in [2] have studied a LoRa based system focusing on localization algorithms for LoRa. In contrast to the above works, in this paper, we focus on the human-computer interaction aspects of such a system. The authors of [3] employ IoT in conjunction with an Unmanned Aerial Vehicle (UAV) for SAR missions. Specifically, the usage of UAVs provides supporting information to rescuers. In this paper, the focus is given on wearable device-based localization monitoring, without the costly UAV technology employed. In [4] the authors provide a study on the feasibility of machine learning algorithms used to GPS data to anticipate the potential paths of dementia patients. The authors propose that prediction models for each individual may be generated based on the frequency with which the user wears the wearable device, and therefore GPS data is gathered. In addition, in the [5], the authors built a GPS-based fall detection system to broadcast the position where the individual fell. The primary drawback of the works [4][5] is that, in contrast to LoRa, GPS quickly consumes the battery of the IoT device.

The goal of this research work is to create a SAR system based on LoRa using wearable devices. In contrast to other similar systems, in this paper, a human-centered approach has been followed to understand the stakeholder's requirements and needs, following the *Norman Interaction Model* and *Design Thinking* frameworks. Moreover, heuristic evaluation was conducted, and a small-scale experiment was conducted with a small number of participants and a questionnaire was disseminated to them. It is important to note that the experiment's goal was not the fully understand the users, so the results did not reach statistical significance but to expose some more usability issues to be improved in the next iterations. Also, some mechanisms of energy consumption were integrated from our previous works such as [6]-[10].

The structure of the paper is the following: the next section explains the motivation of the work. Section III gives an overview of the IoT concepts and explains the wireless technology that is used. Section IV gives an overview of the SAR domain, for a better understanding of the reader about the scenario use. Section V provides information about the HCI-based procedure of the implementation. In section VI the system parts and architecture are presented, and in Section VII the evaluation process of the interface is presented. Lastly, the conclusion and future work is presented.

II. MOTIVATION

Alzheimer's disease (AD) and other causes of dementia are major public health concerns. There are reportedly about 5.4 million people in the United States who have dementia, with 70-80% of all people with dementia in the United States being cared for at home by a family member [12] with 15 million nurses providing an estimated 18.2 billion hours of treatment annually. It is projected that 60% of dementia patients will wander [12]. Wandering can occur as a result of a person with dementia, such as Alzheimer's, being unable to recall his or her name or address, and becoming disoriented even in familiar surroundings. Wandering and getting lost can happen during the mild, moderate, or serious stages of AD and can be risky (leading to falls and injuries, institutionalization, and death) as well as stressful for families and caregivers [12]. Having dementia over a longer period, the severity of dementia (though wandering can occur at any stage), the prevalence of a sleep disorder, deterioration in day-to-day functioning, and behavioral disturbances such as anxiety and depression are all associated with wandering [13]. Thus, we can conclude that it is of paramount importance to monitor the people suffering from such diseases, to find them when they get lost.

Moreover, ASD affects about one of every 59 children in the United States, a neurodevelopmental condition marked by chronic deficiencies in social cognition and social contact, as well as limited and repeated patterns of conduct. Some people with ASD exhibit maladaptive behaviors, such as wandering/elopement, which is described as leaving a controlled, secure environment without the consent or permission of a caregiver. It is estimated that almost half of children with ASD aged 4 years and older have participated in elopement activity at least once, and of those who have eloped, about one-quarter went missing for a period of time that worried caregivers. Children with ASD are at a higher risk of serious injury or death as a result of this action. Drowning, in fact, has been found to be one of the leading causes of death among people with ASD, and wandering was cited as the most prevalent activity that resulted in drowning deaths. In a convenience survey of 1218 children with ASD aged 4 to 17 years, 24 percent had a history of elopement and were in danger of drowning [14].

According to the 2011 Pathways research survey [15], more than 25% of parents of children with ASD used fencing, gates, locks, alarms, or other barriers to avoid elopement in the previous year; 3.5% of parents reported using an electronic tracking system for their infant. The tracking systems are handheld systems that use a variety of technologies, such as GPS technology, wireless networks, Bluetooth, or radiofrequency communications, to locate a child's location in real-time. Any monitoring system can also be configured to define safe zones, giving parents the option of being alerted if their child enters a potentially dangerous environment, such as a swimming pool. Although these features cannot physically prevent elopement, tracking systems can likely increase parents' quality of life by giving them peace of mind in understanding that they may be able to react to elopement episodes more easily and locate their children. Andersen et al. [14] conducted a 2019 report to assess the efficacy, burden, and cost of multiple elopement avoidance measures in a cohort of children with ASD. They discovered that only 6% of households have ever used GPS trackers, and they confirmed that GPS trackers were considered by parents to be less reliable, more difficult to adopt, and more costly than certain physical approaches. They did, however, just look at GPS trackers, while this kind of system can use a range of technologies. Furthermore, their sample of GPS-enabled children was limited (n=534), significantly restricting the accuracy (and presumably generalizability) of their results.

III. INTERNET OF THINGS

There is a lot of discussions nowadays about various innovations that take place in the field of computer engineering and informatics, one of these being the IoT. IoT is mainly multi-parametric, and for this reason, a plethora of technologies, protocols, and prototypes are used in order to support the notion of IoT. Some features with which categorization of the wireless technologies can be done are the communication range, the energy consumption, etc. Thus, wireless technologies can be categorized into technologies of short-range communication, cellular technologies, and LPWAN.

The LPWAN technologies come to fulfill the gap between short-range communication technologies and cellular technologies, as their main features are the energy-efficiency, long-range communication, and low cost, usually compromising the latency and throughput. LPWANs are designed to co-operate with existing short-range radio and cellular IoT networks; though, the user or application must decide which network(s) to use, according to the application's needs and requirements. LPWANs are usually accepted to have a target range of a few kilometers in urban areas and tens of kilometers in rural areas around 10 km in Line of Sight (LoS) conditions. One important LPWAN technology is called LoRa [19].

LoRa technology is a broader term that consists of two main parts. The first one is called LoRa that defines the physical layer of the technology and the modulation technique. The other part called Long Range Wide Area Network (LoRaWAN) refers to the open specification protocol developed by the LoRa Alliance which is an inclusive community in which any person or organization is welcome to participate. LoRa is predominantly a manufacturing-driven business model, with Semtech transceivers being the only ones available, in contrast to Sigfox that follows a subscriber business model or the NB-IoT that operates in the licensed spectrum.

IV. SEARCH AND RESCUE

In this section, the requirements in terms of the hardware, and other constraints are being discussed. First of all, a requirement is that the wearable device that the person should wear. This device should support a technology that can connect to the internet, in many cases such as in suburban conditions where broadband or cellular wireless technologies are out of range. Also, this device should support all the necessary sensors that help in the decision of the emergency state, such sensors could be heart rate sensors, etc. Furthermore, all the networking components and technologies such as cellular towers, femtocells, LoRa Gateway should be present, or the operator of such a SAR system should take special care in order for the wearable device to be able to have supplementary modules that support different technologies.

Another part that is of paramount importance in such systems is localization accuracy. Especially, in the wild and places with mountainous environments, a difference in the localization could be costly to the SAR operations. This can happen as an error of a 500m radius could make the rescuers climb a hill, or descend a canyon, wasting both valuable resources but most importantly, wasting vital time as the person that has been lost can be in danger. Also, the data rate is important, too. In the scenarios where the person that is missing is for example suffering from ASD, the person can move freely, something that leads to a new problem: the need for almost real-time monitoring. One technology that can provide real-time localization with high accuracy is the well-known and widely used GPS. The GPS, formerly known as Navstar, is a satellite-based radio navigation system, that is widely used.

One of the drawbacks of GPS use for SAR scenarios is the fact that is highly energy-consuming. Despite its high accuracy, the battery life of the energy-constrained wearable devices is reduced dramatically, when the GPS module is enabled. In order to understand the importance of the large battery lifetime and consequently the energy consumption, it is good to examine the [20]. The [20] studies the existence of a rule for the selection of SAR operations based on the search time duration, in order to maximize the rescue of the living missing people. For a large number of survivors n = 1439, the average value of the search duration is 7.9 hours with a maximum duration of 323 hours or about 13 days. Specifically, by an estimated cut-off point of 51 hours, almost all the survivors have been located, whereas by 100 hours almost all the lost persons, dead or alive have been located (not rescued). Therefore, the battery life must be large enough to give the necessary time to the rescuers to locate and rescue the people. It is worth noting that it is important for the SAR operations to have "contact" with the wearable device, even though the wearable device's battery is not fully charged.

V. SYSTEM ARCHITECTURE

In this section, the system architecture is presented. The system consists of 4 main parts: a) End Devices (ED); in this study the wearable is based on Dialog's DA 14861 platform with a LoRa module integrated. b) The Gateway (GW), which is a device responsible for translating the packets transmitted through LoRa to Internet packets and vice versa. The GW relays the LoRa packets to the respective Network Server (NS). c) The NS is a server responsible to supervise and set the network parameters. d) The Application Server (AS). In Figure 1, a typical deployment of LoRa system is presented, showing each LoRa component. Figure 2 shows a DA 14864 wearable device incorporating a LoRa module. Figure 2 shows a LoRa GW that is placed on the University of Patras Campus.

As far as the web application is concerned, the main technical aspect of the application is the web framework called Flask. As far as the front-end development is concerned HyperText Markup Language 5 (HTML), Cascading Style Sheets 3 (CSS), Bootstrap 4, JavaScript ES6, and jQuery 3.5.1 were used. For the Relational Database Management System (RDMS) the SQLite 3 technology has been used. As far as the maps in the web application are concerned the Leaflet has been used. The Leaflet is an open-source JavaScript library for creating mobile-friendly interactive maps. Figure 3 shows the homepage of the web application.

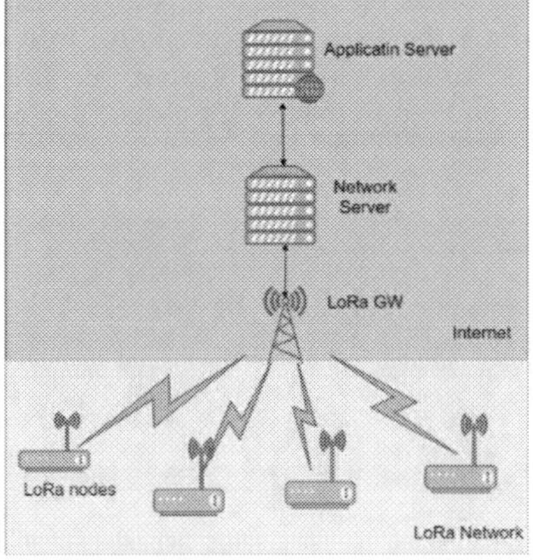

Figure 1. LoRa deployment architecture.

Figure 2. Left: a DA 14861 wearable device, Right: a LoRa GW in the University of Patras campus

The basic scenarios that the system provide to the user are the following: a) The user logs in to the system, b) definition of the allowed region, c) Location monitoring, d) Set the wearable device's state to an emergency/normal state, 7) See past packet information.

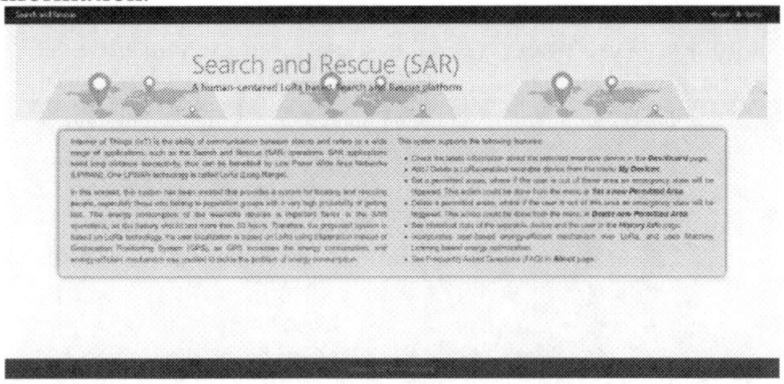

Figure 3. The homepage of the web application.

When a user enters the website, the homepage is the first thing that is presented (Figure 3). When the user logs in, a page is showed with a personalized message to the user informing about the last selected wearable device. Then, the user is redirected to the Dashboard page. On this page the user can find a leaflet map where the latest position of the person has the wearable device, having a tooltip showing the current state of the user (e.g., normal state or emergency state) and the timestamp of the latest LoRa packet. Moreover, below the map, a table is presented where the latest information of the user and the sensor measurements such as the HR, and the pedometer. The Dashboard page is presented in Figure 4. Also, there is a button with which the user can click it in order to set the wearable device to the emergency state, or to cancel the emergency state and return to the normal state again.

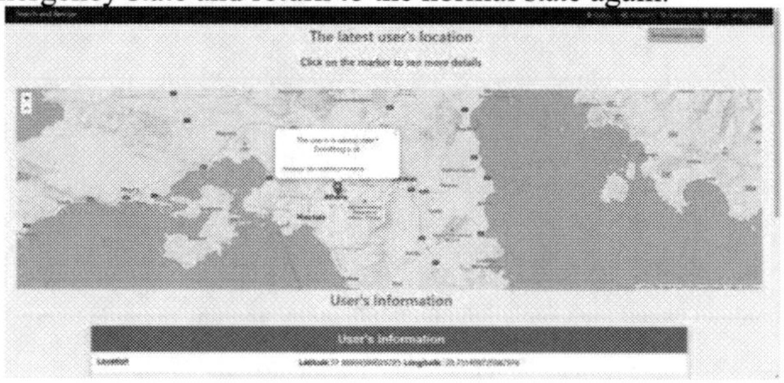

Figure 4. Dashboard

If the user needs to add a new region in which the person suffering from dementia or ASD should move, and if this person exits this region then, the emergency state is triggered. The user should click "Actions" ->"Set permitted Area". On this web page, there is text giving guidelines to the user on how to add a permitted area Figure 5. Next, there is a map, in which the user can draw a circle, representing the permitted area. Then a tooltip type form is presented in which the user can add a Title and a Description. Furthermore, the user can check the previously added permitted areas through the "Check your permitted areas". On this page, the user can see in the map the boundaries of the permitted regions and by clicking on the circles the user can see the respective details and information. Also, the user can check the packet history via the "History" webpage. In this page, the user can see the history of the packets received in a tabular. In the navigational bar the user can spot and click the option "About" where the user can see the Frequently Asked Questions (FAQ). Lastly, the user in order to logout has to click on the logout option in the navigational bar. When the user clicks on the logout option a popup modal is shown that asks for the user's confirmation.

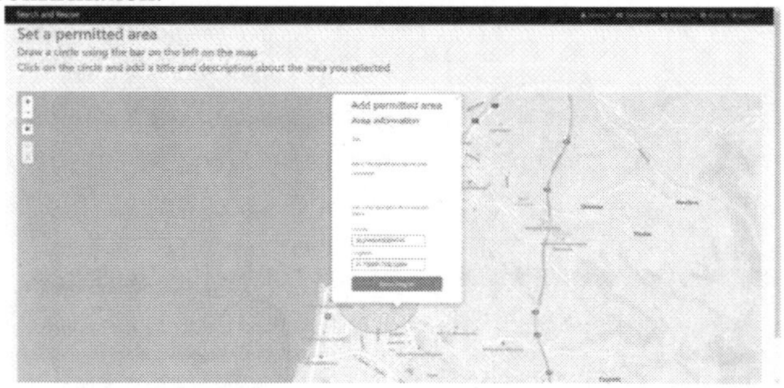

Figure 5. First page in the *"Add new allowed region"* scenario.

VI. HCI Approach And Evaluation

The main goal of computer systems is to be designed under a user-centered approach to help people use them effectively and easily. Every computer system has a target group and for this reason, it has to follow the appropriate design that will satisfy the need and capabilities of that group. Designers of that system think that people have a certain task in their mind, and they have to deliver them a system without complexity. Furthermore, it is very important to make people feel that have control of this system. System designers must know how to translate user's needs into system capabilities and the first step in this process happens with a good design of a system interface. A well-designed interface allows people to interact with the system and deal with any difficulties without external help while at the same time they have full control of the machine. For this reason, the topic of user-centered design has become the most important concept in the design of interactive systems. The keyword, in this case, is the term usability [21].

Usability criteria

The following ten usability criteria were isolated from work by Nielsen.

- The first principle is the visibility of system status.
- Match between the system and the physical world.
- User control and freedom.
- Consistency and standards.
- Error prevention.
- Recognition rather than recall.
- Flexibility and Efficiency of use.
- Aesthetic and Minimalistic Design.
- Help users recognize, diagnose and recover from errors.
- Help and documentation are the last principles.

An evaluation based on basic heuristics and the new can give valuable results about website usability and how can an existing one be more usable and user-friendly.

Heuristic evaluation is a usability engineering method that helps designers find out weak spots and usability problems in their designs. For the evaluation problem generally, a small group of evaluators for the different background are needed. Each evaluator is given sufficient time to test the design in form of mockups or prototypes, find usability problems, write them down on a catalog and also propose a change. When the evaluation process is done for all the evaluators then, they are allowed to communicate with each other and discuss their findings. This procedure is important because in this way the evaluation process is independent and unbiased. Table I presents the problems and the heuristics that were violated in each problem.

In May 2021 the evaluation process of the Search and Rescue prototype took place in the office of the Laboratory of Distributed Systems and Telematics at Rio, Patras. The evaluation team consisted of three people: two HCI Master level graduates and one engineer specialist on monitoring systems with a background in Business and Management Administration. Each evaluator has a certain time of arrival and in 40 minutes it had to evaluate the prototype alone only with the company of the website's designer that had the role of observer. The reason that the evaluation occurred on prototypes instead of simply mock-ups was that prototypes allowed the changes between different pages of the website to achieve the feel of a real functional site.

Evaluators were given a heuristic evaluation sheet that was relevant to the 10 heuristics. There they could note issues and problems that would arise and in the next frame their recommendation about how the interface could be better. Also, on the left side of the sheet, they could note the severity score for each one of the heuristics. The severity follows a particular scale:

- 0-I don't agree this is a usability problem at all.
- 1-Cosmetic problems only needed not to be fixed unless extra time is available on the project.
- 2-Minor usability problem: fixing this should be given low priority.
- 3-Major usability problem: important to fix, so should be given high priority.
- 4-Usability catastrophe: imperative to fix this before the product can be released.

TABLE I. LIST OF THE ERRORS DURING THE HEURISTIC EVALUATION.

Problems	Heuristic violated
1. First screen	*Aesthetic and minimalistic design*
2. Menu actions	*Connection between physical and digital world*
3. Set a permitted area	*Aesthetic and minimalistic design*
4. Check the permitted area	*Consistency of the system*
5. Add permitted area	*Help and documentation + navigation*
6.Registration of new area, wearables list and addition of wearable device	*Error prevention*
7. History	*Aesthetic design*
8. Emergency button	*Connection between physical and digital world*
9. Emergency state	*Visibility of system status*
10. Window segmentation	*Minimalistic design*
11. Redirecting between pages	*Navigation*
12. Design of pages and menu	*Responsive design*

In the Table II an example of the problems found in the heuristic is presented, and particularly the ninth problem is presented. In Figure 4 the screen after the heuristic evaluation is presented.

After the heuristic evaluation, the necessary improvements were made. After this, another iteration was made, but at this time a usability questionnaire was given to each one of 10 random participants, who are frequent internet users that were called to test the prototype online, and then, they answered the questionnaire. This happened in order to test if there are more problems with the interfaces. The study uses a standard questionnaire that could help with the formulation and validation of the questions. More particular the questionnaire that was used was the SUS questionnaire (System Usability Scale).

TABLE II. PROBLEM NO 9.

Issue	When the user clicks on the emergency button, the system triggers an alarm that means that one of the subjects with the wearable device on it has been lost. In the prototype form what the system did was to notifying users by making the whole screen red on every page (Figure 6). This change bothered all the participants that did not understand what the meaning of the red color was. This action violated the heuristic of visibility of system status as well as consistency and standards. The red screen when the set emergency state is active disturbs users
Problem Severity	5
Recommendation	Find an alternative way of showing danger and emergency Figure 7

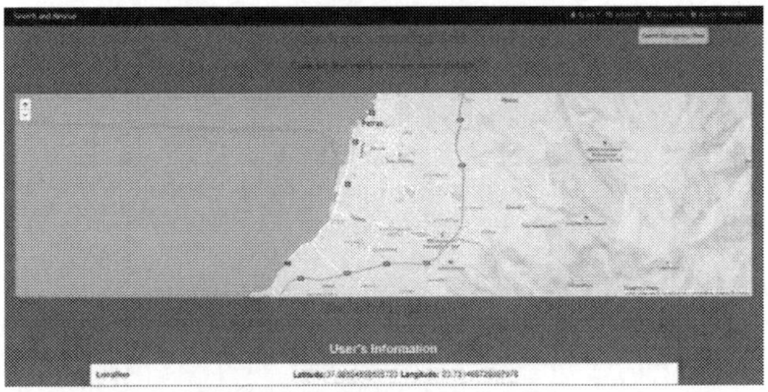

Figure 6. Initial emergency state case.

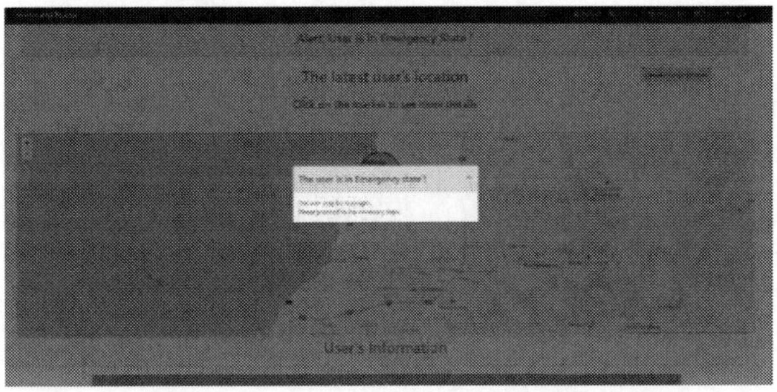

Figure 7. Emergency state alert after evaluation.

The purpose of the work was not to make a statistical analysis but to use the questionnaire as an additional means of evaluation. After all, the number of participants as was mentioned above was small. Considering this situation, the answers that are presented are the most characteristic ones. In the first question, 50% of participants agree that they wanted to use more frequently a system like Search and Rescue because of the purpose it serves, and the rest 50% were divided into neutral and disagree answers. This discrepancy occurred because apart from the three participants from the evaluation process that had an academic background the other participants were high school graduates that use frequently websites and the internet. In the second question "I found Search and Rescue website unnecessary complex" three of the participants were neutral with a scale of 3, five strongly disagree with a 4 scale score and the other two participants answer strongly agree with a scale of 2.

The fact that 30% of the participants' score was 3 and above reveals in combination with the comments through an evaluation process that i) some users were not familiar with a technical website that is aiming at one certain purpose. The heuristic evaluation process had great results as the majority of the users feel that the system is not complex. Something that arise also from the answer in questions 8 and 9. In question 8 all of the ten responds were neutral while in the question 9 only 70% of the participants strongly agree (5) about how confident they were with the use of the website when only 30% of the answers were divided into neutral and disagree. The fact that they were engaged with internet websites it was sufficient enough to make them feel confident about the use of this particular website. Then we calculated the score of the questionnaire, and the score was 72.5. The general guideline for SUS questionnaires classifies it with grade B, which means that the designed system is good and is also greater than the average grade of 68.

VII. Conclusion and Future Work

As mentioned in the previous sections, the need for an IoT-based SAR system has been understood and explained, in order to save the lives of people that have a high probability to go missing. The benefits of such a system can be of paramount importance for the person that goes missing, for the peace of mind of the caretakers and the people that are responsible for the people such as in the case of people suffering from dementia or ASD. Also, emerging technologies, such as the LoRa technology can help to create SAR systems due to many factors, such as it can transmit over long distances and keeps the energy consumption at low levels.

For future work, the examination of different wireless technologies such as the Sigfox or 5th Generation networks will be taken into consideration. Also, after the COVID 19 pandemic is over an ethnographic study should be designed in institutions for people suffering from AD or dementia. Finally, another aspect that can be studied and examined is the legal part of the system that concerns people that can not be fully aware of legal concepts, for example, a person who suffers from dementia can not practically agree or disagree if the person that is responsible about the safety has the right to monitor the position and other vital personal information.

References

[1] C. Bouras, A. Gkamas, V. Kokkinos, and N. Papachristos, "Real-Time Geolocation Approach through LoRa on Internet of Things," 2021 International Conference on Information Networking (ICOIN), 2021, pp. 186-191, doi: 10.1109/ICOIN50884.2021.9333860.

[2] G. M. Bianco, R. Giuliano, G. Marrocco, F. Mazzenga, and A. Mejia-Aguilar, "LoRa System for Search and Rescue: Path-Loss Models and Procedures in Mountain Scenarios," in IEEE Internet of Things Journal, vol. 8, no. 3, pp. 1985-1999, 1 Feb.1, 2021, doi: 10.1109/JIOT.2020.3017044.

[3] S. Kashihara, M. A. Wicaksono, D. Fall, and M. Niswar, "Supportive Information to Find Victims from Aerial Video in Search and Rescue Operation," 2019 IEEE International Conference on Internet of Things and Intelligence System (IoTaIS), BALI, Indonesia, 2019, pp. 56-61, doi: 10.1109/IoTaIS47347.2019.8980435.

[4] J. Wojtusiak and R. M. Nia, Location prediction using GPS trackers: Can machine learning help locate the missing people with dementia?, Internet of Things, 2019, 100035, ISSN 2542-6605, https://doi.org/10.1016/j.iot.2019.01.002.

[5] S. Nooruddin, M. M. Islam, and F. A. Sharna, An IoT based device-type invariant fall detection system, Internet of Things, Volume 9, 2020, 100130, ISSN 2542-6605, https://doi.org/10.1016/j.iot.2019.100130.

[6] C. J. Bouras, A. Gkamas, S. A. K. Salgado, and N. Papachristos, "A Comparative Study of Machine Learning Models for Spreading Factor Selection in LoRa Networks:," International Journal of Wireless Networks and Broadband Technologies, vol. 10, no. 2, pp. 100–121, Jul. 2021, doi: 10.4018/IJWNBT.2021070106.

[7] C. Bouras, A. Gkamas, S. A. K. Salgado, and N. Papachristos, "Spreading Factor Selection Mechanism for Transmission over LoRa Networks", in 28th International Conference on Telecommunications (ICT 2021), June 1 - 3, 2021, London, UK , 2021

[8] C. Bouras, A. Gkamas, and S. A. K. Salgado, "Energy efficient mechanism for LoRa networks," Internet of Things, vol. 13, p. 100360, Mar. 2021, doi: 10.1016/j.iot.2021.100360.

[9] C. Bouras, A. Gkamas, and S. Aniceto Katsampiris Salgado, "Exploring the energy efficiency for Search and Rescue operations over LoRa," 2021 11th IFIP International Conference on New Technologies, Mobility and Security (NTMS), 2021, pp. 1-5, doi: 10.1109/NTMS49979.2021.9432652.

[10] C. Bouras, A. Gkamas, S. A. Katsampiris Salgado, and N. Papachristos, "Spreading Factor Analysis for LoRa Networks: A Supervised Learning Approach," in Trends and Applications in Information Systems and Technologies, vol. 1365, Á. Rocha, H. Adeli, G. Dzemyda, F. Moreira, and A. M. Ramalho Correia, Eds. Cham: Springer International Publishing, 2021, pp. 344–353. doi: 10.1007/978-3-030-72657-7_33.

[11] "Alzheimer's Association": https://www.alz.org/help-support/caregiving/stages-behaviors/wandering#who [retrieved: October, 2021].

[12] "Mayo Clinic": https://www.mayoclinic.org/healthy-lifestyle/caregivers/in-depth/alzheimers-caregiver/art-20045847 [retrieved: October, 2021].

[13] N. Ali et al., "Risk assessment of wandering behavior in mild dementia: Risk factors of wandering behavior," Int J Geriatr Psychiatry, vol. 31, no. 4, pp. 367–374, Apr. 2016, doi: 10.1002/gps.4336.

[14] C. Anderson et al., "Occurrence and Family Impact of Elopement in Children With Autism Spectrum Disorders," PEDIATRICS, vol. 130, no. 5, pp. 870–877, Nov. 2012, doi: 10.1542/peds.2012-0762.

[15] C. E. Rice et al., "Reported Wandering Behavior among Children with Autism Spectrum Disorder and/or Intellectual Disability," The Journal of Pediatrics, vol. 174, pp. 232-239.e2, Jul. 2016, doi: 10.1016/j.jpeds.2016.03.047.

[16] A. L. Adams et al., "Search Is a Time-Critical Event: When Search and Rescue Missions May Become Futile," Wilderness & Environmental Medicine, vol. 18, no. 2, pp. 95–101, Jun. 2007, doi: 10.1580/06-weme-or-035r1.1.

[17] J. Long and A. Whitefield, Cognitive Ergonomics and Human-Computer Interaction, Cambridge: Cambridge University Press, 1989.

[18] A. Lavric and V. Popa, "Internet of Things and LoRa™ Low-Power Wide-Area Networks: A survey," 2017 International Symposium on Signals, Circuits and Systems (ISSCS), Iasi, Romania, 2017, pp. 1-5, doi: 10.1109/ISSCS.2017.8034915.

[19] "LoRa": https://lora-alliance.org/ [retrieved: October, 2021]

[20] A. L. Adams et al., "Search Is a Time-Critical Event: When Search and Rescue Missions May Become Futile," Wilderness & Environmental Medicine, vol. 18, no. 2, pp. 95–101, Jun. 2007, doi: 10.1580/06-weme-or-035r1.1.

[21] R. DePaula, "A new era in human computer interaction: the challenges of technology as a social proxy," in Proceedings of the Latin American conference on Human-computer interaction - CLIHC '03, Rio de Janeiro, Brazil, 2003, pp. 219–222. doi: 10.1145/944519.944543.

Study on the Performance of Sensitive Part of Bridge Type Ultra-Thin Film Hydrogen Sensor

Takahiro Mori, Shoki Wakabayashi, Jin Wang, Kenji Sakai, Keiji Tsukada, Toshihiko Kiwa
Graduate School Interdisciplinary Science and Engineering in Health Systems
Okayama University
3-1-1 Tsushima-naka, Kita-ku, Okayama City, Japan
E-mail: p7lz3cav@s.okayama-u.ac.jp, pgju8212@s.okayama-u.ac.jp, wangjin@okayama-u.ac.jp, sakai-k@okayama-u.ac.jp, tsukada@cc.okayama-u.ac.jp, kiwa@okayama-u.ac.jp

Kenji Kondoh, Takuya Takahashi, Makoto Nakagawa, Naohiro Ueda
RICOH Electronic Devices
13-1 Himemuro-cho, Ikeda City, Osaka, Japan
E-mail: kenji.kondoh@n-redc.co.jp, takuya.takahashi@n-redc.co.jp, makoto.nakagawa@n-redc.co.jp, naohiro.ueda@n-redc.co.jp

***Abstract*—A ultra-thin film hydrogen sensor has been developed to deal with effect of the environment, such as temperature. The performance of the hydrogen sensor was evaluated from the dependence of the sensing area, temperature, and the gas selectivity.**

Keywords-hydrogen sensor; ultra-thin film; platinum; bridge circuit.

I. INTRODUCTION

A large amount of CO_2 emission of fossil fuels leads us to develop new clean energies, including solar, wind, and hydrogen energy. Especially, hydrogen energy is expected because hydrogen energy can be supplied stably. To develop more secure hydrogen gas supply and utilization technology, early detection of hydrogen gas leakage with high-sensitive hydrogen sensors is required. Recently, hydrogen sensors operating at room temperature, which can operate with low-energy consumption, have been developed. In our group, we have developed a Pt ultra-thin-film hydrogen sensor [1][2]. The electrical resistance changed by dissociation of hydrogen molecules on the surface of the film and injection of electrons into the film. In this study, the developed sensor was diagonally aligned as two components with different resistances which forms a Wheatstone bridge circuit fabricated on the Si substrates and the output voltage of the brigade circuit was measured. Because the resistivity changes by the environmental effect, such as temperature is canceled, so robust detection against the environmental change could be realized. The surface area dependence of the sensitives and the gas selectivity were also evaluated here. In addition, the effects of humidity on the hydrogen sensor were investigated.

II. EXPERIMENTAL

The Pt ultra-thin-film hydrogen sensor is based on the catalytic reaction between Pt and hydrogen. When Pt reacts with hydrogen, electrical resistance is reduced. This change is measured as a voltage. Figure 1 shows the structure of the

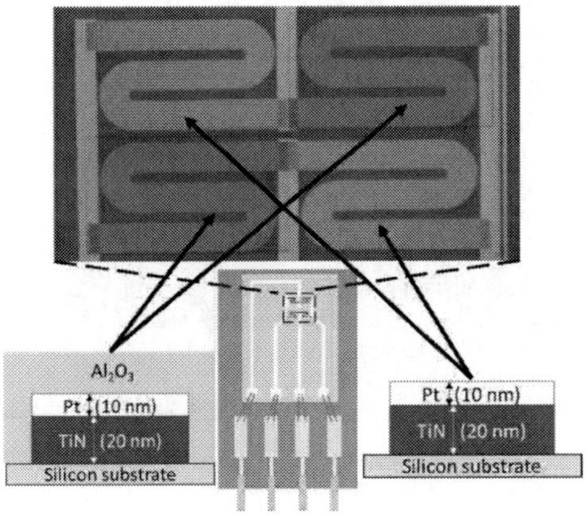

Figure 1. Structure of hydrogen sensor.

TABLE I. SHAPE OF HYDROGEN SENSOR

Sensing area of hydrogen sensor		
Width (μm)	*Length (μm)*	*Area (mm²)*
20	270	5.40×10^{-3}
20	440	8.80×10^{-3}
100	2650	0.265
150	2700	0.405
100	4400	0.440

hydrogen sensor. The hydrogen sensor has a Pt thin film on a silicon substrate with TiN layer. Thus, the Pt thin films formed a Wheatstone bridge circuit. Two diagonal parts of the bridge was coated with alumina to prevent the reaction of hydrogens. By the wire bonding and connectors, the hydrogen sensor was connected to a power supply and measuring instruments. Table 1 shows the shape of one of the four sensing area of the hydrogen sensors. *Width* is the width of the sensing area. *Length* is the length along the electric current of the sensing area. *Area* is the product of *Width* and *Length*.

The output voltage by the Wheatstone bridge circuits of the Pt ultra-thin-film hydrogen sensor can be given by.

$$V = -rE / (200 - r), \quad (1)$$

where V is output voltage, E is supply voltage, and r is rate change of resistance of the sensor without environmental effect, such as temperature. Both resistivities of the coated and non-coated parts of Pt thin film could be changed by the direct environmental effect, therefore the output voltage of the bridge was canceled, while only coated parts were changed by exposure of hydrogen, therefore, the output voltage was changed depends on reactions of the hydrogen.

In this experiment, hydrogen gas was balanced by artificial mixed air which consists of 80%-N_2 and 20%-O_2.

A hot plate was used to heat the copper plate on which the sensor was placed and sealed.

A gas divider was used to adjust the humidity by mixing the gas that was dipped in water and the gas that was not dipped in water.

III. RESULTS AND DISCUSSION

The hydrogen sensor was exposed to hydrogen gas for 5 minutes. Figure 2 shows the sensor response to the hydrogen gas. From this result, the sensor can detect hydrogen gas with a concentration of above 0.1%.

The hydrogen sensor with different area of sensing region was exposed to 1% hydrogen gas for 5 minutes. Figure 3 shows the relationship between the maximum value of the voltage change and the sensing area. The slope estimated by the linear fit was approximately 2.3 mV/mm^2.

The output voltages of the sensor under the temperature between 30 and 90 °C was also and the range of dispersion was 0.31 mV, which was less than 2% of the voltage response of the sensor for 1%-hydrogen gas exposure.

When the humidity was changed from 20% to 70%, the response of hydrogen sensor is significantly decreased. At 20% of humidity, the output voltage was changed 9.5 mV. At 70% of humidity, output voltage of the sensor was changed 2.8 mV.

The output voltages of the sensor for 1%-CH_4, C_2H_6 and CO_2 gas was evaluated to be less than 0.1 mV for all gas types.

IV. CONCLUSION

We developed a highly sensitive and selectivity Pt ultra-thin-film hydrogen sensor. The effect of temperature for Pt could be removed by forming Wheatstone bridge circuits. However, it is difficult to eliminate the effect of humidity. Therefore, we use a sensor package to reduce the effect of humidity.

REFERENCES

[1] K. Tsukada, H. Inoue, F. Katayama, K. Sakai, and T. Kiwa, "Ultrathin-film hydrogen gas sensor with nanostructurally modified surface" JJAP, Vol.51, p.015701, 2012.

[2] K. Tsukada, S. Takeichi, K. Sakai, and T. Kiwa, "Ultrathin-film hydrogen gas sensor with nanostructurally modified surface" JJAP, Vol.53, p.076701, 2014.

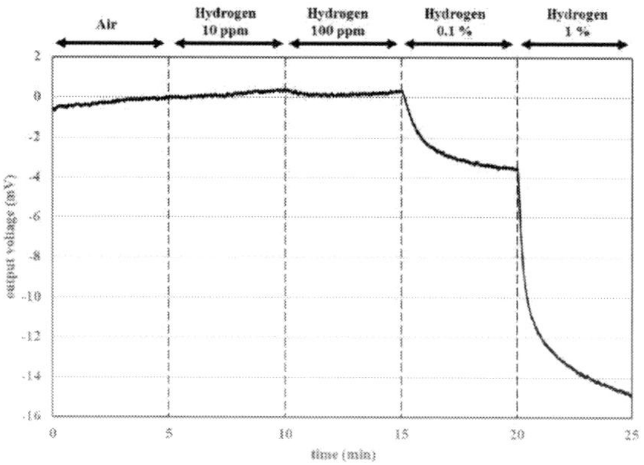

Figure 2. Hydrogen concentration.

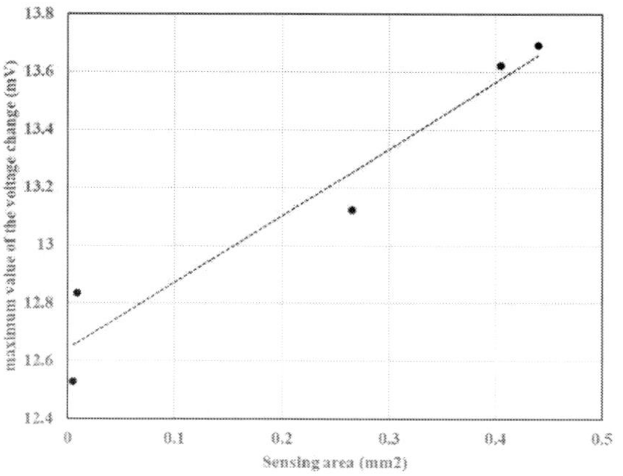

Figure 3. Relationship between sensing area and sensitivity.

Vehicular Visible Light Communication in a Two-Way-Two-Way Traffic Light Controlled Crossroad

Manuel Augusto Vieira, Manuela Vieira, Paula Louro,
ADETC/ISEL/IPL,
R. Conselheiro Emídio Navarro, 1959-007
Lisboa, Portugal
CTS-UNINOVA
Quinta da Torre, Monte da Caparica, 2829-516,
Caparica, Portugal

e-mail: mv@isel.ipl.pt, mv@isel.pt, plouro@deetc.isel.pt

Mirtes de Lima, Pedro Vieira
ADETC/ISEL/IPL,
R. Conselheiro Emídio Navarro, 1959-007
Lisboa, Portugal
Instituto das Telecomunicações
Instituto Superior Técnico, 1049-001,
Lisboa, Portugal
e-mail: A43891@alunos.isel.pt, pvieira@deetc.isel.pt

***Abstract*—The concept of request/response and relative pose estimation for the management of the trajectory is used, in a two-way-two-way traffic lights controlled crossroad, using Vehicular Visible Light Communication (V-VLC). The connected vehicles receive information from the network and interact with each other and with the infrastructure. In parallel, an Intersection Manager (IM) coordinates the crossroad and interacts with the vehicles using the temporal/space relative pose concepts. V-VLC is performed using the street lamps, the traffic signaling and the headlamps to broadcast the information. Data is encoded, modulated and converted into light signals emitted by the transmitters. As receivers and decoders, optical sensors with light filtering properties are used. Cooperative localization is realized in a distributed way with the incorporation of the indirect vehicle-to-vehicle relative pose estimation method. A phasing traffic flow is developed, as Proof of Concept (PoC) and a generic model of cooperative transmission is analysed. Results expresses that the vehicle's behavior (successive poses) is mainly influenced by the manoeuvre permission and presence of other vehicles.**

Keywords- Vehicular Communication; Light Fidelity, Visible Light Communication, white LEDs, SiC photodetectors, OOK modulation scheme, Traffic control.

I. Introduction

High-end models of last generation vehicles nowadays are equipped with hundreds of embedded computers and sensors which allow them to perceive their surroundings, and interact with it in semi-autonomous, and eventually, fully-autonomous fashion. Although at a slower pace, the road infrastructure has evolved as well, with adaptive traffic lights. Next step in the evolution course of transportation systems is to adopt the concept of communication and enable information exchange between vehicles and with infrastructure (V2I) shifting the paradigm from autonomous driving to cooperative driving by taking advantage of Vehicle-to-Everything (V2X) communications [1] [2]. The objective is to increase the safety and throughput of traffic intersections using cooperative driving [3] [4].

Vehicular Communication Systems are a type of network in which vehicles and roadside units are the communicating nodes, providing each other with information, such as safety warnings and traffic information [5].Vehicular networking applications can take advantage of the LED-equipped lighting modules and transportation infrastructure to realize V-VLC. Here, the communication can be performed using the street lamps, the traffic signaling and the headlamps.

The goal is to develop a cooperative system that supports guidance services. An edge/fog based architecture is proposed. Here, the streetlights and traffic lights, through VLC, report its geographical positions and specific information to the drivers and its infrastructure is reused to embed the edge/fog nodes in them. Using this architecture, an Intersection Manager (IM) can increase the throughput of the intersection by exchanging information and directing the incoming Connected Autonomous Vehicles [6] [7] [8] [9]. Cooperative localization is realized in a distributed way with the incorporation of the indirect Vehicle-to-Vehicle (V2V) relative pose estimation method. The vehicle gathers relevant data from neighboring vehicles and estimates the relative pose of them. In this paper a V2X traffic scenario is stablished and bidirectional communication between the infrastructure and the vehicles is tested, using the VLC request/response concept. Tetra-chromatic white sources are used to broadcasting the geolocation and traffic information. The receiver modules include a light controlled filter [10] recovering the transmitted information.

This paper is organized as follows. After the introduction, in Section 2, the V-VLC system is described and the scenario, architecture, communication protocol, coding/decoding techniques analyzed. In Section 3, the experiential results are reported and the system evaluation performed. A phasing traffic flow diagram based on V-VLC is developed, as PoC, to control the arrival of vehicles to the intersection. Finally, in Section 4, the main conclusions are presented.

II. VEHICULAR VISIBLE LIGHT COMMUNICATION SYSTEM

A. *Scenario and architecture*

The V-VLC make use of outdoor light sources (street lamps and traffic lights) as the access points, which can serve for both lighting and communication purposes, providing drivers with outdoor wireless communications. The system is composed by two modules: the transmitter and the receiver located at the infrastructures and at the driving cars. The block diagram of the V-VLC system is presented in Figure 1.

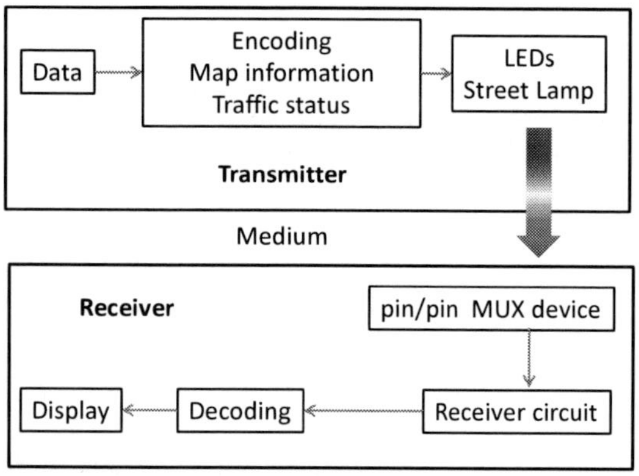

Figure 1. Block diagram of the VLC system.

To realize both the communication and the street illumination, white light tetra-chromatic sources are used providing a different data channel for each chip. At each node, only one chip of the LED is modulated for data transmission, the Red (R: 626 nm), the Green (G: 530 nm), the Blue (B: 470 nm) or the Violet (V) while the others provide constant current for white perception.

Data is encoded, modulated and converted into light signals emitted by the transmitters. Modulation and digital-to-analog conversion of the information bits is done using signal processing techniques. The signal is propagating through the optical channel and a VLC receiver, at the reception end of the communication link, is responsible to extract the data from the modulated light beam. It transforms the light signal into an electrical signal that is subsequently decoded to extract the transmitted information. The core element of a receiver is a Silicon-Carbon (SiC) photodetector. This component converts the optical power into electrical current. The VLC photosensitive receiver is a double pin/pin photodetector based on a tandem heterostructure, p-i'(a-SiC:H)-n/p-i(a-Si:H)-n sandwiched between two conductive transparent contacts [10]. Due to its tandem structure, the device is an optical controlled filter able to identify the wavelengths and intensities of the impinging optical signals. Its quick response enables the possibility of high speed communications. The generated photocurrent is processed using a transimpedance circuit obtaining a proportional voltage. The obtained voltage is then processed until the data signal is reconstructed at the data processing unit (digital conversion, decoding and decision [11, 12]).

A V2X communication link, in a traffic light controlled crossroad, was simulated.

In Figure 2a the lighting plan and generated joint footprints in the crossroad region (LED array=RGBV modulated color spots) is displayed. To build the I2V it is proposed a simplified cluster of unit square cells in an orthogonal topology that fills all the service area [12, 13]. The grid size was chosen in order to avoid an overlap in the receiver from the data from adjacent grid points. The geometric scenario used in the experimental results uses a smaller size square grid (2 cm), to improve its practicality. Each transmitter, $X_{i,j}$, carries its own color, X, (RGBV) as well as its horizontal and vertical ID position in the surrounding network (*i,j*). In the PoC, was assumed that the crossroad is located in the intersection of line 4 with column 3, and the emitters at the nodes along the roadside. To receive the I2V information from several transmitters, the receiver must be located at the overlap of the circles that set the transmission range (radial) of each transmitter. The nine possible overlaps, defined as fingerprint regions, are also displayed in Figure 2a for each unit cell. Thus, each LED sends a message that includes the synchronism, its physical ID and the traffic information. When a probe vehicle enters the streetlight's capture range, the receiver replies to the light signal, and assigns an unique ID and the traffic message [13]. At each moment, *t*, the receiver identifies the footprint, finds it centroid and stores it as the reference point. All observations for a single section are jointly analyzed to produce an estimate of the occupied lane, direction and travel time along the considered section. The received message, acts twofold: as a positioning system and as a data receiver.

In Figure 2b we propose a draft of a mesh cellular hybrid structure to create a gateway-less system without any external gateways needed [14]. As illustrated the street lights, in this architecture, are equipped with one of two types of nodes: A "mesh" controller that connects with other nodes in its vicinity. These controllers can forward messages to the vehicles (I2V) in the mesh, effectively acting like routers nodes in the network. A "mesh/cellular" hybrid controller, that is also equipped with a modem provides IP base connectivity to the Intersection Manager (IM) services. These nodes acts as border-router and can be used for edge computing. The proposed short-range mesh network enables edge computing and device-to-cloud communication, by ensuring a secure communication from a street light controller to the edge computer or datacenter, through a neighbor traffic light controller with an active cellular connection.

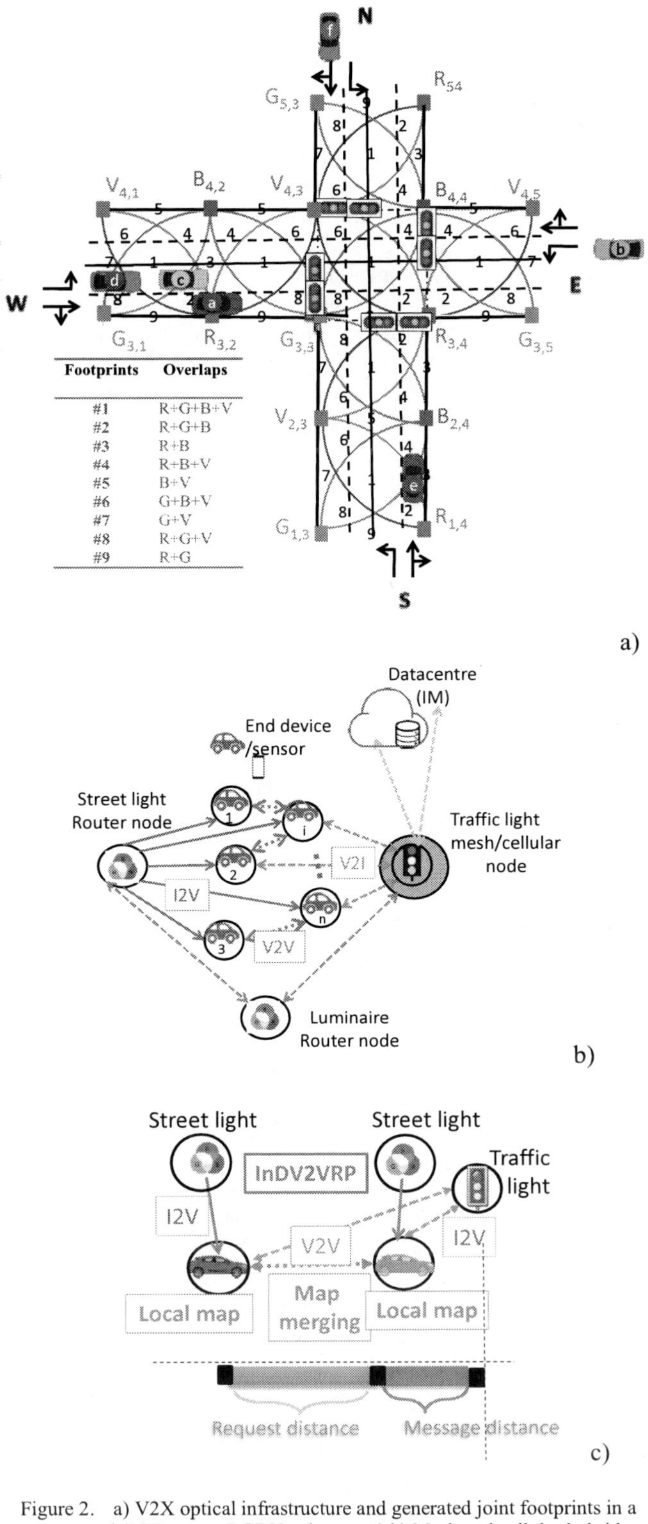

Figure 2. a) V2X optical infrastructure and generated joint footprints in a crossroad (LED array=RGBV color spots).b) Mesh and cellular hybrid architecture. c) Graphical representation of the simultaneous localization and mapping problem.

B. Multi-vehicle cooperative localization

The combined estimation of both position and orientation (pose estimation) of the vehicle is important to path definition. In a two-dimensional coordinate systems the pose, $q(t) = [x(t), y(t), \delta(t)]$, is defined by position (x,y) and orientation angle δ, with respect to the coordinate axes. Let's consider that $q_i(t,t')$ represents the pose of vehicle *i* at time *t′* relative to the pose of the same vehicle at time *t* and $q_{ij}(t)$ denotes the pose of vehicle *j* relative to the pose of vehicle *i* at time *t*. These three types of information $q_i(t)$, $q_i(t,t')$and $q_{ij}(t)$ compose the basic elements of a pose graph for multi-vehicle cooperative localization [15].

An Indirect V2V Relative Pose Estimation (InDV2VRPE) method is proposed and exemplified in Figure 2c. Here, when two vehicles are in neighborhood, the geometric relationship between them can be indirectly inferred via a chain of geometric relationships among both vehicles positions and local maps. Let´s consider two neighboring vehicles. Both vehicles, having self-localization ability based on I2V street lamps communication perform local Simultaneous Localization and Mapping (SLAM). The follower vehicle can be localized by itself, as in single vehicle localization, $q_i(t)$, and can also be localized by combining the localization result of vehicle leader and the relative localization estimate between the two vehicles, $q_{ij}(t)$. For a vehicle with several neighboring vehicles, it uses the indirect V2V relative pose estimation method to estimate the relative pose of each neighboring vehicle one by one and takes advantage of the data of each neighboring vehicle.

C. Color phasing diagrams

Four traffic flows were considered (Figure 2a): One from West (W) with three vehicles (*a, c, d*) approaching the crossroad, Vehicle *a* with straight movement and Vehicle *c* and Vehicle *d* with left turn only. In the second flow, Vehicle *b* from East (E), approaches the intersection with left turn only. In the third flow, Vehicle *e*, oncoming from South (S), has e right-turn approach. Finally, in the fourth flow, Vehicle *f*, coming from North, goes straight.

For the intersection manager crossing coordination, the vehicle and the IM exchange information through two specific types of messages, "request" (V2I) and "response" (I2V) as exemplified in Figure 2b. Inside the request distance, an approach "request" is sent, using as emitter the headlights. To receive the "requests", two different receivers are located at the same traffic light, facing the cross roads (local controller of the traffic light). Concretely, when one head vehicle enters in the infrastructure´s capture range of one of the receivers (request distance) the request message is received and decoded by the receiver facing the lane which is interconnected to the Intersection Manager. Those messages contain the assigned ID positions, speeds, and flow directions of the vehicles. The "request" contains all the information that is necessary for a vehicle's space-time reservation for its intersection crossing. Intersection manager uses this information to convert it in a sequence of timed rectangular spaces that each assigned vehicle needs to occupy the intersection. An intersection manager's acknowledge is sent from the traffic signal over the facing receiver to the in car application of the head vehicle. The response includes both the infrastructure and the vehicle identifications and the "confirmed vehicle" message. Once the response is received (message distance in Figure 2c), the vehicle is required to follow the occupancy trajectories (footprint regions, Figure 2a) provided by the intersection manager. If a request has any potential risk of collision with all other vehicles that have already been approved to cross the intersection, the control manager only sends back to the vehicle (V2I) the "response" after the risk of conflict is exceeded. The use of both navigation and lane control signs to communicate lane restrictions is demanding. Downstream from that location (request distance), lane restrictions should be obeyed. Vehicles may receive their intentions (*e.g.*, whether they will turn left or continue straight and turn right) or specifically the need to interact with a trafic controler at a nearby crossroad (message distance). In the sequence, a traffic message coming from a transmitter nearby the crossroad will inform the drivers of the location of their destination (*i.e.*, the intended intersection exit leg).

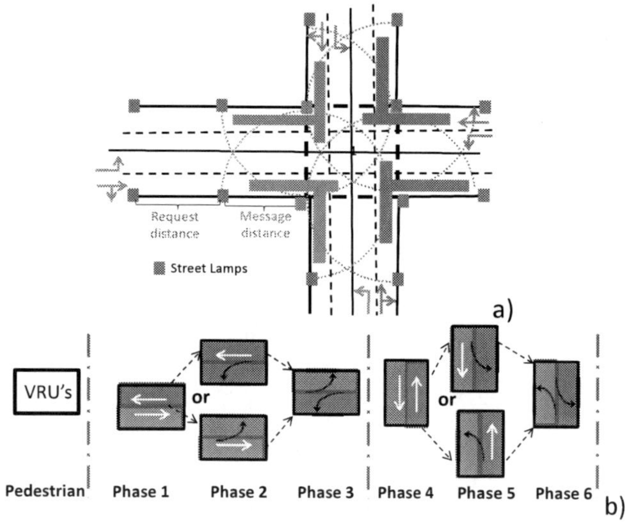

Figure 3: a) Physical area, color poses and channelization. b) Representation of a phasing diagram.

In the proposed architecture (Figure 2b), the major operational requirement of IM is the ability to register synchronized measurements in a common frame of reference. The effective solution is to maintain a buffer of time-stamped measurements and register them as a batch using a temporal sliding window. The vehicles can use such techniques to find their "color poses" at regular time intervals. We have assumed four "color poses" linked with the radial range of the modulated light in the crossroad nodes (dotted arcs in Figure 3a). As depicted in Figure 3a, where the physical area and channelization are shown, the West straight, South left turn and West right turn manoeuvres correspond to the "Green pose". "Red poses" are related with South straight, East left turn and South right turn manoeuvres, "Blue poses with East straight, North left turn and East right turn and finally "violet poses with North straight, West left turn and North right turn manoeuvres, In Figure 3b, a color phasing diagram is displayed. Here, since two movements can proceed simultaneously without conflict hence two of the timing functions will always have simultaneous control.

D. VLC Communication protocol and coding/decoding techniques

An on-off keying (OOK) modulation scheme was used to code the information. Synchronous transmissions based on a 64- bits data frame are analysed.
An example of the used codification to drive the headlamps LEDs of a vehicle, coming from N, located in in footprint #1 ($R_{3,4,}$ $G_{3,3,}$ $B_{4,4,}$ and V_{43}) moving to South is illustrated in Figure 4a.

Different control fields are used depending on the driver motivation. All messages, in a frame, start with the header labelled as Sync, a block of 5 bits. The same synchronization header [10101], in an ON-OFF pattern, is imposed simultaneously to all emitters. The next block (ID) gives the location (*x, y* coordinates) of the emitters inside the array ($X_{i,j,k}$). Cell's IDs are encoded using a 4 bits binary representation for the decimal number. So, the next 8 bits are assigned, respectively, to the *x* and *y* coordinates (*i, j*) of the emitter in the array. If the message is diffused by the IM transmitter, a pattern [0000]) follows this identification, if it is a request (R) a pattern [00] is used. The steering angle (δ) completes the pose in a frame time. Eight steering angles along the cardinal points and coded with the same number of the footprints in the unit cell (Figure 2a) are possible from a start point to the next goal. The last block is used to transmit the traffic message. A stop bit is used at the end of each frame.

The decimal numbers assigned to each ID block are pointed out in the Figure. Results show that, in network, $R_{3,4,S}$; $G_{3,3,S}$; $B_{4,4,S}$ and $V_{4,3,S}$ are the transmitted node packets, in a time slot, from the crossroad. In this location, the driver receives his request message [pose, and traffic needs] from the infrastructure. This allows it movement across the crossroad to South (violet code 9, δ=270º), directly from the current point (#1) to the goal point (#9).
The calibration of the receiver supplies an additional tool to enhance the decoding task. The calibration procedure is exemplified in Figure 4b. Here the MUX signal obtained at the receiver as well as the coded transmitted optical signals is displayed.

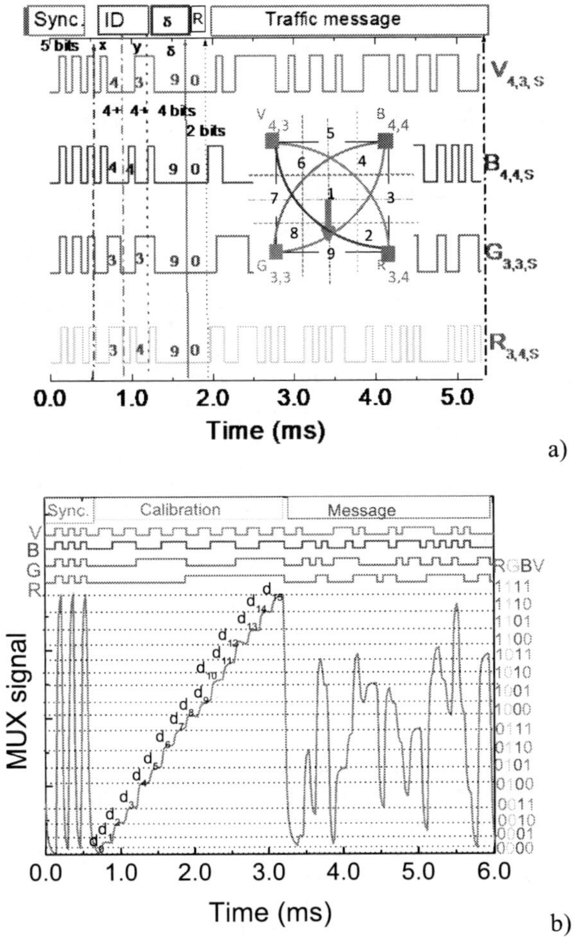

Figure 4 a) Frame structure representation of a request message. b) MUX/DEMUX signal of the calibrated cell. In the same frame of time a random signal is superimposed.

The message, in the frame, start with the header labelled as Sync, a block of 5 bits. In the second block, labelled as calibration, the joint transmission of four calibrated R, G, B and V optical signals is imposed. The bit sequence for this block was chosen to allow all the *on/off* sixteen possible combinations of the four RGBV input channels (2^4). Finally a random message was transmitted. All the ordered levels (d_0-d_{15}) are pointed out at the correspondent levels and are displayed as horizontal dotted lines. In the right hand side the match between MUX levels and the [RGBV] binary code assigned to each level is shown. Comparing the calibrated levels (d_0-d_{15}) with the different assigned 4-digit binary [RGBV] codes, ascribed to each level, the decoding is straightforward and the message decoded. The footprint position comes directly from the synchronism block, where all the received channels are, simultaneously, *on* or *off*. The pose of the mobile receiver (x,y, δ) in the network comes directly from the next 12 decoded bits. Finally, the received traffic message is decoded based on the last MUX levels.

III. V2X Cooperative System Evaluation

Figure 5a displays the MUX signals assigned to a two IM response messages received by Vehicle *a*, driving the right lane, that enters Cell $C_{4,2}$ by the enter #2 ($t'_{1,a}$, Phase1, green pose), goes straight to E to position #8 ($t'_{2,a}$; Phase1, green pose).

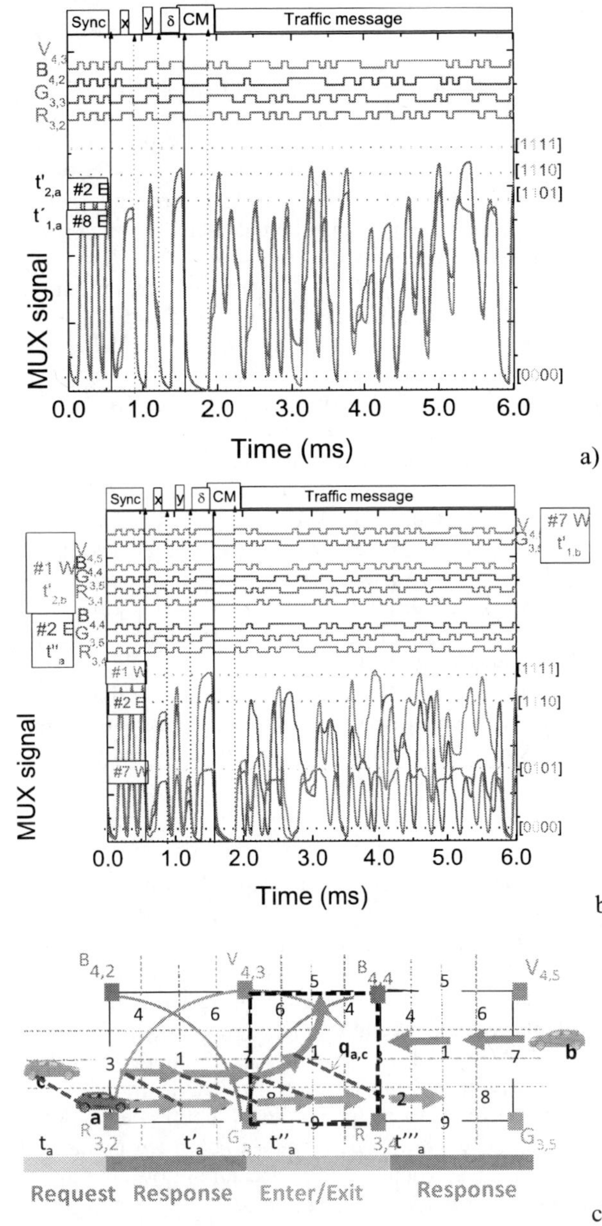

Figure 5. Normalized MUX signal responses and the assigned decoded messages acquired by vehicles *a, b, c* at different response times. On the top the transmitted channels packets [R, G, B, V] are decoded. a) Before the crossroad. b) After the cross road. c) Movement of the cars, in the successive moments, with their colorful poses (color arrows) and q_{ac} spatial relative poses (dot lines).

Then, this vehicle enters the crossroad through #8 (t''$_a$) and leaves it in the exit #2 at t'''$_a$, keeping always the same direction (E). In Figure 5b, vehicle *b* approaches the intersection after having asked permission to cross it and only receives authorization when the vehicle *a* has left the intersection (end of Phase 2). Then, Phase 3 begins with vehicle *b* heading to the intersection (W) (pose red) while vehicle *a* follows its destination towards E (pose green). In Figure 5c, the movement of the cars, in the successive moments, is shown through their colorful poses (color arrows) and q_{ac} spatial relative poses along the time (dot lines). Results show that, as the receiver moves between generated point regions, the received information pattern changes. The vehicle speed can be calculated by measuring the actual travelled distance overtime, using the ID´s transmitters tracking. Two measurements are required: distance and elapsed time. The distance is fixed while the elapsed time will be obtained through the instants where the number of received channels changes. The receivers compute the geographical position in the successive instants (path) and infer the vehicle's speed. In the following, this data will be transmitted to another leader vehicle through the V2V communication or to control manager (IM) at the traffic light through V2I. When two vehicles are in neighborhood and in different lanes, the geometric relationship between them can ($q_{i,j}$) (dotted lines in Figure 5c) can be inferred through local SLAM fusing their self-localizations via a chain of geometric relationships among the vehicles poses and the local maps.

For a vehicle with several neighboring vehicles, the mesh node uses the indirect V2V relative pose estimations method taking advantage of the data of each neighboring vehicle.

IV. CONCLUSIONS

This paper presents a new concept of request/response for the redesign and management of a trajectory in a two-way-two-way traffic lights controlled crossroad, using VLC between connected cars. A simulated traffic scenario was presented and a generic model of cooperative transmission for vehicular communication services was established. As a PoC, a phasing of traffic flows is suggested. The simulated/experimental results confirmed that the proposed cooperative VLC architecture is suitable for the intended applications. The introduction of VLC between connected vehicles and the surrounding infrastructure allows the direct monitoring of relative speed thresholds and inter-vehicle spacing increasing the safety.

ACKNOWLEDGEMENTS

This work was sponsored by FCT – Fundação para a Ciência e a Tecnologia, within the Research Unit CTS – Center of Technology and Systems, reference UIDB/00066/2020. The project IPL/IDI&CA/2020/Geo-Loc/ISEL, is also acknowledge.

REFEEENCES

[1] G. Karagiannis et al.: A Survey and Tutorial on Requirements, Architectures, Challenges, Standards and Solutions," IEEE Communications Surveys & Tutorials, vol. 13, no. 4, pp. 584–616, (2011).

[2] A. Memedi, and F. Dressler, "Vehicular Visible Light Communications: A Survey," in IEEE Communications Surveys & Tutorials, vol. 23, no. 1, pp. 161-181, (2021).

[3] N. Cheng, et al., "Big data driven vehicular networks," IEEE Network, vol. 32, no. 6, pp. 160–167, (Nov. 2018).

[4] P. Singh, G. Singh, and A. Singh, "Implementing Visible Light Communication in intelligent traffic management to resolve traffic logjams,"-Int. J. Comput. Eng. Res., 2015 - academia.edu pp.13-17 (2015).

[5] S. Yousefi, E. Altman, R. El-Azouzi, and M. Fathy, "Analytical Model for Connectivity in Vehicular Ad Hoc Networks," IEEE Transactions on Vehicular Technology, 57, 3341-3356 (2008).

[6] D. Elliott, W. Keen, and L. Miao, "Recent advances in connected and automated vehicles" Journal of Traffic and Transportation Engineering, Vol. 6, Issue 2, 109-131(2019).

[7] N. Jitendra, and Bajpai, "Emerging vehicle technologies & the search for urban mobility solutions,Urban, Planning and Transport Research, 4:1, 83-100, (2016).

[8] Azimi, R., Bhatia, G., Rajkumar, R., and Mudalige, P., "V2V-Intersection Management at Roundabouts," SAE Int. J. Passeng. Cars - Mech. Syst. 6(2):681-690, (2013).

[9] Wang, N., Qiao, Y., Wang, W., Tang, S., and Shen, J., "Visible Light Communication based Intelligent Traffic Light System: Designing and Implementation,"2018 Asia Communications and Photonics Conference (ACP) DOI: 10.1109/ACP.2018.8595791(2018).

[10] Vieira, M. A., Louro, P., Vieira, M., Fantoni, A., and Steiger-Garção, A., "Light-activated amplification in Si-C tandem devices: A capacitive active filter model," IEEE sensor journal, 12(6), 1755-1762 (2012).

[11] M. A. Vieira, M.Vieira, V. Silva, P. Louro, J. Costa, "Optical signal processing for data error detection and correction using a-SiCH technology," Phys. Status Solidi C 12 (12), 1393–1400 (2015).

[12] Vieira, M. A., Vieira, M., Louro, P., Vieira, P., "Bi-directional communication between infrastructures and vehicles through visible light," Proc. SPIE 11207, Fourth International Conference on Applications of Optics and Photonics, 112070C (3 October 2019).

[13] M. A. Vieira, M. Vieira, P. Vieira, P. Louro, "Vehicle-to-Vehicle and Infrastructure-to-Vehicle Communication in the Visible Range," Sensors & Transducers, 218 (12), 40-48 (2017).

[14] A. Yousefpour, et al., "All one needs to know about fog computing and related edge computing paradigms: A complete survey", Journal of Systems Architecture,Volume 98, pp. 289-330 (2019).

[15] M. A. Vieira, M. Vieira, P. Louro, P Vieira, "Vehicular visible light communication in a traffic controlled intersection," Proc. SPIE 11772, Optical Sensors 2021, 117720K (18 April 2021).

Indoor Self-localization and Wayfinding Services using Visible Light Communication: A model

Manuela Vieira, Manuel Augusto Vieira, Paula Louro,
DEETC/ISEL/IPL,
R. Conselheiro Emídio Navarro, 1959-007
Lisboa, Portugal
CTS-UNINOVA
Quinta da Torre, Monte da Caparica, 2829-516,
Caparica, Portugal

e-mail: mv@isel.ipl.pt, mv@isel.pt, plouro@deetc.isel.pt,

João Rodrigues, Pedro Vieira
ADETC/ISEL/IPL,
R. Conselheiro Emídio Navarro, 1959-007
Lisboa, Portugal
Instituto das Telecomunicações
Instituto Superior Técnico, 1049-001,
Lisboa, Portugal
e-mail: A42101@alunos.isel.pt, pvieira@isel.pt

***Abstract*— Visible Light Communication (VLC) is a promising technology that can jointly be used to accomplish the typical lighting functionalities of the Light-Emitting Diodes (LEDs) and data transmission, where light intensity can be modulated on a high rate that cannot be noticed by the human eye. A VLC cooperative system that supports guidance services and uses an edge/fog based architecture for wayfinding services is presented. The dynamic navigation system is composed of several transmitters (luminaries) which send the map information and path messages required to wayfinding. Each luminaire for downlink transmission is equipped with one two type of controllers: mesh controller and cellular controllers to forward messages to other devices in the vicinity or to the central manager services. Data from the luminaires is encoded, modulated and converted into light signals emitted by the transmitters. Tetra-chromatic white sources, located in ceiling landmarks, are used providing a different data channel for each chip. Mobile optical receivers, collect the data, extracts theirs location to perform positioning and, concomitantly, the transmitted data from each transmitter. Uplink transmission is implemented and the best route to navigate through venue calculated. The results show that the system allows determining the position of a mobile target inside the network, to infer the travel direction along the time and to interact with information received optimizing the route towards the destination.**

Keywords- Visible Light Communication; Indoor navigation; Bidirectional Communication; Wayfinding services; Optical sensors; Multiplexing/demultiplexing techniques.

I. INTRODUCTION

Nowadays, wireless networks have seen a demand for increased data rate requirements. For a realistic coverage with the data rate requirements, a large bandwidth is needed which remains a limiting factor when compared with the RF communication technologies. The advancement in data streaming and multimedia quality has an adverse effect on the available radio spectrum, which is soon set to hit a roadblock. Consequently, research has started exploring alternate wireless transmission technologies to meet the ever-increasing demand. In this context, the huge bandwidth available in the unlicensed electromagnetic spectrum in the optical domain is seen as a promising solution to the spectrum crunch. Visible Light Communication (VLC) makes use of the higher frequencies in the visual band and extends the capabilities of data transmission using general light sources [1][2]. It transmits data by high-speed switching or flickering at a rate that is not perceivable to the naked eye. VLC has been regarded as an additional communication technology to fulfill the high data rate demands and as a new affiliate in the beyond fifth-generation (5G) heterogeneous networks. It can be easily used in indoor environments using the existing LED lighting infrastructure with few modifications [3] [4]. This means that the LEDs are twofold by providing illumination as well as communication. Therefore, communications within personal working/living spaces are highly demanded. Multi-device connectivity can tell users, from any device, where they are, where they need to be and what they need to do when they get there. Research has shown that compared to outdoors, people tend to lose orientation a lot easier within complex buildings [5] [6]. Fine-grained indoor localization can be useful, enabling several applications [7] [8].

To support people's wayfinding activities this paper proposes a method able to generate ceiling landmark route instructions using VLC. Tetra-chromatic white sources are used providing a different data channel for each chip and offers the possibility of Wavelength Division Multiplexing (WDM), which enhances the transmission data rate. The system is composed of several transmitters (LEDs luminaries) which send the map information and path messages required to wayfinding. Data is encoded, modulated and converted into light signals emitted by the transmitters. Every mobile terminal is equipped with a receiver module for receiving the mapped information generated from the ceiling light and displays this information in the mobile terminal. The receiver modules includes a photodetector based on a tandem a-SiC:H/a-Si:H pin/pin light controlled filter that multiplexes the different optical channels, performs different filtering processes and finally decodes the encoded signals, recovering the transmitted information [9] [10] [11]. This kind of receiver has proved to be adequate when used in large indoor environments with a 2D building model [12]. The proposed LED aided system involves wireless communication, smart sensoring and optical sources network, building up a transdisciplinary approach framed in cyber-physical systems.

The paper is organized as follows. After the introduction (Section I), in Section II, a VLC scenario, architecture and building model are established and the dynamic navigation system explained. In Section III, models for the VLC link are presented and in Section IV, the communication protocol and the encoding/decoding techniques are analyzed and the wayfinding evaluation discussed. Finally, in Section V, conclusions are addressed.

II. Scenario, Architecture and Building model

A. Scenario

When we are looking for the shortest route to a place, we want to be guided on a direct, shortest path to our destination. A destination can be targeted by user request to a Central Manager (CM).

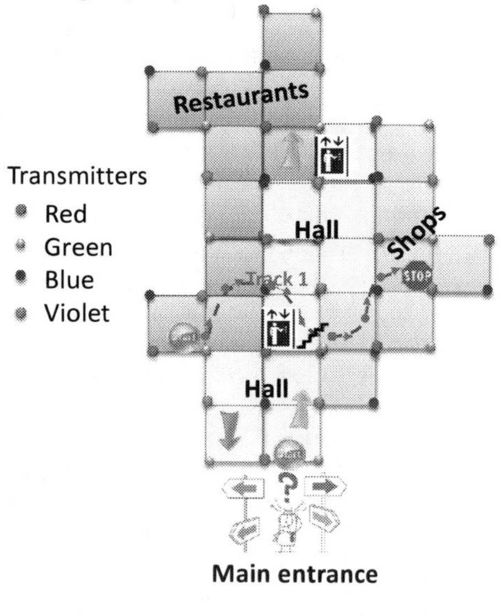

Figure 1. Optical infrastructure and indoor layout. Proposed scenario: a user navigates from outdoor to indoor. It sends a request message to find the right track and, in the available time, he adds customized points of interest (wayfinding services). The requested information is sent by the emitters at the ceiling to its receiver.

So, self-localization is a fundamental issue since the person must be able to estimate its position and orientation (pose) within a map of the environment it is navigating.

The scenario simulated is a 3D complex building. Different users are considered (Figure 1). Depending on the time available, they can find a friend, shop, have a meal or rest. When arriving, they notify the CM of their localization (x, y, z), asking for help to find the right track for their needs (wayfinding services). A code identifies each user. If a user wishes to find a friend both need previously to combine a common code for the schedule meeting. The first arriving initiates the alert notification to be triggered when the other is in his floor vicinity and generates a buddy list for the meeting. The buddy finder service uses the location information from the network's VLC location from both users to determine their proximity and sends a response message with the location and path of the meeting point avoiding crowded regions and minimizing the path.

We consider the path to be a geometric representation of a plan to move from a start pose to a goal pose. Let us we consider a person navigating in a 2D environment (Figure 1). Its non-omnidirectional configuration is defined by position (x, y, z) and orientation angle, δ, with respect to the coordinate axes. $q(t) = [x(t), y(t), z(t), \delta(t)]$ denote its pose at time t, in a global reference frame. In cooperative positioning systems, persons are divided into two groups, the stationary persons and the moving persons. Let's consider that $q_i(t,t')$ represents the pose of person *i* at time *t′* relative to the pose of the same person at time *t* and $q_{ij}(t)$ denotes the pose of person *j* relative to the pose of person *i* at time *t*. $q_i(t,t')$ is null for people standing still and non-zero if they move. These three types of information $q_i(t)$, $q_i(t,t')$ and $q_{ij}(t)$ compose the basic elements of a pose graph for multi-person cooperative localization.

B. Mesh cellular hybrid structure

In Figure 2, the proposed architecture is illustrated. A mesh cellular hybrid structure to create a gateway-less system is proposed. This network configuration is wireless and ad-hoc. It spans all devices, is wire free, demonstrate resiliency to physical obstructions and adapt to changes in the transmission medium. A mesh network is a good fit because it dynamically reconfigures itself and grows to the size of any installation [13]. As illustrated in Figure 2, the luminaires, in this architecture, are equipped with one of two types of nodes: A "mesh" controller that connects with other nodes in its vicinity. These controllers can forward messages to other devices (I2D) in the mesh, effectively acting like routers nodes in the network. A "mesh/cellular" hybrid controller, that is also equipped with a modem providing IP base connectivity to the central manager services (CM). These nodes act as border-router and can be used for edge computing. Under this architecture, the short-range mesh network purpose is twofold: enable edge computing and device-to-cloud communication, by ensuring a secure communication from a luminaire controller to the edge computer or datacenter (I2CM), through a neighbor luminaire controller with an active cellular connection; and enable peer-to-peer communication ($I2I_{IP}$), to exchange information between smart devices.

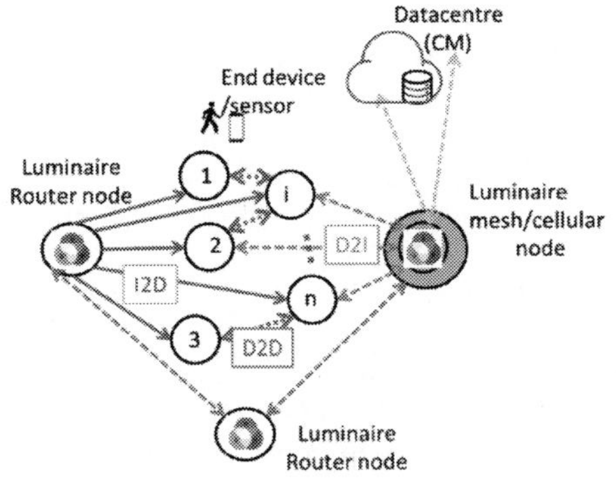

Figure 2. Mesh and cellular hybrid architecture.

To estimate each person track the pure pursuit approach [14] [15] is used. The principle took into account the curvature required for the mobile receiver to steer from its current position to its intended position. By specifying a look-ahead distance, it defines the radius of an imaginary circle. This allows to iteratively construct the intermediate arcs between itself and its goal position as it moved, thus, obtaining the required trajectory for it to reach its objective position (see Figure 1).

C. Building model

Building a geometry model of interiors of buildings is complex since the interior structure has to be seen as an aggregation of several different types of objects (rooms, stairs, etc.) with different shapes. In the proposed architecture the logical model is easier since represents each room/crossing/exit with a node (Figure 1), and a path as the links between nodes. By integrating floor number information into the previous 2D system, the overall performance of the system will not be significantly affected. The user positions can be represented as P (x, y, z) by providing the horizontal positions (x, y) and the correct floor number z. The ground floor is level 0 and the user can go both below (z<0) and above (z>0) from there. In this study, the 3D model generation is based on footprints of a multi-level building that are collected from available sources (luminaires) and are displayed on the user receiver for user orientation. It is a requirement that the destination can be targeted by user request to the CM and that floor changes are notified. The indoor route throughout the building is presented to the user by a responding message transmitted by the ceiling luminaires that work also either as router or mesk/celular nodes (Figure 2). With this request/response concept, the generated landmark-based instructions help the user to unambiguously identify the correct decision point where a change of direction (pose) is needed, as well as offer information for the user to confirm that he/she is on the right way.

III. VLC LINK MODELS

The principal components of the VLC system are the LEDs which act as the communication sources and the SiC WDM devices that serve as receiving elements as pointed out in Figure 3. Data from the sender is converted into an intermediate data representation, byte format, and converted into light signals emitted by the transmitter module. The data bit stream is input to a modulator where an ON–OFF KEYING (OOK) modulation is utilized. Here, a bit one is represented by an optical pulse that occupies the entire bit duration, while a bit zero is represented by the absence of an optical pulse.

LEDs are modeled as Lambertian source where the luminance is distributed uniformly in all directions, whereas the luminous intensity is different in all directions. The luminous intensity for a Lambertian source is given by Equation 1. [16]:

$$I(\emptyset) = I_N(\cos \emptyset)^m \tag{1}$$

Where m is the order derived from a Lambertian pattern, I_N is the maximum luminous intensity in the axial direction and , ϕ is the angle of irradiance. The Lambertian order m is given by:

$$m = -\frac{\ln(2)}{\ln \cos(\emptyset_{1/2})} \tag{2}$$

For the proposed system, the commercial white LEDs were designed for illumination purposes, exhibiting a wide half intensity angle ($\phi_{1/2}$) of 60º. Thus, the Lambertian order m is 1.

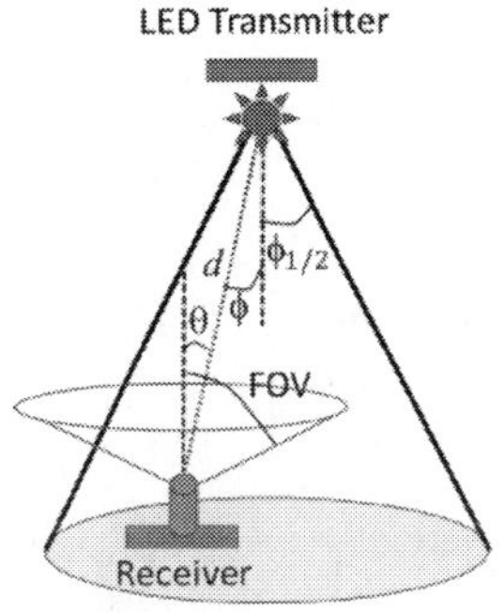

Figure 3. – Geometry of the relative position of the transmitter and receiver units.

The light signal is received by the WDM photodetector that detects the on/off states of the LEDs, generates a binary sequence of the received signals and convert data into the original format. For simplicity, we will consider a line of sight (LoS) connection for both VLC links, which corresponds to the existence of straight visibility between the transmitter and the receiver. In Figure , it is plotted the geometry of the transmitter and receiver relative position, with emphasis to the main parameters used for characterization of the LED source and the photodiode receiver (angles of irradiance and illumination, transmitter's semi-angle at half-power and field of view). The Lambertian model is used for LED light distribution and MatLab simulations are used to infer the signal coverage of the LED in the illuminated indoors space [17] [18].

Lighting in large environments is designed to illuminate the entire space in a uniform way. Ceiling plans for the LED array layout is shown in Figure 4.

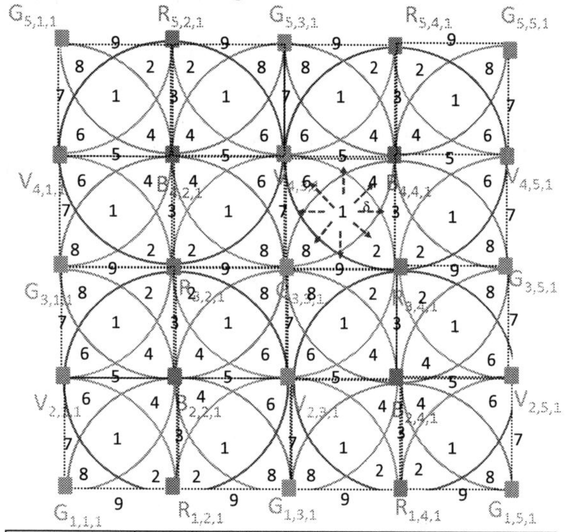

Footprint regions	#1	#2	#3	#4	#5	#6	#7	#8	#9
Square topology	RGBV	RGB	RB	RBV	BV	GBV	GV	RGV	RG

Steering angle code	1	2	3	4	5	6	7	8	9
Square topology (δ)	-	(SE)º	(E)	(NE)	(N)	(NW)	(W)	(SW)	(S)

Figure 4. Illustration of the optical scenarios (RGBV =modulated LEDs spots). Clusters of cells in square topology .

A square lattice topology was considered. Here, cells have squares shapes to form an orthogonal shaped constellation with the modulated RGBV LEDs at the nodes.

The LEDs emit light when the energy levels change in the semiconductor diode. The wavelength depends on the semiconductor material used to form the LED chip. For data transmission, commercially available polychromatic white LEDs were used at the nodes of the network. On each node only one chip is modulated for data transmission and carries useful information while the others are only supplied with DC to maintain white color illumination. Red (R; 626 nm), Green (G; 530 nm), Blue (B; 470 nm) and violet (V; 390 nm) LEDs, are used [19] [20].

Since lighting and wireless data communication is combined, each luminaire for downlink transmission become a single cell, in which the optical access point (AP) is located in the ceiling and the mobile users are scattered within the overlap discs of each cells underneath. So, each node, $X_{i,j}$, carries its own color, X, (RGBV) as well as its ID position in the network (i,j). The grid sizes were chosen to avoid overlap in the receiver from adjacent grid points. To receive the information from several transmitters, the receiver must be positioned where the circles from each transmitter overlaps, producing at the receiver, a multiplexed (MUX) signal that, after demultiplexing, acts twofold as a positioning system and a data transmitter. The device receives multiple signals, finds the centroid of the received coordinates and stores it as the reference point position. Nine reference points, for each unit cell, are identified giving a fine grained resolution in the localization of the mobile device across each cell. The overlap regions (footprints) are pointed out in Figure 4.

Planning the route to follow from the current position to a goal point is achieved with the help of a CM linked to the ceiling landmarks (Figure 2). To compute the point-to-point along a path, we need the data along the path. The input of the aided navigation system is the coded signal sent by the transmitters to an identify user, and includes its position in the network *P(x, y, z)*, inside the unit cell and the steering angle, δ, that guides the user across his path. In Figure 4, the steering angles are pointed out as dotted arrows and the associated codes displayed.

IV. COMMUNICATION PROTOCOL AND DECODING TECHNIQUE

In Figure 5, the MUX/DEMUX signals from two users, that have request wayfinding services, are displayed.

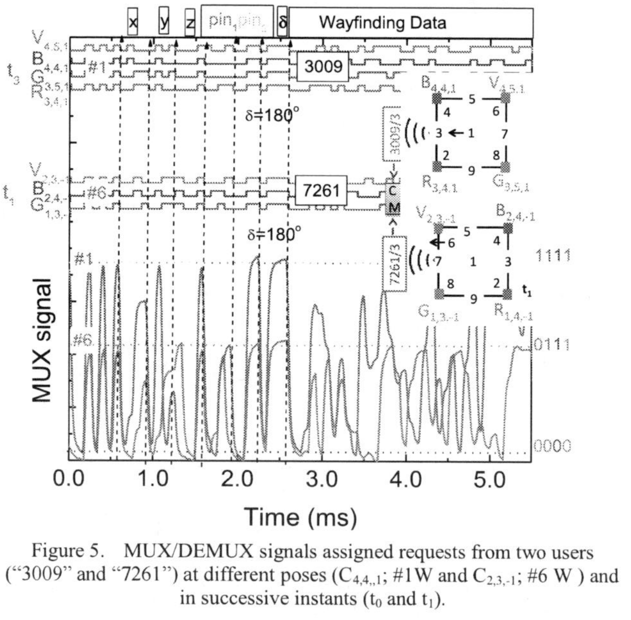

Figure 5. MUX/DEMUX signals assigned requests from two users ("3009" and "7261") at different poses ($C_{4,4,,1}$; #1W and $C_{2,3,-1}$; #6 W) and in successive instants (t_0 and t_1).

In the right side, the match between the MUX signals and the 4-binary codes are pointed out (horizontal dotted lines). On the top the decoded channels packets are shown [R, G, B, V]. The visualized cells, paths and the reference points (footprints) are also shown as inserts.

The data was coded using an On-Off keying (OOK) modulation in a 64-bits word, divided into five blocks. All messages, in a frame, start with the header labelled as Sync, a block of 5 bits. The same synchronization header [10101], in an ON-OFF pattern, is imposed simultaneously to all emitters. The next block (ID) gives the geolocation (*x,y,z* coordinates) of the emitters inside the array ($X_{i,j,k}$). Cell's IDs are encoded using a 4 bits binary representation for the decimal number. The first bit represents the number's sign: setting that bit to *0* is for a positive number, and setting it to *1* for a negative number, the remaining 3 bits indicate the absolute value of the coordinate. So, the next 12 (4+4+4) bits in are assigned, respectively, to the *x*, *y* and *z* coordinates (*i, j, k*) of the emitter in the array.

In the proposed architecture, bi-directional communication is available through the mesh/cellular nodes. Each user sends to the local controller a "request" message with his pose (x,y,z, δ), user code (pin_1) and also adds its needs (code meeting and wayfinding data). If the message is diffused by the CM transmitter, a pattern [0000] precedes this identification. When bidirectional communication is required, the user has to register by choosing a user name (pin_1) with 4 decimal numbers, each one associated to a colour channel. So, to compose the decimal code each digit (0-9) has its own colour, codified in a 4-binary bit code. If buddy friend services are required a 4-binary code of the meeting (pin_2) has to be inserted. The coded steering angle (δ) completes the pose in a frame time (Table 2). The codes assigned to the pin_2 and to δ be the same in all the channels. If no wayfinding services are required these last three blocks are set at zero and the user only receives its own location. The last block is used to transmit the wayfinding message. A stop bit is used at the end of each frame.

The calibration of the receiver supplies an additional tool to enhance the decoding task and includes the simultaneous modulation of the four RGBV emitters in the cell [21]. The resultant optical signal is a combination of the all the possible optical excitation (2^4), which results in 16 possible photocurrent levels at the photodetector. Under these conditions, when all possible signal output levels are well distinct, it is possible to infer the corresponding input optical states.

Taking into account the frame structure, results from Figure 5, show that the user located at $C_{2,3,-1}$, arrived first (t_1), identified himself ("7261") and has informed the controller of his intention to find a friend for a scheduled meeting ([0011]; 3). Then, a buddy list was generated and includes all the users who have the same meeting codes. User "3009" arrives later sends the alert notification ($C_{4,4,1}$; t_3) to be triggered when his friend is in his floor vicinity, identifies himself ("3009") and uses the same code, in the buddy wayfinding services (code 3), to track the best way to his meeting. After this second request, the buddy finder service uses the location information from both user devices to determine the proximity of their owners and sends a response message with the best route to the meeting.

Figure 6, shows the decoded messages from the two users as they travel to the pre-scheduled meeting. The trajectory followed (poses) is shown on the right side of the figure. At the top the figure the simulated scenario is illustrated.

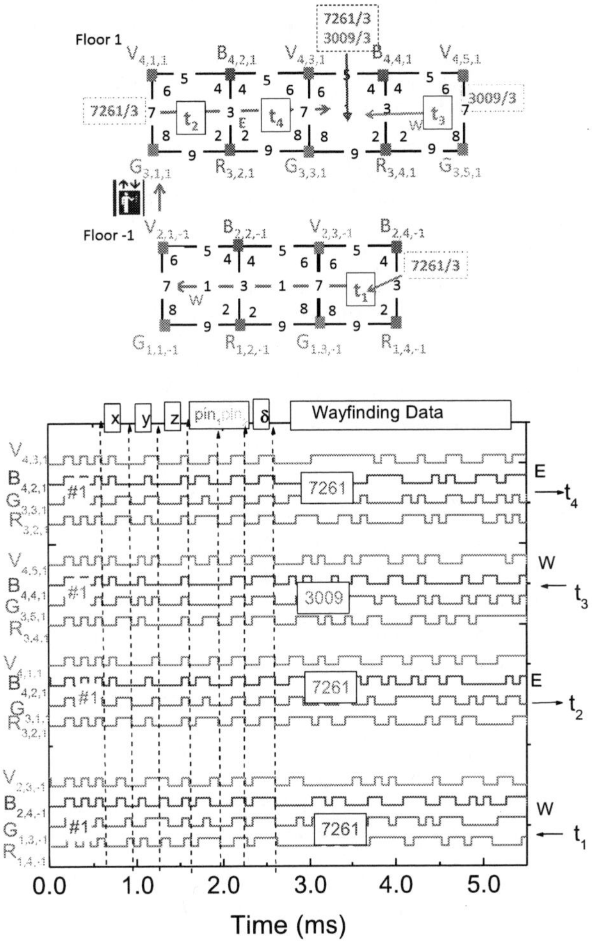

Figure 6. Decoded messages from the two users as they travel to a pre-scheduled meeting.

Data shows that user "7621" starts (t_1) his journey on floor -1, $C_{2,3,-1}$; #1W, goes up to floor 1 in $C_{2,1,-1}$ and at t_2 he arrives at $C_{4,1,1}$ heading for E. During his journey, user "3009" from $C_{4,4,1}$ #1 asks the CM (t_3) to forward him to the scheduled meeting and follows course to W. At t_4 both friends join in $C_{4,3,1}$.

The existence of congested zones can be locally detected by the "mesh / cellular" hybrid controller (Figure 1a), which is also equipped with a modem providing IP base connectivity to the central manager. The hybrid controller integrates the number of requests and individual poses, q_i *(t),* received during the same time interval. Once the individual poses are known, the relative poses, q_{ij} *(t)* are calculated. An alert notifies the user of the best route.

V. CONCLUSIONS

A VLC multi-person cooperative localization dynamic LED-assisted positioning and navigation system was proposed based on ceiling landmark route instructions using VLC. A 3D building model for large indoor environments was presented, and a VLC scenario in a multilevel building was established. The communication protocol was presented. Bi-directional communication between the infrastructure and the mobile receiver was analyzed. Global results show that the location of a mobile receiver, concomitant with data transmission is achieved. The dynamic LED-aided VLC navigation system enables to determine the position of a mobile target inside the network, to infer the travel direction along the time and to interact with received information.

The VLC system, when applied to large building, can help to find the shortest path to a place, guiding the users on a direct, shortest path to their destinations.

ACKNOWLEDGEMENTS

This work was sponsored by FCT – Fundação para a Ciência e a Tecnologia, within the Research Unit CTS – Center of Technology and Systems, reference UIDB/00066/2020. The project IPL/IDI&CA/2020/Geo-Loc/ISEL, is also acknowledge.

REFERENCES

[1] E.Ozgur, E. Dinc, and O. B. Akan, "Communicate to illuminate: State-of-the-art and research challenges for visible light communications," Physical Communication 17 pp. 72–85, (2015).

[2] C. Yang and H. R. Shao, "WiFi-based indoor positioning," IEEE Commun. Mag., vol. 53, no. 3, pp. 150–157 (Mar. 2015).

[3] D. Tsonev, et al. "A 3-Gb/s single-LED OFDM-based wireless VLC link using a Gallium Nitride µLED," IEEE Photon. Technol. Lett. 26 (7), pp.637–640 (2014).

[4] D. O'Brien et al. "Indoor visible light communications: challenges and prospects," Proc. SPIE 7091, 709106 (2008).

[5] H.-H. Liu and Y.-N. Yang,"WiFi-based indoor positioning for multi-floor environment," Proceedings of the IEEE Region 10 Conference on Trends and Development in Converging Technology Towards (TENCON '11)November 2011Bali,Indonesia59760110.1109/TENCON.2011.61291752-s2.0-84863014825 (2011).

[6] Y. Wang, H. Li, X. Luo, Q. Sun, and J. Liu, "A 3D Fingerprinting Positioning Method Based on Cellular Networks," International Journal of Distributed Sensor Networks, (2014).

[7] M. Vieira, M. A. Vieira, P. Louro, P. Vieira, and A. Fantoni, "Fine-grained indoor localization: optical sensing and detection," Proc. SPIE 10680, Optical Sensing and Detection V, 106800H (9 May 2018).

[8] A. Jovicic, J. Li, and T. Richardson, "Visible light communication: opportunities, challenges and the path to market," Communications Magazine, IEEE, vol. 51, no. 12, pp. 26–32 (2013).

[9] M. A. Vieira, M. Vieira, P. Louro, V. Silva, P. Vieira, "Optical signal processing for indoor positioning using a-SiCH technology," Opt. Eng. 55 (10), 107105 (2016), doi: 10.1117/1.OE.55.10.107105 (2016).

[10] M. A. Vieira, M. Vieira, P. Vieira, P. Louro, "Optical signal processing for a smart vehicle lighting system using a-SiCH technology," Proc. SPIE 10231, Optical Sensors 2017, 102311L (2017);

[11] M. Vieira, M.A. Vieira, P. Louro, A. Fantoni, and Steiger-A. Garção, "Light-activated amplification in Si-C tandem devices: A capacitive active filter model," IEEE sensor journal, 12, NO. 6, 1755-1762 (2012).

[12] M. A. Vieira, M. Vieira, P. Louro, V. Silva, P. Vieira, "Optical signal processing for indoor positioning using a-SiCH technology," Opt. Eng. 55 (10), 107105 (2016), doi: 10.1117/1.OE.55.10.107105 (2016).

[13] A. Yousefpour et al."All one needs to know about fog computing and related edge computing paradigms: A complete survey", Journal of Systems Architecture,Volume 98, pp. 289-330 (2019).

[14] R. Rajamani "Dynamic Vehicle and control" Mechanical Engineering Series, ISBN 978-1-4614-1433-9 (2012).

[15] J. Ackermann, J. Guldner, W. Sienel, R. Steinhauser, and V. Utkin, "Linear and Nonlinear Controller Design for Robust Automatic Steering" IEEE Transactions on Control Systems Technology (Volume: 3, Issue: 1, Mar 1995), pp. 132 – 143, DOI: 10.1109/87.370719 (1995).

[16] Y. Zhu, W. Liang, J. Zhang, and Y. Zhang, "Space-Collaborative Constellation Designs for MIMO Indoor Visible Light Communications," IEEE Photonics Technology Letters, vol. 27, no. 15, pp. 1667–1670, (2015).

[17] Y. Qiu, H. Chen and W. Meng, "Channel modeling for visible light communications—a survey", Wirel. Commun. Mob. Comput. 2016; 16:2016–2034,(2016)

[18] S. Raza, et al. "Optical Wireless Channel Characterization For Indoor Visible Light Communications", Indian Journal of Science and Technology, Vol 8 (22), DOI: 10.17485/ijst/2015/v8i22/70605, 2015

[19] M. Vieira, M. A. Vieira., P. Louro., P. Vieira, A. Fantoni, "Fine-grained indoor localization: optical sensing and detection," Proc. SPIE 10680, Optical Sensing and Detection V, 106800H (9 May 2018).

[20] M. Vieira, M. A. Vieira., P. Louro., P. Vieira, A. Fantoni, "Light-emitting diodes aided indoor localization using visible light communication technology," Opt. Eng. 57(8), 087105 (2018).

[21] M. Vieira, M. A. Vieira, P. Louro, A. Fantoni, and P. Vieira "Location and wayfinding services through visible light in crowded buildings", Proc. SPIE 11772, Optical Sensors 2021, 117721V (2021).

A Wearable Internet of Things Device for Bio-signals Real Time Monitoring of Elderly People

Panagiotis Pikasis, Grigoris Kaltsas
microSENSES Laboratory, Department of Electrical and Electronics Engineering, University of West Attica, Ancient Olive – Grove Campus, 12243 Athens, Greece
email: mscres-1@uniwa.gr, G. Kaltsas@uniwa.gr

***Abstract*—Monitoring of elderly health in real time could be vital in the event of emergency medical incidents and could possibly result in saving a person's life. Researchers are focusing on the field of monitoring vital signs in real time via biosensors with non-invasive methods, followed by processing and assessment of the acquired data. Due to Internet of Things technology, vital signs could be gathered and distributed in real time to multiple users simultaneously. The main indicators of vital signs involve measurements of skin temperature, heart rate, blood pressure respiration rate, oxygen saturation, PH level, calories, etc. In this paper, we present a novel approach of a wearable device fabricated in a flexible substrate that can measure such bioindicators and notify caregivers in order to assist an elderly person in a potential emergency situation. In this paper a wearable vital sign monitoring wearable device is presented in order to monitor the physiological state in real time.**

Keywords- Internet of Things; homecare elderly; elderly care; wearable monitoring; health monitoring system.

I. INTRODUCTION

Recent technological advances that brought about the Internet of Things revolution that we are experiencing today [1], can provide efficient and innovative solutions to issues related to elderly care, taking in the average life expectancy [2]. Elderly care facilities are investing in human resources to provide high quality treatment to elderly people in need, which in many cases is a must for people with continuous medical treatment. Caregivers must spend multiple hours measuring and recording vital signs of people with high probability of human errors through this process. The cost for such an institution is highly raised due to the numerous personnel needed and the fees for the boarders are raised proportionally. Towards this direction, researches have been carried out in order to integrate wearable technology in the continuous monitoring and precision measuring of the user's vital indicators [3].

Wearables have been a growing technology in recent decades. More and more are getting involved in our daily life in the forms of smartwatches, bands, Virtual Reality glasses, etc. This technology provides an easy-to-access method to precise recording of vital signs with low cost [4].

In addition, measuring and monitoring by a sensor device could provide stable, long term, continues medical records without requiring personnel and expensive medical equipment; moreover, it provides extended freedom of movement to the user. These medical records could be stored in cloud services 24/7 and prove to be a useful tool for future state of health analysis or even for early diagnosis of potentially harmful diseases.

The paper is organized as follows. Section II describes recent advances on wearable systems and devices. Section III presents in the first part the wearable device fabricated for the purpose of this research and in the second part the monitoring system designed for the same reason. Section IV presents the results of the measurements and the corresponding procedure. Finally, conclusions and future research directions are drawn in Section IV.

II. BACKGROUND

Several research groups have already fabricated wearable devices for continuous real time monitoring of vital signs with non- invasive technics.

Duran-Vega et al. [5] created a system for monitoring and storing vital signs called "Abuelometro" to assist in an elderly care facility. Using the Hexiwear biometric [6] wearable device, a platform was fabricated, able to monitor skin temperature, heart rate and oxygen saturation in real time, as well as additional data, such as exercise time, sleep time, meal time etc. Relatives and caregivers could have access to that information and would be notified in case of an emergency condition.

Kumar et al. [7] demonstrated a wearable device measuring blood vessel change via an optical device in real time using the Photoplethysmography method. The system is separated in 4 main parts, the sensor device, the gateway the smartphone app and the cloud server. The device communicates with MiWi and BLE protocols to a smartphone app through a gateway and the data are uploaded to the cloud where they stored and visualized.

Cohen et al. [8] demonstrated a ring sensor device able to measure blood pressure and heart rate using transmission Photoplethysmography technique. In their device, an LDR and a LED were used to observe the pulses using transmission Photoplethysmography while a microcontroller was reading the change in the LDR resistance. The accuracy of the device prediction exceeds over 90% compared to an average real for both systolic and diastolic pressure.

Zheng et al. [9] demonstrated a cuff-less wearable system using pulse arrival time measurements for monitoring blood pressure in order to obtain and diagnose hypertension.

Wearable contained of optical Photoplethysmography sensor parted from a led and a photodiode and two pieces of Electrocardiography patches sewed on the inner side of the armband. The receiving signal is amplified and filtered before it reaches the microcontroller. After that, data can be stored and transmitted via Bluetooth to a smartphone app. The system was tested on both healthy and hypertense subjects.

Gao et al. [10] demonstrated a wearable device capable of performing perspiration analysis by sampling human sweat and measuring sweat metabolites such as glucose and lactose and electrolytes such as potassium and sodium ions. The device was placed in a flexible substrate in order to achieve contact with human body and a skin temperature sensor was used in order to monitor thermal shift. A microcontroller was implemented for gathering all the measurements and sending the corresponding data to a smartphone app via a Bluetooth module. The aim of the researchers was to monitor the physiological state of an athlete in real time.

The devices mentioned above are using Internet of Things technology to gather data from the biosensor in order to determine and present the physiological state of the user. Despite vital signs, it is common to monitor information such as environmental conditions, the kinetic changes, or the time and duration of the measurements taken from the user. Research is continuing in the integration of new biosensor to wearable systems in order to improve the quality of the measurements and the variety of vital signs collected.

III. WEARABLE DEVICE

In this section an overview of our approach and the corresponding monitoring system will be presented.

A. Overview of the present approach

The wearable device fabricated for the purposes of this research consisted of both vital sign and environmental sensors. The criteria for choosing the sensors are driven by the main specifications of the device, which can be analyzed as follows: At least two user's vital signs of the user must be monitored, non-invasive methods must be implemented, and the device should be flexible and easily fit. Furthermore, the final device should be low cost and expandable.

A schematic indicating the main parts of the proposed device is illustrated in Figure 1. The device implements a microcontroller (atmega328p) in order to collect measurements, perform calculations and send data via a Wi-Fi module to a MQTT server in real time. The device is powered by 2 Li-po batteries of 400mAh in series.

All data collected by the microcontroller are processed and send in real time to the Wi-Fi module placed in the flexible substrate. The Wi-Fi module (esp8266) is constantly connected to the internet and posting the measurement received by the MCU to a MQTT cloud server. The measurements are shortly stored on the server and posted to all the subscribers.

In order to build the device, a commercial Kapton substrate was chosen since it provides stability in high temperatures and can be commonly found in many thicknesses and covering metal layers. A Vishay PT100 thermistor (100-ohm PTS SMD flat chip temperature dependent resistor) was integrated in the above-mentioned substrate for skin temperature monitoring. A simple passive linear circuit of a voltage divider was used for this purpose, with a resistor and a thermistor in series, and the output was connected to an ADC channel of the microcontroller. The voltage divider transfer function was used for the calculation of the thermistor resistance value.

The person's heartbeat (also referred as 'pulse') can commonly be measured on the wrist or neck. The pulse of a person is measured by counting the number of heart beats in one minute. Beats per minute measurements were calculated using a non-invasive, optical sensor, using the Photoplethysmography method [11] to determine the heart rate of the user. Specifically, the HRM-2511E optical sensor was utilized, which is a transmissive sensor with a phototransistor output, emitting at 950nm. The sensor system consists of an infrared LED and a photodiode pair in a transmissive topology (LED is placed opposite of the photodiode, with the finger in between). A proportion of light passes through the finger to the photodiode is absorbed by the hemoglobin (a protein in red blood cells carrying oxygen) resulting to a pulsation relevant to the heart rate. The corresponding principle of operation is presented in Figure 2a (depicted by [12]). The recorded signal of the photodiode after been filtered by a high pass - low pass filter and amplified, ends up to the ADC channel of the microcontroller.

Additionally, a 3-axis accelerometer (ADXL362) with a 12-bit output resolution was used for precise monitoring of the person's movements. An environmental sensor (HIH6130) was used to measure humidity and environmental temperature in order to acquire data regarding the user's background conditions. All the parts of the system were fabricated on a flexible substrate (Polyimide), so that the device could easily fit on a person's wrist.

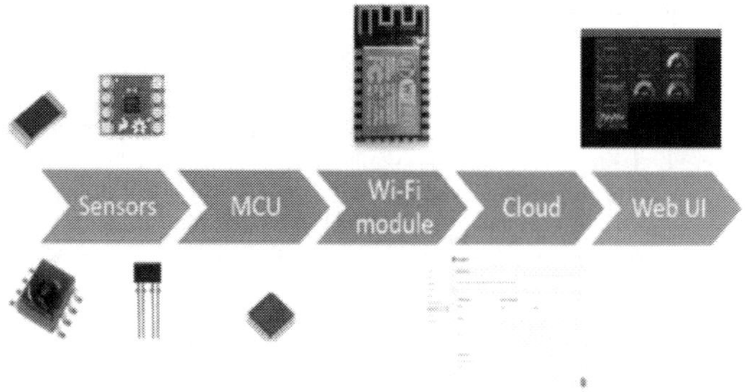

Figure 1. Schematic of the main components involved in the device.

a)

b)

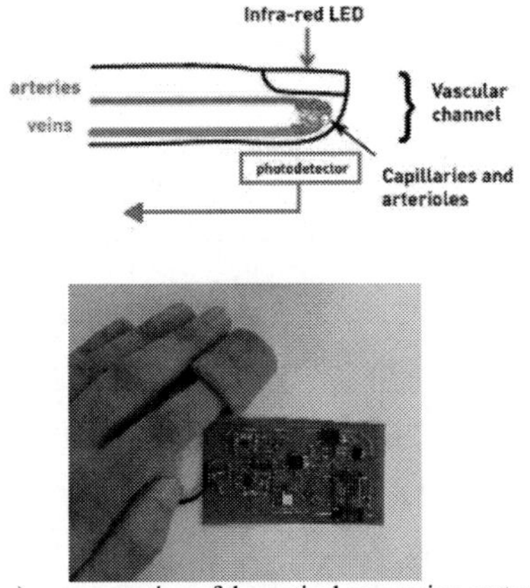

Figure 2. a) representation of the optical measuring system principle [11], b) Wearable device.

B. *Monitoring System*

A software written in C, using Arduino and public libraries was developed in order to achieve communication among the integrated ICs.

Several protocols were used for the communication of the atmega328p microcontroller with the various peripherals. More specifically UART was used for esp8266 connection, SPI was utilized for ADXL362 communication and I2C was implemented for HIH6130 connection.

Real time monitoring system is based on the MQTT protocol. The WIFI module (subscriber) is publishing data on an MQTT server (Broker). We used the MQTT cloud server of Amazon as a Broker and our device publishes data on it.

The Node-RED online platform [13] was utilized (as a Subscriber), to receive the data acquired by the server. A custom user interface called FRED was created for the data transferring, visualization and storage. More specifically, we develop an interface to visualize the sensor readings, create a user's archive, and alert the caregivers regarding the user condition, when potential danger situation is detected. In this way, relatives and caregivers could monitor vital signs of elder people and become alert to act in case of an emergency.

Figure 3 shows a typical representation of the device output when it is connected to a user.

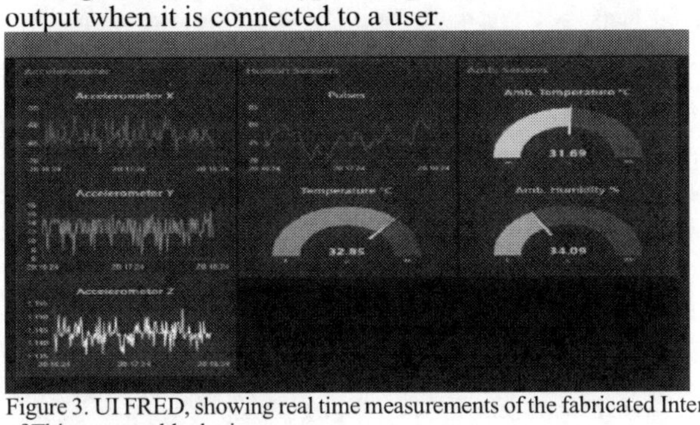

Figure 3. UI FRED, showing real time measurements of the fabricated Internet of Things wearable device.

IV. RESULTS

In order to demonstrate the validity of the proposed device, commercial systems were utilized for reference purposes. In our case, the optical sensor's measurements were compared to a commercial band, a Xiaomi Mi smart band integrated with a 3-axis accelerometer sensor, a 3-axis gyroscope, a Photoplethysmography heart rate sensor and a Bluetooth 5 BLE module. The temperature sensor measurements were compared to a digital infrared thermometer, Mastech MS6522B, simultaneously in four different daily routine tasks. During Sleep, at Lunch time, at Rest time and during casually exercise. For both test scenarios, a series of measurements were taken, up to 1 minute, and the final result was the average for each task. This process was repeated 3 times, over 3 different days to improve the reliability of the corresponding evaluation.

Table 1 and Table 2 present the results for the optical sensor and skin temperature evaluation, while Figure 4 illustrates the corresponding raw data of the accelerometers' signals in all axis.

Additionally, further processing of the acquiring data could occur in order to extract more bio-parameters. For example, by integrating a burnt calory counter in the measurements of the 3-axis sensor stored in the UI platform via the use of open-source algorithms, we can determine calories burn. Furthermore, by processing the measuring data acquired from the optical sensor, the systolic and diastolic pressure [8] can be extracted from the average maximum and minimum bits per minute.

Although the system design was successfully performed, there were some limitations that were faced during the procedure. The main limitations were focused on the process complexity and time, Moreover, the fitting of the optical sensor was also an issue mainly in terms of device robustness.

V. CONCLUSION AND FUTURE WORK

A system for monitoring vital signs of elderly in real time was presented. The system is capable of performing real-time vital signs monitoring and transferring them to an Internet of Things platform for future medical processing and analysis. The device is low-cost and could easily be fitted to a wristband for daily use due to its flexible substrate. The main parts used for the device include several sensors, namely: a thermistor, a reflective sensor combined by an IR transmitter and a phototransistor, an environmental sensor and an accelerometer. Those parts were connected directly to the MCU, which processes and transmits the data via a Wi-Fi module to a Web server using the MQTT communication protocol and presented the results in a web UI.

The measurements took place for 4 different body states and during 3 different days. The preliminary data demonstrate the ability of the device to successfully monitor predefined biosignals and its potential to discriminate among various activities of people.

TABLE I. BAND – WEARABLE DEVICE COMPARISON MEASURING BEATS PER MINUTE .

	Days	Xiaomi Band	Wearable device
Lunch	Day- 1	78.3	79.3
	Day- 2	80.6	81
	Day- 3	79.6	79.3
Rest	Day- 1	77.3	77.6
	Day- 2	75.2	76.8
	Day- 3	72.4	72.2
Exercise	Day- 1	91.2	91.1
	Day- 2	95.5	94.2
	Day- 3	103.1	102.7
Sleep	Day- 1	68.5	68.6
	Day- 2	64.3	64.7
	Day- 3	70.1	70.4

TABLE II. DIGITAL INFRARED THERMOMETER – WEARABLE DEVICE COMPARISON MEASURING SKIN TEMPERATURE

	Days	Mastech MS6522B	Wearable device
Lunch	Day- 1	34.1	33.2
	Day- 2	33	33.3
	Day- 3	32	32.3
Rest	Day- 1	33.1	33.4
	Day- 2	32.2	32.5
	Day- 3	32.9	32.8
Exercise	Day- 1	33.3	33.3
	Day- 2	35.3	34.1
	Day- 3	34.3	33.1
Sleep	Day- 1	32.4	32.7
	Day- 2	32.8	33.2
	Day- 3	32.2	32.6

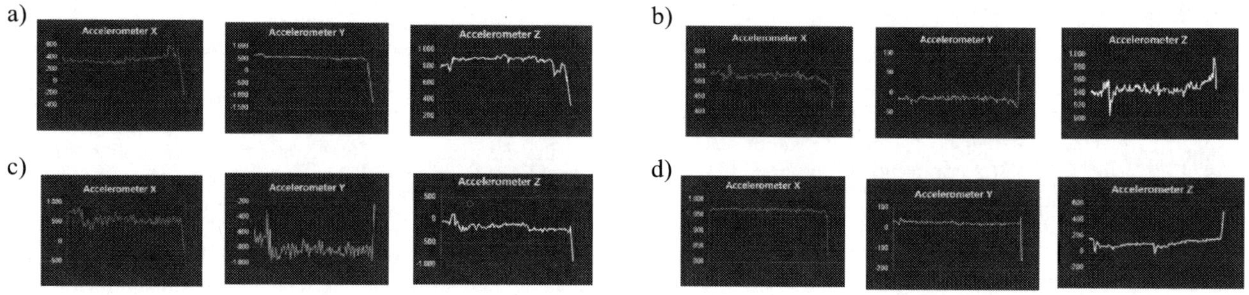

Figure 4. Visual representation of accelerometer during: a) lunch, b) rest, c) exercise, d) sleep

REFERENCES

[1] Rafiullah Khan, Sarmad Ullah Khan, Rifaqat Zaheer and Shahid Khan, “Future Internet: The Internet of Things Architecture, Possible Applications and Key Challenges”, 2012 10th International Conference on Frontiers of Information Technology - Future Internet: The Internet of Things Architecture, Possible Applications and Key Challenges. , (), 257–260. , DOI:10.1109/FIT.2012.53

[2] Shyamal Patel, Hyung-Soon Park, P. Bonato, L. Chan and M. Rodgers, “A review of wearable sensors and systems with application in rehabilitation”, JNER 2012, 9(1), 21–0. ,DOI:10.1186/1743-0003-9-21

[3] Mohanraj Karunanithi, “Monitoring technology for the elderly patient”, Expert Review of Medical Devices 4(2), 267–277. DOI:10.1586/17434440.4.2.267

[4] Marcello Cinque, Antonio Coronato and Alessandro Testa “Dependable Services for Mobile Health Monitoring Systems” , International Journal of Ambient Computing and Intelligence, IJACI ,2012 4(1)

[5] Luis A. Durán-Vega, Pedro C. Santana-Mancilla, Raymundo Buenrostro-Mariscal and Juan Contreras Castillo, “An IoT System for Remote Health Monitoring in Elderly Adults through a Wearable Device and Mobile Application”, Geriatrics (Basel). 2019 Jun; 4(2): 34. DOI: 10.3390/geriatrics4020034

[6] Hexiwear IoT and Wearables Development Platform 2018. http://www.hexiwear.com (accessed on 17 October 2021).

[7] Sanjeev Kumar, John Buckley, John Barton and Melusine Pigeon, “A Wristwatch-Based Wireless Sensor Platform for IoT Health Monitoring Applications”, MDPI Sensors 2020, 20(6) - 1675 DOI:10.3390/s20061675

[8] Zachary Cohen and Shyqyri Haxha, “Optical Based Sensor Prototype for Continuous Monitoring of the Blood Pressure“ ,IEEE SENSORS JOURNAL Materials Science 2017 1 – 1 , DOI:10.1109/JSEN.2017.2704098

[9] Yali Zheng, Carmen C. Y. Poon , Bryan P. Yan and James Y. W. Lau, “Pulse Arrival Time Based Cuff-Less and 24-H Wearable Blood Pressure Monitoring and its Diagnostic Value in Hypertension”, Journal of Medical Systems, 40(9), 195 DOI:10.1007/s10916-016-0558-6

[10] Wei Gao, Sam Emaminejad, Hnin Yin Yin Nyein and Samyuktha Challa, S, “Fully integrated wearable sensor arrays for multiplexed in situ perspiration analysis.” Nature, 529(7587), 509–514. DOI: 10.1038/nature16521

[11] Toshiyo Tamura , Yuka Maeda , Masaki Sekine and Masaki Yoshida, “Wearable Photoplethysmographic Sensors Past and Present”, MDPI electronic, 2014, DOI:10.3390/electronics302028

[12] Scott Wilkes, Gerard Stansby, Andrew Sims and Shona Haining, “Peripheral arterial disease: diagnostic challenges and how photoplethysmography may help”, British Journal of General Practice 2015, 65(635)- 323, https://doi.org/10.3399/bjgp15X685489

[13] https://fred.sensetecnic.com/ (accessed on 17 October 2021

PdAu Based Resistive Hydrogen Sensor in Anaerobic Environment

Clément Occelli, Tomas Fiorido, Carine Perrin-Pellegrino, Jean-Luc Seguin
Aix-Marseille Univ, Univ Toulon, CNRS, IM2NP
Marseille, 13397, France
e-mails : {clement.occelli, tomas.fiorido, carine.perrin-pellegrino and jean-luc.seguin}@im2np.fr

***Abstract*—Hydrogen is a promising gas for greenhouse gas emission reduction but also a reactive one. Thus, sensor for hydrogen detection in various atmospheres is mandatory. While leak sensors in air environments have been widely studied, only few researches have been done for hydrogen detection in anaerobic environments. In this work, the electrical resistance variation of a PdAu alloy as a sensitive film, is studied at various temperatures for hydrogen exposures in an anaerobic (N_2) environment. The $Pd_{0.8}Au_{0.2}$ alloy was deposited on a Si/SiO_2 substrate using magnetron sputtering followed by annealing at 200°C in N_2. The sensor was then tested at various temperatures for 0.3% H_2 exposure, the best operating temperature was found to be 50°C. Finally, sensor was able to detect at 50°C, concentrations from 0.3 to 3% H_2. These preliminary results are promising for further development of hydrogen sensors in anaerobic environment.**

Keywords-Hydrogen; PdAu; Resistive sensor; Anaerobic.

I. INTRODUCTION

The current context of climate change and the drive for sustainable development require the reduction of greenhouse gas emissions through the introduction of new technologies with minimal or no carbon emissions. Hydrogen gas has been identified as a very attractive energy carrier, since its combustion and its use to produce electricity generate only water as by-products [1]–[3]. As a result, a fast-growing hydrogen economy, based on the replacement of fossil fuels by hydrogen, will become a reality in several countries. Hydrogen is the lightest of chemical elements and the smallest molecule, having a great propensity to leak. Furthermore, hydrogen is a colourless, odourless, and tasteless gas, which has low auto ignition concentration in air (4 to 75%). Hence, high sensitivity hydrogen sensors, able to detect any leakage of hydrogen, are essentials wherever hydrogen is produced, transported and used. Gas pipelines are considered as a way to transport hydrogen (as a hydrogen/natural gas mixture) toward the end user, avoiding construction of new costly infrastructures and facilitate long term storage [4]–[6]. Gas impurities such as humidity and SO_2 are kept to a minimum limiting the corrosion and fragilization of pipelines [7] [8]. As a result, output gas can be considered as almost perfectly dry. While sensors for the detection of hydrogen leaks into the air have been widely studied for decades [9]–[11], no comprehensive study has yet been published on the measurement of high hydrogen concentrations in an oxygen-deprived atmosphere. To our knowledge, only two papers have focused on the anaerobic operation of hydrogen sensors [12] [13].

The main sensor technology able to measure selectively high hydrogen concentrations is Palladium (Pd) based thin film resistive sensors [10] [14]. Indeed, the Pd surface atoms decompose the adsorbed hydrogen molecules, and atomic hydrogen is easily absorbed into the Pd bulk to form Pd hydride. The absorbed hydrogen atoms cause changes in the crystal structure of the metal and an increase of electrical resistivity due to scattering of free electrons by the absorbed hydrogen atoms. However, the absorption of hydrogen causes an expansion of the Pd crystal lattice, leading to hysteresis in the sensor response and crack formation and delamination from the substrate.

One solution to avoid these serious drawbacks is to introduce, into Pd, metal atoms with an atomic radius larger than that of Pd atoms, e.g., Gold (Au) atoms. Hence, Au atoms, which occupy Pd lattice sites, slightly expand the Pd lattice, thereby reducing the strain induced energy barrier created upon hydrogen absorption, and thus hysteresis. As a result, hysteresis shrinks symmetrically and disappears about 20-25 % Au at room temperature [15] [16].

PdAu alloys were mainly used to realize optical sensors showing interesting performances [15], [17]–[19], but optical sensors are more complex and expensive than resistive sensors.

In this paper, we present preliminary results on the fabrication, characterisation and dry anaerobic sensing properties of a $Pd_{0.8}Au_{0.2}$ resistive hydrogen sensor. The paper is structured as follow: in section II we will describe the sensor fabrication and the experimental setup used for sensing characterization; then, in section III, the sensing results under various temperatures and hydrogen exposures will be discussed. Finally, in section IV, a conclusion is drawn with an insight of future work.

II. DESCRIPTION OF APPROACH AND TECHNIQUES

A. *Sensor fabrication*

PdAu deposition was made by radio frequency magnetron sputtering. Prior to the sensor fabrication, SiO_2/Si substrates were cleaned in an ultrasonic acetone bath followed by an alcohol and deionized water rinsing. Two cleaned substrates were placed in the sputtering chamber: one for structural characterization (sample A), the other for sensor realization (sample B). To allow rapid characterisation of hydrogen sensing, a simple basic sensor was made using a shadow mask consisting of a thin sheet of steel mechanically drilled. A picture of a typical fabricated sensor is shown in Fig. 1. The chamber was first pumped to a vacuum of 5 x 10^{-9} bar, then a thin titanium layer was deposited to promote adherence to the substrate as reported by several authors [20] [21]. The sputtering was performed on a Pd target partially covered by Au disks, at an argon pressure of $15x10^{-6}$ bar. Once deposition completed, the samples were annealed at 200°C in N_2 gas for several hours, since 200°C was found to be the best annealing temperature as described in [22]. Finally, a 120nm thick film was obtained, measurements were performed using a Dektak XT profilometer.

B. *Experimental Setup for Sensor Characterization*

The sensor was tested in a chamber of approximately 0.3 litre. Sensor was positioned on a heating plate with a Pt100

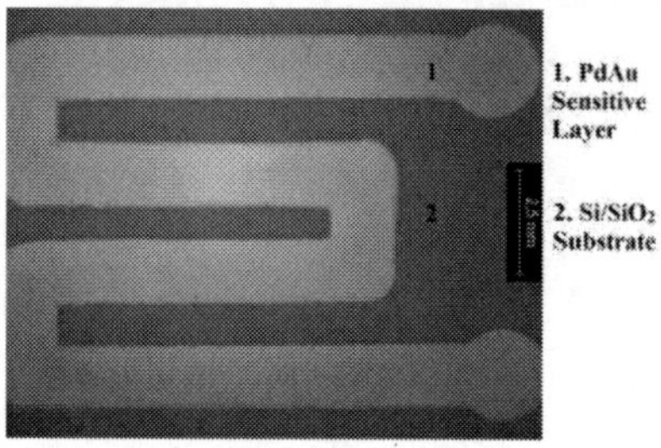

Figure 1. Optical microscope picture of a PdAu sensor made by sputtering.

(class B accuracy) temperature sensor attached next to it. The electrical resistance of the sensing film was measured by a Keithley Sourcemeter 2450 and recorded on a personal computer by a homemade software, every 0.5s. A programmable commercial gas mixing system was used for flow regulation. A continuous dry nitrogen (N_2) flow was used as baseline for every electrical measurement presented below. Hydrogen (H_2) concentrations were obtained by mixing a 3% H_2 in N_2 bottle with a pure N_2 bottle (used for baseline). Every H_2 exposure last 25 min. A 100sccm gas flow at atmospheric pressure was used on every experiment. As electrical resistance varies with temperature, only the sensor response (R_s) is calculated and presented in this work, using (1), were R_0 is the value of sensor stable base line resistance under constant temperature and pure nitrogen flow (value taken once, before any H_2 exposure), and R is the value of the sensor electrical resistance under H_2 exposure. The response and recovery time presented bellow are respectively defined as the time needed to reach 90% of the maximal R_s value for a given H_2 exposure (T_{90}) and as the time needed to return from stable R_s value to 10% of the stable baseline when hydrogen gas was stopped (T_{10}).

$$R_s\ (\%) = [(R - R_0)/R_0]\times 100 \qquad (1)$$

III. PHYSICOCHEMICAL AND ELECTRICAL CHARACTERIZATION

A. Chemical composition

Scanning Electron Microscopy (SEM) analysis was performed with a Zeiss Gemini SEM 500 ultra-high resolution Field Emission Scanning Electron Microscope (FESEM). For chemical analyses (Energy Dispersive X-ray Spectroscopy (EDS)), an Energy Dispersive Analysis of X-rays (EDAX) Octane Silicon Drift Detector (129 eV energy resolution for Manganese) was used at 15 kV, with a magnification of 10k on 3um x 3um area. Fig. 2 shows X-ray line spectra performed on sample A, with detected elements such as Palladium (Pd), Gold (Au), Silicon (Si) and Carbon (C). Four measurements were performed revealing an estimated alloy composition of 80% Pd and 20% Au.

Visual surface sample inspection is shown in Fig. 3, using SEM 100k magnification. No major variation is observed for surface morphology after annealing. Surface is composed of zones with small grains and zones of merged grains.

B. X Ray diffraction

The sample A microstructure was examined by X-ray diffraction, prior and after annealing was performed. The diagrams have been carried out with a theta-theta configuration and CuKα radiation (λ=0.154 nm) using an Empyrean diffractometer, equipped with a rapid detector,

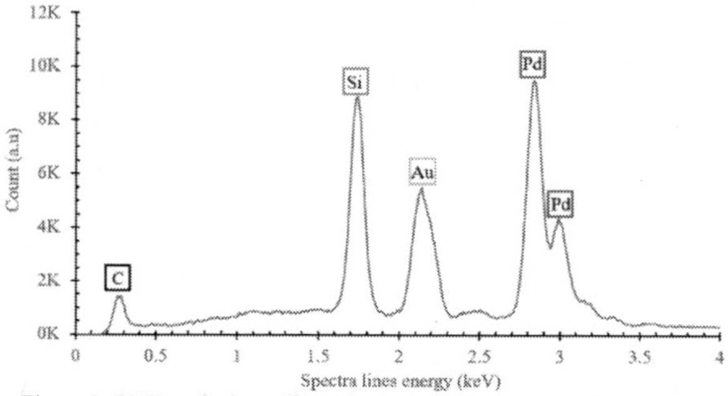

Figure 2. EDX analysis performed on sample A, for ease of reading, Au peak at 9.72 keV is not displayed.

using a 2° offset to avoid to be aligned with Si substrate. The average crystallite grain size (G_s) was estimated using the Scherrer formula (2).

$$G_s = [0.89\times\lambda]/[\beta\times cos\theta] \qquad (2)$$

Where λ is the X-ray wavelength, β the FWHM of (111) peak and θ the diffraction angle. Fig. 4 evidences that, for our sputtering parameters and film thickness, the film crystallizes mainly with a (111) preferred orientation and this trend is kept even after annealing. Small diffraction peaks are detected for the (311) and (222) planes; * symbol refers to SiO_2/Si substrate diffraction peak. Heat treatment has a noticeable impact on the microstructure with an increase of the crystallinity as (111) peak intensity grows from 13700 to almost 19400 counts. But, as suggested by Fig. 3, the grain size estimated from the Scherrer formula seems to be stable about 20 ±1 nm. Otherwise, the 2θ angle shift of the diffraction peaks is suggesting stress relaxation during the heat treatment.

C. Temperature influence on sensor response to hydrogen

Temperature of measurement is of crucial importance as it both affects sensor performance in term of response/recovery time and sensitivity. Furthermore, for practical applications, high operating temperatures are power consuming and hazardous for explosive environment [23]. Response/recovery time is usually reported to decrease with increasing temperature of measurement. Regarding sensor response to H_2 exposure, data vary. Some authors see their response dropping [24] [25], others increasing [20] [25] [26].

Figure 3. SEM photo of the surface aspect of sample A, before (1) and after annealing (2).

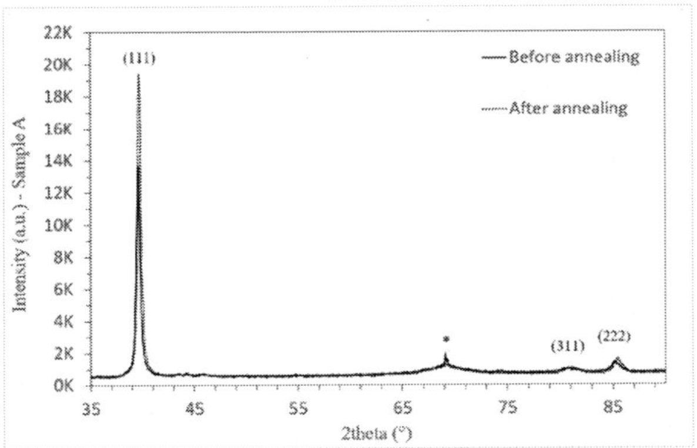

Figure 4. XRD diagram of sample A before and after annealing (λ=0.154 nm). The star indicates the trace of the Si substrate diffraction peak.

Fig. 5 shows the sensor response to 0.3% H_2 in N_2 exposure, at various temperatures. Response and recovery time as well as response amplitude are decreasing with increasing temperature. The response (T_{90}) and recovery time (T_{10}) are respectively 6min50s and 68min at 25°C, 5min40s and 17min30s at 100°C. Those results are in line with previous literature. Regarding sensor amplitude, it can be seen that upon heating, the maximal response value to 0.3% H_2 exposure diminishes and signal tends to become noisy, thus sensor will be less sensitive to H_2 variations. Yet, sensor was found to be operative for hydrogen detection in an anaerobic environment at all temperatures, 1.9% being the maximal response, obtained at 25°C and 0.5% being the lowest response, obtained at 100°C. Best operative temperature was found to be 50°C as it combines sufficient short response and recovery time (6min20s and 21min40s respectively), good sensitivity with 1.3% response toward 0.3% H_2 and a clear signal. Response and recovery time as well as sensor response are plotted for all temperatures in Fig. 6 and Fig. 7 respectively.

The sensor response dropping with increasing temperature can be explained as follows. The hydrogen absorption capacity of Pd and its alloys is linked to their Fermi level and the number of free d-states at this level [27] [28]. When increasing temperature, the number of low energy free d-sites tends to diminish as Fermi level rises, thus, more and more energy is needed for octahedral site occupation. For a given H_2 concentration, less site occupation will occur at elevated temperature, resulting in a lower response amplitude.

Finally, sensor sensitivity to others H_2 concentrations was investigated with a 1.5% and 3% H_2 exposure, results are

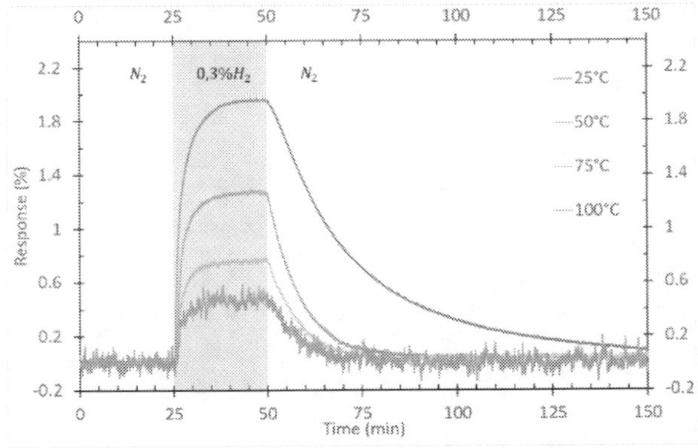

Figure 5. Sensor responses to 0.3% H_2 in N_2 at various temperatures

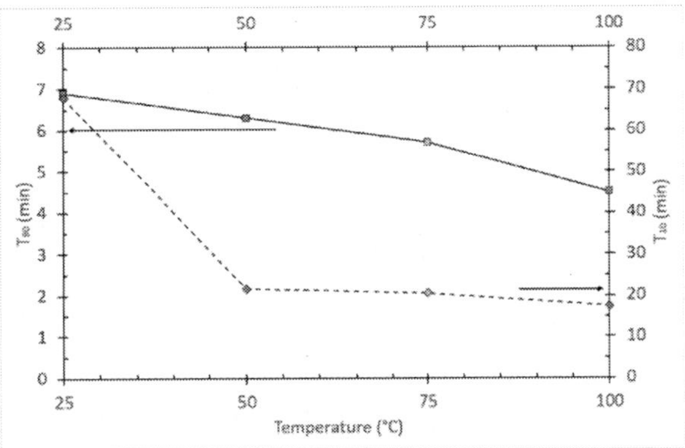

Figure 6. Plot of response (T_{90}) and recovery (T_{10}) time of sensor for 0.3% H_2 in N_2 at various temperatures.

presented in Fig. 8. Response amplitude is 2.6% for 1.5% H_2 and 3.4% for 3% H_2. Response and recovery time are respectively 6min20s and 20min20s for 1.5% H_2, 6min and 20min40s for 3% H_2. Those data show that our sensor was able to detect hydrogen from low to high concentration with a stable baseline.

Regarding response time, literature usually shows response/recovery time in the order of a few tens of seconds for the same material. An explanation for such difference with our minutes order response time could be due to : (1) thickness and width of our sensor design, simulation [29] show that expanding sensor volume largely increases reaction time; (2) low gas flow compare to cell volume. Fick's second law is usually used to ascribe the hydrogen diffusion dependence to H_2 partial pressure [29]. Thus, a long filling time results in a non-maximal kinetic of diffusion in the sensing layer. Recent work put in evidence long filling time of our cross chamber [30], validating above hypothesis.

IV. CONCLUSION AND FURTHER WORK

In summary, we have fabricated a resistive hydrogen sensor, using $Pd_{0.8}Au_{0.2}$ alloy as sensitive film, by magnetron sputtering and tested it in an anaerobic environment at different temperatures. DRX analysis shows the preferential growth along the (111) plane. Thermal treatment increased the film crystallinity, while grain size remains at 20 ±1 nm. The best operating temperature was found to be at 50°C as it combines a relative fast response and recovery time, a sufficient response amplitude to 0.3% H_2 in N_2 and a clear and exploitable signal. Sensor was also able to detect hydrogen from low (0.3%) to high concentration (3%). After this preliminary work showing PdAu alloy ability to measure hydrogen in an anaerobic atmosphere, the next steps of the study will concern :

- Characterisation of the sensitivity and selectivity
- Improving response and recovery times
- Testing the effect of different Au contents in the alloy under anaerobic atmospheres containing up to 3%H_2.

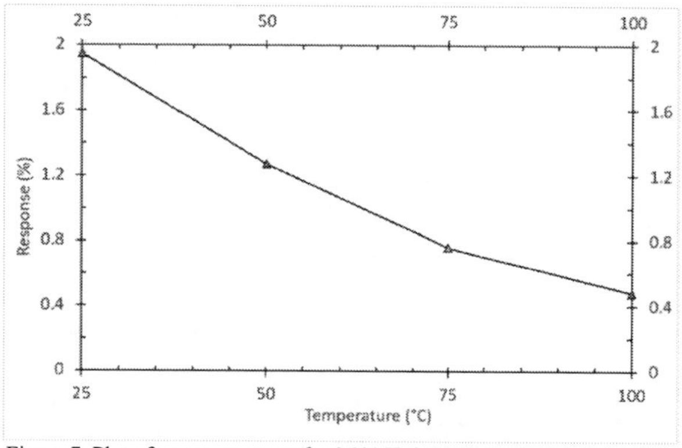

Figure 7. Plot of sensor response for 0.3% H_2 in N_2 at various temperatures.

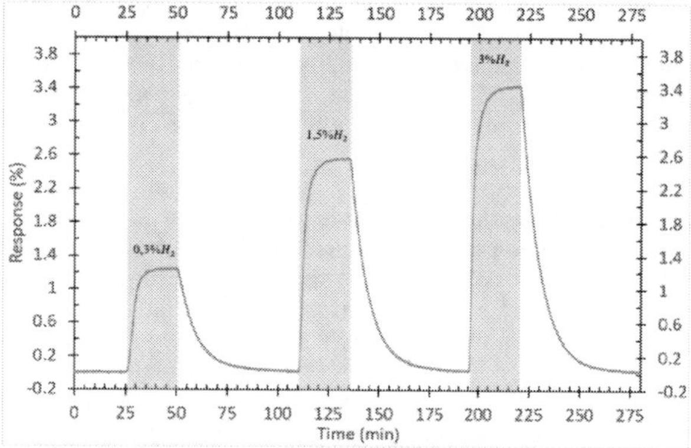

Figure 8. Sensor responses to 0.3%, 1.5% and 3% H_2 in N_2 at 50°C.

ACKNOWLEDGMENT

The authors thank Soilihi Moindjie, Jean-Jacques Furter, CP2M laboratory for their technical support and Khaoula El Ouazzani for performing XRD.

Clément Occelli would like to thank Région Sud of France and CMR Group for financial support.

References

[1] A. Demirbas, 'Future hydrogen economy and policy', Energy Sources, Part B: Economics, Planning, and Policy, vol. 12, no. 2, pp. 172–181, Feb. 2017, doi: 10.1080/15567249.2014.950394.

[2] Z. Abdin et al., 'Hydrogen as an energy vector', Renewable and Sustainable Energy Reviews, vol. 120, p. 109620, Mar. 2020, doi: 10.1016/j.rser.2019.109620.

[3] C. Acar and I. Dincer, 'Review and evaluation of hydrogen production options for better environment', Journal of Cleaner Production, vol. 218, pp. 835–849, May 2019, doi: 10.1016/j.jclepro.2019.02.046.

[4] D. Haeseldonckx and W. D'haeseleer, 'The use of the natural-gas pipeline infrastructure for hydrogen transport in a changing market structure', International Journal of Hydrogen Energy, vol. 32, no. 10, pp. 1381–1386, Jul. 2007, doi: 10.1016/j.ijhydene.2006.10.018.

[5] A. Maroufmashat and M. Fowler, 'Transition of Future Energy System Infrastructure; through Power-to-Gas Pathways', Energies, vol. 10, no. 8, p. 1089, Jul. 2017, doi: 10.3390/en10081089.

[6] M. Kong et al., 'Investigation of Mixing Behavior of Hydrogen Blended to Natural Gas in Gas Network', Sustainability, vol. 13, no. 8, p. 4255, Apr. 2021, doi: 10.3390/su13084255.

[7] A. S. Ruhl and A. Kranzmann, 'Investigation of corrosive effects of sulphur dioxide, oxygen and water vapour on pipeline steels', International Journal of Greenhouse Gas Control, vol. 13, pp. 9–16, Mar. 2013, doi: 10.1016/j.ijggc.2012.12.007.

[8] S. Younus Ahmed, P. Gandhidasan, and A. A. Al-Farayedhi, 'Pipeline drying using dehumidified air with low dew point temperature', Applied Thermal Engineering, vol. 18, no. 5, pp. 231–244, Jan. 1998, doi: 10.1016/S1359-4311(97)00083-5.

[9] Y. Luo, C. Zhang, B. Zheng, X. Geng, and M. Debliquy, 'Hydrogen sensors based on noble metal doped metal-oxide semiconductor: A review', International Journal of Hydrogen Energy, vol. 42, no. 31, pp. 20386–20397, Aug. 2017, doi: 10.1016/j.ijhydene.2017.06.066.

[10] W.-T. Koo et al., 'Chemiresistive Hydrogen Sensors: Fundamentals, Recent Advances, and Challenges', ACS Nano, vol. 14, no. 11, pp. 14284–14322, Nov. 2020, doi: 10.1021/acsnano.0c05307.

[11] T. Hübert, L. Boon-Brett, G. Black, and U. Banach, 'Hydrogen sensors – A review', Sensors and Actuators B: Chemical, vol. 157, no. 2, pp. 329–352, Oct. 2011, doi: 10.1016/j.snb.2011.04.070.

[12] W. J. Buttner et al., 'Inter-laboratory assessment of hydrogen safety sensors performance under anaerobic conditions', International Journal of Hydrogen Energy, vol. 37, no. 22, pp. 17540–17548, Nov. 2012, doi: 10.1016/j.ijhydene.2012.03.165.

[13] Y. Du et al., 'Aerobic and anaerobic H2 sensing sensors fabricated by diffusion membranes depositing on Pt-ZnO film', Sensors and Actuators B: Chemical, vol. 252, pp. 239–250, Nov. 2017, doi: 10.1016/j.snb.2017.06.005.

[14] A. Mirzaei et al., 'An overview on how Pd on resistive-based nanomaterial gas sensors can enhance response toward hydrogen gas', International Journal of Hydrogen Energy, p. S0360319919320944, Jun. 2019, doi: 10.1016/j.ijhydene.2019.05.180.

[15] C. Wadell et al., and C. Langhammer, 'Hysteresis-Free Nanoplasmonic Pd–Au Alloy Hydrogen Sensors', Nano Lett., vol. 15, no. 5, pp. 3563–3570, May 2015, doi: 10.1021/acs.nanolett.5b01053.

[16] S. Luo, D. Wang, and T. B. Flanagan, 'Thermodynamics of Hydrogen in fcc Pd–Au Alloys', J. Phys. Chem. B, vol. 114, no. 18, pp. 6117–6125, May 2010, doi: 10.1021/jp100858r.

[17] Z. Zhao, M. A. Carpenter, H. Xia, and D. Welch, 'All-optical hydrogen sensor based on a high alloy content palladium thin film', Sensors and Actuators B: Chemical, vol. 113, no. 1, pp. 532–538, Jan. 2006, doi: 10.1016/j.snb.2005.03.070.

[18] R. J. Westerwaal et al., 'Nanostructured Pd–Au based fiber optic sensors for probing hydrogen concentrations in gas mixtures', International Journal of Hydrogen Energy, vol. 38, no. 10, pp. 4201–4212, Apr. 2013, doi: 10.1016/j.ijhydene.2012.12.146.

[19] L. J. Bannenberg et al., 'Direct Comparison of PdAu Alloy Thin Films and Nanoparticles upon Hydrogen Exposure', ACS Appl. Mater. Interfaces, vol. 11, no. 17, pp. 15489–15497, May 2019, doi: 10.1021/acsami.8b22455.

[20] Q. Liu, J. Yao, Y. Wang, Y. Sun, and G. Ding, 'Temperature dependent response/recovery characteristics of Pd/Ni thin film based hydrogen sensor', Sensors and Actuators B: Chemical, vol. 290, pp. 544–550, Jul. 2019, doi: 10.1016/j.snb.2019.04.024.

[21] M. W. Jenkins, R. C. Hughes, and S. V. Patel, 'Stabilizing the response of Pd/Ni alloy films to hydrogen with Ti adhesion layers', Boston, MA, Feb. 2001, p. 99. doi: 10.1117/12.417437.

[22] Z. Zhao and M. A. Carpenter, 'Annealing enhanced hydrogen absorption in nanocrystalline Pd/Au sensing films', Journal of Applied Physics, vol. 97, no. 12, p. 124301, Jun. 2005, doi: 10.1063/1.1927690.

[23] I. Darmadi, F. A. A. Nugroho, and C. Langhammer, 'High-Performance Nanostructured Palladium-Based Hydrogen Sensors—Current Limitations and Strategies for Their Mitigation', ACS Sens., p. acssensors.0c02019, Nov. 2020, doi: 10.1021/acssensors.0c02019.

[24] M. Wang and Y. Feng, 'Palladium–silver thin film for hydrogen sensing', Sensors and Actuators B: Chemical, vol. 123, no. 1, pp. 101–106, Apr. 2007, doi: 10.1016/j.snb.2006.07.030.

[25] K. Yu et al., 'Enhanced accuracy of palladium-nickel alloy based hydrogen sensor by in situ temperature compensation', Sensors and Actuators B: Chemical, vol. 299, p. 126989, Nov. 2019, doi: 10.1016/j.snb.2019.126989.

[26] B. Sharma and J.-S. Kim, 'Pd/Ag alloy as an application for hydrogen sensing', International Journal of Hydrogen Energy, vol. 42, no. 40, pp. 25446–25452, Oct. 2017, doi: 10.1016/j.ijhydene.2017.08.142.

[27] M. Hara et al., 'Evaluation of terminal composition of palladium–silver hydrides in plateau region by electronic structure calculations', Journal of Alloys and Compounds, vol. 580, pp. S202–S206, Dec. 2013, doi: 10.1016/j.jallcom.2013.03.095.

[28] S. Akamaru, M. Hara, N. Nunomura, and M. Matsuyama, 'Effect of substituting elements on hydrogen uptake for Pd–Rh–H and Pd–Ag–H systems evaluated by magnetic susceptibility measurement', International Journal of Hydrogen Energy, vol. 38, no. 18, pp. 7569–7575, Jun. 2013, doi: sakamoto.

[29] Y. Liu, Y. Li, P. Huang, H. Song, and G. Zhang, 'Modeling of hydrogen atom diffusion and response behavior of hydrogen sensors in Pd–Y alloy nanofilm', Scientific Reports, vol. 6, no. 1, pp. 1–9, Nov. 2016, doi: 10.1038/srep37043.

[30] F.-E. Annanouch et al., 'Hydrodynamic evaluation of gas testing chamber: Simulation, experiment', Sensors and Actuators B: Chemical, vol. 290, pp. 598–606, Jul. 2019, doi: 10.1016/j.snb.2019.04.023.

Signal Accuracy of Terahertz Chemical Microscope for Lung Cancer Cell Detection

Yuichi Yoshida, Xue Ding, Kohei Iwatsuki, Jin Wang, Kenji Sakai, Toshihiko Kiwa
Graduate School of Interdisciplinary Science and Engineering in Health Systems,
Okayama University
Okayama, Japan
e-mail: (pjaa6rfb, pm7g9k5d, prsd3x9h)@s.okayama-u.ac.jp
(wangjin, sakai-k, kiwa)@okayama-u.ac.jp

Sayaka Tsuji
Faculty of Engineering,
Okayama University
Okayama, Japan
e-mail: proc9afb@s.okayama-u.ac.jp

Hirofumi Inoue
Graduate School of Medicine Dentistry and Pharmaceutical Sciences,
Okayama University
Okayama, Japan
e-mail: inoue-h1@cc.okayama-u.ac.jp

***Abstract*—It is essential to evaluate the number of cancer cells to analyze cancer genome for cancer genomic medicine. However, it takes a long time, and pathologists' skills are needed to evaluate it. Our group has developed and proposed a Terahertz Chemical Microscope (TCM) to evaluate it easily and fast. In this study, antibodies were immobilized by covalent bonding and avidin-biotin reaction to detect cancer cells, and their immobilizing methods were compared. The results suggest that signal accuracy is improved to detect lung cancer cells using avidin-biotin reaction.**

Keywords-terahertz chemical microscope; terahertz; immobilizing antibody; cancer cell

I. INTRODUCTION

Recently, cancer genomic medicine has been attracted to be a cancer treatment to reduce the physical burden of patients in cancer treatments. The cancer genome is analyzed, and individualized treatment is provided to each cancer patient. In order to provide cancer patients with this treatment, it is essential to analyze the cancer genome. Before analyzing the cancer genome, it is essential to evaluate the number of cancer cells in a specimen tissue to analyze the cancer genome efficiently. In general, the evaluation is done by treating the specimen tissue with Formalin-Fixed Paraffin-Embedded (FFPE) and observing it with a microscope by pathologists. However, in FFPE, the recommended time to fix the specimen tissue is from 24 to 48 hours [1], so it takes at least 2 or 3 days to evaluate. Also, evaluation precision depends on the pathologists' skills to process the tissue by FFPE or distinguish cancer cells from normal cells in the tissue.

Our group has developed and proposed a Terahertz Chemical Microscope (TCM) [2] [3] to evaluate the number of cancer cells in a solution without complex pretreatments as FFPE [4]-[6]. TCM can measure cancer cells in the solution, so little pretreatment is required. Also, TCM can evaluate the number of cancer cells quantitatively. In the TCM, cancer cells are detected using immune reactions. So, it is crucial to immobilize antibodies on a sensing plate used as a terahertz emitter.

In this study, in order to accurate detection terahertz signals, the methods of immobilizing antibodies using covalent bonding [7] [8] and using an avidin- biotin reaction [6] were compared by measuring PC9 and EBC1, which are a human lung adenocarcinoma culture cell and a human lung squamous cell carcinoma culture cell, respectively.

II. EXPERIMENTAL

TCM can detect cancer cells in a solution on a sensing plate by measuring the amplitude of terahertz wave radiated from the sensing plate. Figures 1 (a) and (b) show the processes of immobilizing antibodies using covalent bonding and avidin-biotin reaction respectively. In Figure 1 (a), 20 μg/mL of anti IgG (Antigen Affinity Purified, Bethyl Laboratories, Inc., Montgomery, Alabama, USA) was immobilized on the sensing plate using amino coupling as the covalent bonding [7] [8] for 17 h at 4 °C, and the SiO_2 film surface was blocked using skim milk to prevent nonspecific adsorption for 15 min at 18 °C-25 °C. Cytokeratin, AE1/AE3 (Agilent Technologies Japan, Ltd., Tokyo, Japan) which is reacted with various tumors such as adenocarcinoma and squamous cell carcinoma was used as an antibody and it was immobilized by reacting with the anti IgG for 9 h at 4 °C. In Figure 1 (b), 45 μg/mL of avidin (affinity-purified, Vector Laboratories, Inc., Burlingame, California, United States) was immobilized on the sensing plate for 17 h at 4 °C, and the SiO_2 film surface was blocked in the same way as immobilizing the anti IgG. 100 μg/mL of biotin conjugated anti IgG (Antigen Affinity Purified, Bethyl Laboratories, Inc., Montgomery, Alabama, USA) was immobilized for 5 h at 4 °C, and Cytokeratin, AE1/AE3 was immobilized in the same way as the covalent bonding. After that, in the covalent bonding and

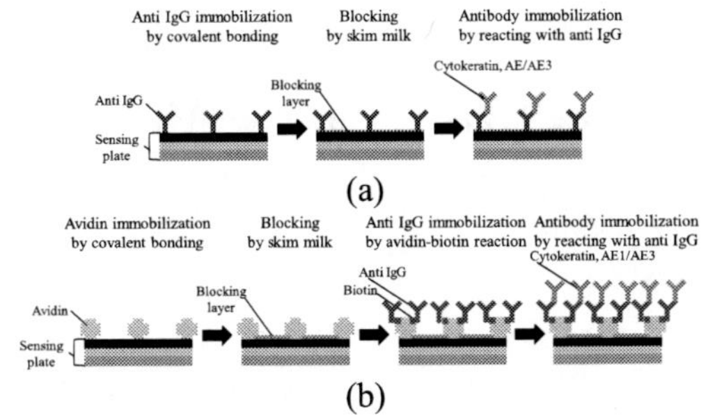

Figure 1. The processes of immobilizing antibodies on the SiO_2 film surface on the sensing plate: (a) Covalent bonding method (b) avidin-biotin reaction method

the avidin-biotin reaction, 6.7×10^6 cell/mL of PC9 and 2.7 $\times$ 10^6 cell/mL of EBC1 reacted with immobilized Cytokeratin, AE/AE3 for 12 h at 4 °C, respectively. The unreacted PC9 and EBC1 were removed by washing 10 times. After Cytokeratin, AE1/AE3 was immobilized on the sensing plate and the unreacted PC9 and EBC1 were washed, the amplitude of terahertz was measured by the TCM. The change of terahertz amplitude was calculated.

III. Results and Discussion

Figure 2 shows the average change of terahertz amplitude before and after the reaction of PC9 and EBC1 in each immobilizing method. Error bars show the standard deviation of the change of terahertz amplitude in 3 samples. In the covalent bonding, the average changes of terahertz amplitude were 0.90±0.66 mV for measuring PC9 and 0.68±0.43 mV for measuring EBC1. In the avidin-biotin reaction, they were 0.82±0.15 mV, 0.33±0.23 mV for measuring PC9 and EBC1, respectively. In both methods, the average changes of terahertz amplitude in measuring EBC1 were lower than measuring PC9, because we think the concentration of EBC1 is lower than that of PC9 and the charge of EBC1 is smaller than that of PC9. Especially in the avidin-biotin reaction, we think that the lower electric charge of EBC1 was not transmitted well, because the distance between the sensing plate and the EBC1 was longer. However, the avidin-biotin reaction was 4.4-fold and 1.9-fold lower standard deviation than the covalent bonding for the measurement of PC9 and EBC1, respectively, because we think that the antibody could be

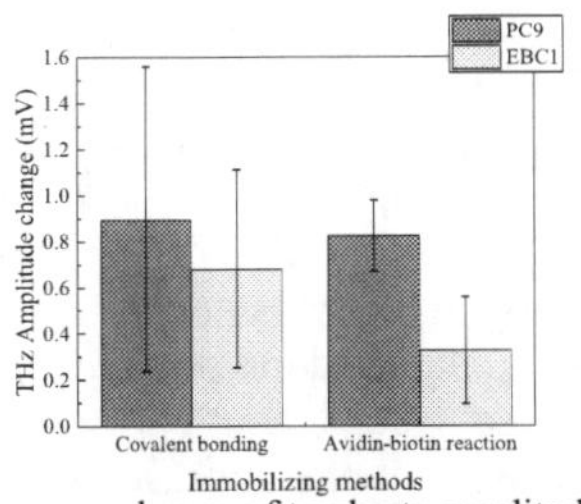

Figure 2. The average change of terahertz amplitude before and after the reaction of lung cancer cells which are PC9 and EBC1 in each immobilizing method

immobilized in higher density using avidin biotin reaction and did not detach from the sensing plate in the process of the reaction of lung cancer cells or washing. This result shows lung cancer cells could be measured accurately by immobilizing antibodies using the avidin-biotin reaction.

IV. Conclusion

Immobilization methods of covalent bonding and avidin-biotin reaction were compared by measuring PC9 and EBC1. In the avidin-biotin reaction, the change of terahertz amplitude was smaller. However, the standard deviation was 4.4-fold and 1.9-fold lower than the covalent bonding. This result suggests that lung cancer cells can be measured accurately by using avidin-biotin reaction and immobilizing the antibody in high density and firmly.

References

[1] R. Thavarajah, V. K. Mudimbaimannar, J. Elizabeth, U. K. Rao, and K. Ranganathan, "Chemical and physical basics of routine formaldehyde fixation," J. Oral Maxillofac. Surg., vol. 16, 3, pp. 400-405, 2012

[2] T. Kiwa et al., "Chemical sensing plate with a laser-terahertz monitoring system," Appl. Opt., vol. 47, 18, pp. 3324-3327, 2008

[3] T. Kiwa, A. Tenma, S. Takahashi, K. Sakai, and K. Tsukada, "Label free immune assay using terahertz chemical microscope," Sens. Actuators B Chem., vol. 187, pp. 8-11, 2013

[4] E. M. Hassan et al., "High-sensitivity detection of metastatic breast cancer cells via terahertz chemical microscopy using aptamers," Sens. Actuators B Chem., vol. 287, 15, pp.595-601, 2019

[5] K. Sato et al., "Detection of lung cancer cells using a terahertz chemical microscope," JSAP-OSA Joint Symposia 2019 Abstracts, OSA Technical Digest, 18-21 Sep., 2019, Hokkaido, Japan, 19p-E215-16, ISBN: 978-4-86348-743-7

[6] Y. Yoshida et al., "Detection Of cancer cells using immune reaction with a terahertz chemical microscope," The 46th IRMMW-THz 2021, 29 Aug.-3 Sep., 2021, online, Mo-AM-5-4 5103240

[7] R. Tero et al., "Fabrication of avidin single molecular layer on silicon oxide surfaces and formation oftethered lipid bilayer membranes," e-J. Surf. Sci. Nanotech., vol. 3, pp. 237-243, 2005

[8] N. Misawa et al., "Orientation of avidin molecules immobilized on COOH-modified SiO2/Si(1 0 0) surfaces," Chem. Phys. Lett., vol. 419, 1-3, pp. 86-90, 2006

Detection of Proteins Associated with Alzheimer's Disease using a Terahertz Chemical Microscope

Kohei Iwatsuki, Yuichi Yoshida, Xue Ding, Jin Wang, Kenji Sakai, Toshihiko Kiwa
Graduate School of Interdisciplinary Science and Engineering in Health Systems
Okayama University
Okayama, Japan
e-mail: (prsd3x9h, pjaa6rfb, pm7g9k5d) @s.okayama-u.ac.jp
(wangjin, sakai-k, kiwa) @okayama-u.ac.jp

Sayaka Tsuji
Faculty of Engineering
Okayama University
Okayama, Japan
e-mail: proc9afb @s.okayama-u.ac.jp

***Abstract*— In recent years, the number of Alzheimer's Disease (AD) has been increasing. We proposed a Terahertz Chemical Microscope (TCM) for early diagnosis of cognitive decline by measuring the concentration of Apolipoprotein AI (ApoA1) and Complement component 3 (C3) in solution as biomarkers for AD using the TCM. As a results, ApoA1 and C3 with the concentration of 0.1 μg/ml and 1.0 μg/ml could be respectively detected by measuring the change in the amplitude of terahertz waves by the TCM.**

Keywords- Terahertz; TCM; Alzheimer's Disease; mild cognitive impairment.

I. INTRODUCTION

In recent years, the number of Alzheimer's Disease (AD) has been increasing as the increase of average life expectancy. Generally, a cognitive function of patients of AD gradually declines. Patients at mild cognitive impairment (MCI) stage, where is the initial stage of AD, have potential to recover by appropriate prevention and treatment. So, early detection and diagnosis of AD is important. Conventionally, imaging systems such as computed tomography (CT), magnetic resonance imaging (MRI), single photon emission computed tomography (SPECT) are used to diagnose. However, these types of modalities are expensive so that diagnostic fees are relatively high. Therefore, primary screening method are essential for early diagnosis of AD.

Practically, detection of concentration of biomarkers, transthyretin (TTR), Apolipoprotein AI (ApoA1) and Complement component 3 (C3), in the blood are measured for the screening [1]. This screening method require multiple testing methods and a large amount of specimens to detect proteins.

In our group, a Terahertz Chemical Microscope (TCM) has been proposed and developed to detect proteins or sugar chains in small amount of liquids [2][3]. In this study, the concentrations of ApoA1 and C3 in solution were measured using the TCM.

Section II describes a schematic of the TCM and experimental procedure. Section III describes the results, and Section IV describes the conclusion.

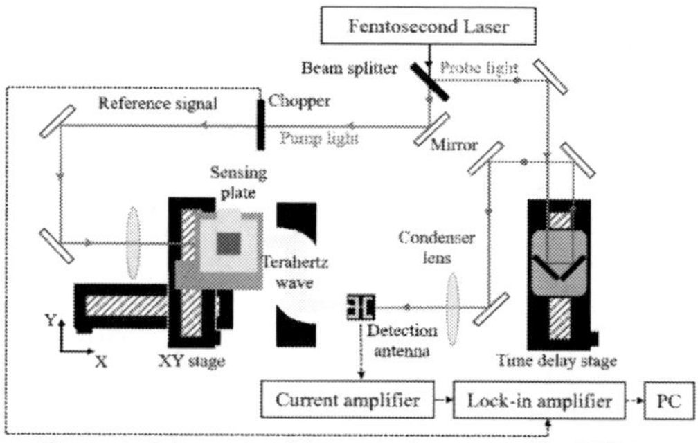

Figure 1. Schematic of the optical system of the TCM.

II. EXPERIMENTAL

The TCM visualize chemical reactions on a sensing plate, which consists of a SiO_2 film and a Si film on a sapphire substrate (Al_2O_3). The thicknesses of the films were a few nm for the SiO_2 film, 500 nm for Si, and 500 μm for the sapphire substrate (Al_2O_3), respectively. When a femtosecond laser is irradiated from the sapphire substrate side to the Si film, terahertz wave is generated in the Si film. The amplitude of terahertz wave depends on the surface potential of Si, which depends on chemical reactions on the sensing plate. Thus, the chemical reaction can be related to the amplitude of terahertz wave radiated from the sensing plate.

Figure 1 shows a schematic of the optical system of the TCM. The femtosecond laser was divided into a pump light and a probe light by a beam splitter, and the pump light was focused onto the substrate side of the sensing plate by an objective lens. The amplitude map of the terahertz wave from the sensing plate was obtained by changing the position of the femtosecond laser across the surface of the sensing plate by moving the XY stage and measuring the amplitude by a photoconductive antenna. The repetition rate of the laser was 82 MHz. And the output power, the center wavelength, and the pulse width of the laser were, respectively, 780 mW, 780 nm, and 100 fs.

Figure 2 shows the protocol to immobilize protein antibodies on the sensing plate to selectively detect antigens. First, the SiO_2 side of the sensing plate was chemically

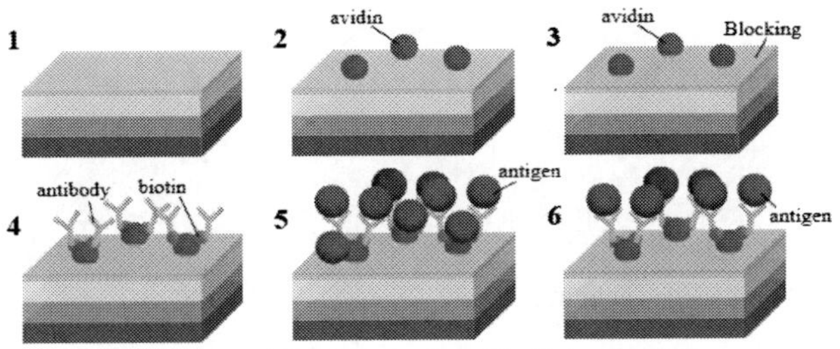

Figure 2. Immobilization protein antibodies and proteins.

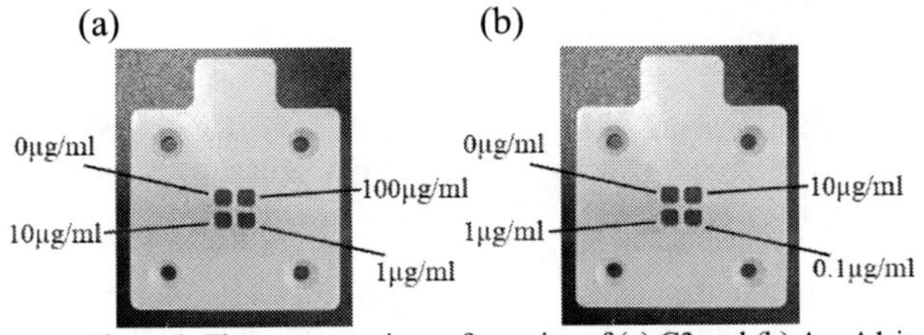

Figure 3. The concentrations of proteins of (a) C3 and (b) ApoA1 in the wells fabricated on the sensing plate.

modified and activated. Then, an avidin was conjugated to the surface of the sensing plate for 24 hours at 4°C. Then, the sensing plate was coated by skim milk to prevent from non-specific reactions on the surface of the sensing plate. After coating, biotin-labeled antibodies were immobilized using avidin-biotin reaction. A human complement C3 antibody (Rabbit, Polyclonal, Biotin conjugate) and Apolipoprotein A1 antibody (Goat, Polyclonal, Biotin conjugate) were respectively used as antibodies for selective detection of C3 and ApoA1. Before measuring the C3 and ApoA1, the amplitude map of the terahertz wave was recorded as a background signal of the TCM. After reacting with C3 and ApoA1, the sensing plate was washed 10 times to remove unbounded antigen. Then, the amplitude map of the terahertz wave was measured to evaluate the change in the amplitude from the background signal.

Figure 3 shows the photos of the solution wells fabricated on the sensing plates and the concentration of (a) C3 and (b) ApoA1 in the wells fabricated on the sensing plate. The volume of each well was 30 μl.

III. RESULTS

Figure 4 shows change in the amplitude of the terahertz waves (a) before and (b) after the reaction of C3 and C3 antibody. The amplitude of the terahertz wave was reduced by the reaction of C3. On the other hand, Figure 5 shows the change in the amplitude of the terahertz waves before and after the reaction of ApoA1 and ApoA1 antibody. The amplitude of terahertz wave increased by the reaction of ApoA1.

The difference between (a) and (b) in Figure 4 and 5 was calculated and then, the values in the each well were averaged. Then, the averaged values were plotted in Figure 6 (a) and (b).

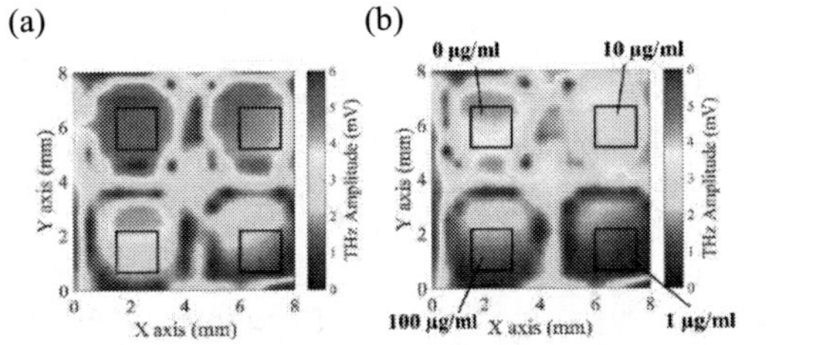

Figure 4. The terahertz maps (a) before and (b) after reaction of C3. The concentrations in the image is the concentration of C3.

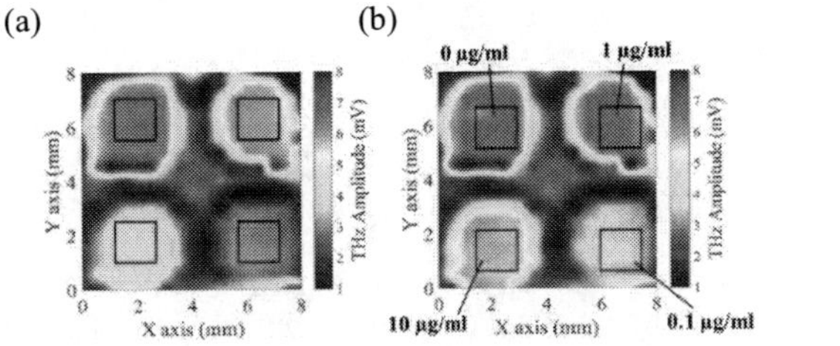

Figure 5. The terahertz maps (a) before and (b) after reaction of ApoA1. The concentrations in the image is the concentration of ApoA1.

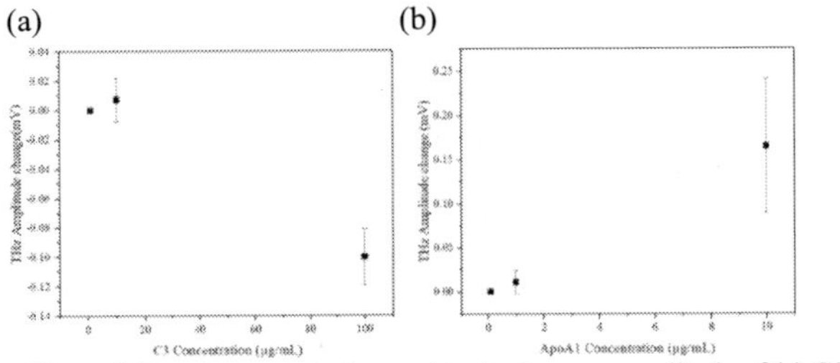

Figure 6. Protein concentration and terahertz wave amplitude of (a) C3 and (b) ApoA1.

One can see that the amplitudes could be related to the concentration of C3 and ApoA1.

IV. CONCLUSION

The TCM has been proposed for early diagnosis of AD by measuring several types of biomarkers. Antibodies (Anti-ApoA1 and Anti-C3) were immobilized on the sensing plate using avidin-biotin conjugation to measure the ApoA1 and C3, respectively. The change in the amplitude of terahertz wave from the sensing plate depended on the concentration of C3 and ApoA1 in the 30 μl solutions with the concentration ranges of from 1 to 100 and from 0.1 to 10 μg/ml, respectively. These results suggest the TCM is one of potential tools for AD diagnosis.

REFERENCES

[1] K. Uchida et al., "Amyloid-β sequester proteins as blood-based biomarkers of cognitive decline.", Amst., 1(2), pp. 270-280, 2015.

[2] T. Kiwa et al., "Chemical sensing plate with a laser-terahertz monitoring system", Appl. Opt., 47(18), pp. 3324-3327, 2008.

[3] T. Kiwa et al., "Terahertz chemical microscope for label-free detection of protein complex", Appl. Phys. Lett., 96 (21), 211114, 2010.

A Method to Minimize Resonant Frequency Drift of CMUTs Due to Fluid Loading

Thasnim Mohammed, Sazzadur Chowdhury
Department of Electrical and Computer Engineering
University of Windsor
Windsor, Ontario, Canada
e-mail: sazzadur@uwindsor.ca

Abstract— **This paper presents a method to minimize the resonant frequency drift of Capacitive Micromachined Ultrasonic Transducers (CMUTs) due to fluid loading. A unified mathematical model for the resonant frequency of a CMUT that includes the electrostatic spring softening effect and the fluid loading effect due to the coupled fluidic layer has been developed that provides the basis of the proposed approach. The minimization method involves dynamic adjustment of the DC bias voltage to modify the electrostatic spring softening parameter to offset the effects of fluid loading. Analytical and COMSOL based 3D Finite Element Analysis (FEA) results show that the drift in the resonant frequency of a 6 MHz CMUT operated in water can be compensated by adjusting the bias voltage by 2% from its 75% pull-in voltage value to render an improvement of 4% in lateral and axial resolutions in imaging applications. A bias voltage adjustment of 9% of the 75% pull-in voltage value is necessary to achieve an improvement of 20.74% when the CMUT is operated in glycerol.**

Keywords- CMUT; electrostatic spring softening; fluid loading effect; resonant frequency drift; 3D FEA.

I. Introduction

Capacitive micromachined ultrasonic transducers are emerging as a superior alternative to piezoelectric transducers for biomedical imaging, Non-Destructive Evaluation (NDE), and High Intensity Focused Ultrasound (HIFU) applications [1]–[3]. They can be batch fabricated using conventional microfabrication techniques at a lower cost and can be efficiently integrated with CMOS based integrated circuits for control, drive, and signal processing to offer improved Signal-to-Noise Ratio (SNR) with higher fractional bandwidth and thermal stability.

The CMUT is basically a reciprocal electrostatic transducer that relies on capacitance change between a movable and a fixed electrode separated by a small gap to generate or receive ultrasound [4][5]. The space between the electrodes is filled with either vacuum or a thin film of air. The movable electrode is supported at the edges by dielectric support posts.

When a CMUT array operates in a fluidic medium, the coupled fluid layer manifests itself as an inertial mass onto the diaphragm and as a viscous damper depending on the viscosity of the fluidic medium. As these fluid loading effects alter the effective mass of the CMUT diaphragm, a drift of the resonant frequency of the CMUT occurs. As the elements in a CMUT array are designed and fabricated to have a fixed pitch to satisfy the Nyquist criteria of spatial sampling to minimize grating lobes and maximize the main lobe power in beamforming operations, a change in the CMUT resonant frequency compromises the array operation to lower imaging quality.

Serious research is in progress to minimize the fluid loading effects on CMUTs. The fluid loading effects on a circular CMUT cell were investigated in [6], where frequency dependent equivalent density was used as the effective CMUT diaphragm material density to account for the distributed fluid loading. The authors in [6] also presented a dimensional dependence model based on the equivalent density using a finite element method (FEM) based data fitting technique. In another approach [7], linear and nonlinear equivalent circuit models of a CMUT were developed based on electrical, mechanical, and acoustical parameters assuming the CMUT as a piston radiator. The mass loading and waveguiding effects of the fluids were incorporated in the model using data extracted from FEM simulations. The authors in [8] presented a generalized model for surface acoustic wave devices considering the mass and viscous fluid loading. Numerical modeling of fluid interaction with oscillating surfaces is available in [9]. In [10], the sensitivity of a CMUT diaphragm to the dynamic viscosity of the surrounding fluid medium was investigated to realize CMUT based fluid sensors.

In this perspective, this paper presents a method to minimize the resonant frequency drift of a CMUT due to fluid loading by dynamically adjusting the DC bias voltage. The scientific basis of the proposed method lies in the spring softening effect associated with the DC bias voltage applied to a CMUT. Due to an applied DC bias, necessary for CMUT operation in both transmit and receive modes, the effective stiffness of the diaphragm reduces to lower the resonant frequency. As the amount of spring softening (lowering of the stiffness) depends on the DC bias, the DC bias voltage can be dynamically controlled using a suitable microelectronic circuit to adjust the spring softening amount to offset the effect of fluid loading on the resonant frequency. Excellent agreements between lumped element model analysis and 3D electromechanical finite element analysis conducted by the authors show that the method can effectively offset the resonant frequency drift due to fluid loading to validate the hypothesis.

The rest of the paper has been organized in the following

manner: Section II provides the problem statement and theoretical background of the proposed approach, Section III investigates the effect of fluid loading on CMUT resonant frequency in different fluids, Section IV presents the proposed frequency drift compensation method with simulation results of analytical and FEA analysis using COMSOL and finally, Section V provides the concluding remarks.

II. THEORETICAL BACKGROUND

A CMUT array is comprised of several transmit and receive elements as shown in Figure 1(a). Each element in turn is designed to have several CMUT cells connected in parallel [9][11]-[14]. A conceptual cross-section of a typical CMUT cell is shown in Figure 1(b).

Assuming that the stiffness of the diaphragm is linear, the resonant frequency of a CMUT in air can be calculated following

$$f_{res} = \frac{1}{2\pi}\sqrt{\frac{k}{m}} \tag{1}$$

where, k and m are the stiffness and mass of the CMUT diaphragm as shown in Figure 1(b), respectively. Typically, the CMUT diaphragms are constructed to have a circular, hexagonal, or square shape geometry to satisfy the design requirements.

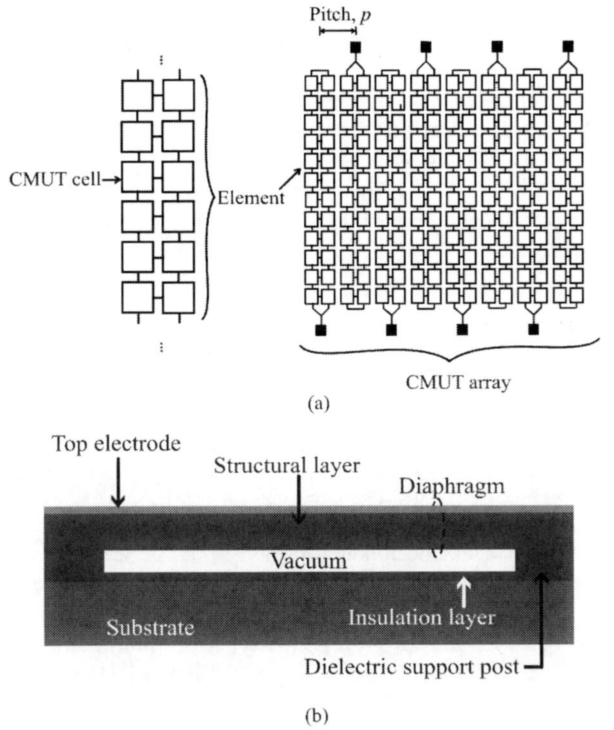

Figure 1. (a) Layout of a CMUT array comprising of array elements. (b) Typical cross-section of a single CMUT cell.

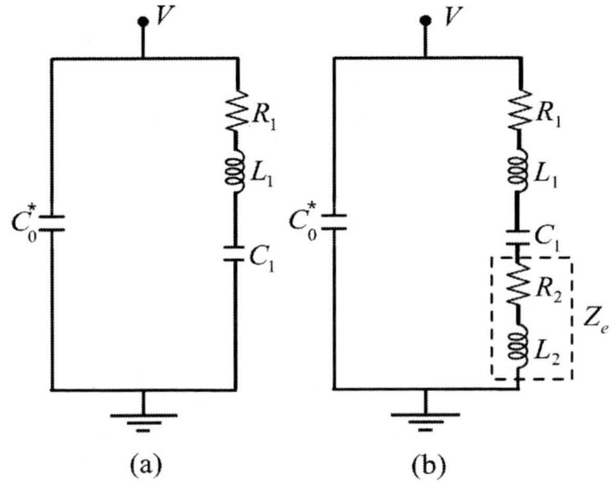

Figure 2. (a) The BVD model of a CMUT without fluid loading. (b) The BVD model of a CMUT with fluid loading. The fluid loading effect is represented by inductance L_2 and resistance R_2.

The array pitch, defined as the distance between corresponding points in the neighboring elements (Figure 1(a)), is optimized following Nyquist criteria of spatial sampling to minimize grating lobes following

$$p \le \frac{\lambda}{2} \tag{2}$$

where, λ is the wavelength corresponding to the center frequency of operation.

The frequency response of a CMUT cell with and without the fluid loading effect can be obtained using the Butterworth-Van Dyke (BVD) model as shown in Figure 2(a) [15]. The BVD model depicts an analog electrical equivalent circuit of a CMUT that includes both electrical and equivalent mechanical lumped element circuit parameters.

In the BVD model, the electrical circuit element is represented by a lumped capacitor C_0^*, and the electrical equivalent of mass m, stiffness k, and damping element b is represented by L_1, C_1, and R_1 respectively. Assuming that the CMUT diaphragm is square, the stiffness k of the diaphragm can be calculated following

$$k = C_r \frac{t_d \sigma_0}{(L/2)^2} + C_b \frac{12 D_{eff}}{(L/2)^4} \tag{3}$$

where C_r =3.45 and C_b =4.06 [16]. The parameters D_{eff}, L, σ_0, and t_d are the effective flexural rigidity, sidelength, residual stress, and thickness of the diaphragm, respectively. The mass of the diaphragm can be calculated from the volume and density of the CMUT diaphragm materials. The parameters R_1, L_1, and C_1 (zero bias equivalent stiffness) can be calculated from [15] following

$$\left.\begin{aligned} C_1 &= \frac{n^2}{k} \\ L_1 &= \frac{m}{n^2} \\ R_1 &= \frac{b}{n^2} \end{aligned}\right\} \quad (4)$$

where, n is the electromechanical transformation ratio.

The coupling of the CMUT diaphragm with a liquid medium alters the CMUT motional impedance contributed by L_1, C_1, and R_1. The adjacent (coupled) liquid layer contributes an additional equivalent damping R_2 due to the fluid viscosity and an additional equivalent fluid mass L_2. The inclusion of these additional mass and damping parameters in the BVD model as shown in Figure 2(b) alters the frequency response of the CMUT. The amount of alteration (drift) depends on the density and viscosity of the fluidic medium.

Following [15], the fluid loading quantities L_2 and R_2 can be approximately calculated from

$$L_2 = \frac{\pi}{4k_s^2\omega_s C_0}\left(\frac{\rho\eta}{2\omega_s\mu_q\rho_q}\right)^{\frac{1}{2}} \quad (5)$$

$$R_2 = \frac{\pi}{4k_s^2 C_0}\left(\frac{\rho\eta}{2\omega_s\mu_q\rho_q}\right)^{\frac{1}{2}} \quad (6)$$

where, ρ, η, μ_q, ρ_q, k_s^2 and ω_s represents the liquid density, shear viscosity of the liquid, diaphragm shear stiffness, mass density of diaphragm, coupling coefficient, and resonant frequency of the circuit in rad/sec, respectively.

The entrained liquid layer of effective height $\delta/2$ is considered for the calculations shown in (5)–(6) where $\delta = \sqrt{2\eta/\omega_s\rho}$ is the depth of penetration of damped shear wave propagating into the liquid by the oscillating surface [15][17]. Thus, the motional impedance Z_{m} in the BVD model of a CMUT including the fluid loading effect (Figure 2(b)) can be expressed as:

$$Z_m = R_1 + R_2 + j\omega L_1 + j\omega L_2 + \frac{1}{j\omega C_1} \quad (7)$$

On the other hand, assuming the small-signal model of a CMUT where the AC actuation signal is much smaller compared to the DC bias voltage ($V_{\mathrm{DC}} >> V_{\mathrm{AC}}$), the spring softening effect due to the applied DC bias voltage reduces the zero bias CMUT diaphragm stiffness k by a factor k_{soft} as given by (8).

$$k_{\mathrm{soft}} = \frac{\varepsilon A V_{\mathrm{DC}}^2}{d_{\mathrm{eff}}^3} \quad (8)$$

where, ε, A, V_{DC}, and d_{eff} denote the permittivity, coupling area of the electrodes, DC bias voltage applied to the CMUT, and the effective electrode gap, respectively. Consequently, the spring softening effect causes a downshift of the resonant frequency of the CMUT diaphragm following

$$f_{\mathrm{res\text{-}ss}} = \frac{1}{2\pi}\sqrt{\frac{k - k_{\mathrm{soft}}}{m}} \quad (9)$$

During an immersion operation, the resonant frequency $f_{\mathrm{res\text{-}ss}}$ as expressed in (9) is further affected by the inertial mass m_{f} contributed by the coupled fluid layer adjacent to the CMUT diaphragm.

Thus, including both the spring softening effect and the fluid loading effect, the resonant frequency $f_{\mathrm{res\text{-}ss\text{-}fl}}$ of the diaphragm can be expressed as

$$f_{\mathrm{res\text{-}ss\text{-}fl}} = \frac{1}{2\pi}\sqrt{\frac{k - k_{\mathrm{soft}}}{m + m_{\mathrm{f}}}} \quad (10)$$

A careful examination of (8) and (10) reveals that the drift in the resonant frequency due to the fluid loading effect m_{f} alone can be minimized by adjusting the spring softening factor k_{soft} which is a function of the bias voltage V_{DC} in small-signal approximation.

A suitable microelectronic circuit can be used to sense the resonant frequency offset and adjust the bias voltage dynamically to control k_{soft} to bring the resonant frequency back to its design value while generating the desired acoustic pressure.

III. Investigation of Fluid Loading Effects

A. *Analytical CMUT Resonant Frequency Calculation with Fluid Loading Effects*

To investigate the proposed approach, a linear CMUT array with a center frequency of 6 MHz has been considered. This center frequency is suitable for cardiac diagnostic imaging as reported in [18]. Individual CMUT cells in the array have been designed to have the same resonant frequency as the array [19]. The element pitch p has been selected following (2) to satisfy the Nyquist criteria of spatial sampling to obtain better directivity with minimum side lobes. The lateral and axial resolution of the CMUT array is given by [1] as:

$$\Delta y = \left(\frac{1.22\lambda}{A_{\mathrm{a}}}\right)S \quad (11)$$

$$\Delta x = \frac{n\lambda}{2} \quad (12)$$

respectively, where, A_a, S and n are the array aperture, the distance between the focus and the array surface at the center of the array, and the number of scanning pulses, respectively. Following (11) and (12), it is necessary for the CMUT and the array physical dimensions to correspond to the same wavelength or center frequency to achieve setpoint axial and lateral resolutions and avoid any deviation from Nyquist criteria of spatial sampling [20][21].

To investigate the effects of viscosity and density of the fluidic medium on the resonant frequency of the CMUT diaphragms, a square shaped CMUT diaphragm with the same 6 MHz center frequency in air as for the array has been investigated.

Typical CMUT diaphragms are fabricated as a multilayer laminate where a thin insulating material is used as the structural layer to provide the necessary mechanical strength and a thin conducting layer is used on the top of the structural layer to enable electrical functionality.

Following [20], bisbenzocyclobutene (BCB) has been used as the structural layer for this analysis. The BCB layer is coated with a thin layer of gold to form the top electrode. Low resistivity silicon has been used to constitute the ground electrode. BCB has also been used to fabricate the dielectric support post. The major physical properties of the selected CMUT materials are listed in Table I.

To obtain the 6 MHz resonant frequency in air using the materials listed in Table I, a diaphragm sidelength of 28 µm, BCB layer thickness of 1.5 µm, and gold layer thickness of 0.1 µm has been determined following [22].

The pull-in voltage of the CMUT has been determined from 3D electromechanical FEA using COMSOL as 395 volts. The frequency responses of the CMUT biased at 295 volts (74.68% of the pull-in voltage) in air, water, engine oil, and glycerol are shown in Figure 3. The physical properties of the fluids are listed in Table II.

The frequency response in air without any DC bias voltage has also been shown in Figure 3. As it can be seen, there is a significant drift in the resonant frequency due to the spring softening effect caused by the bias voltage which

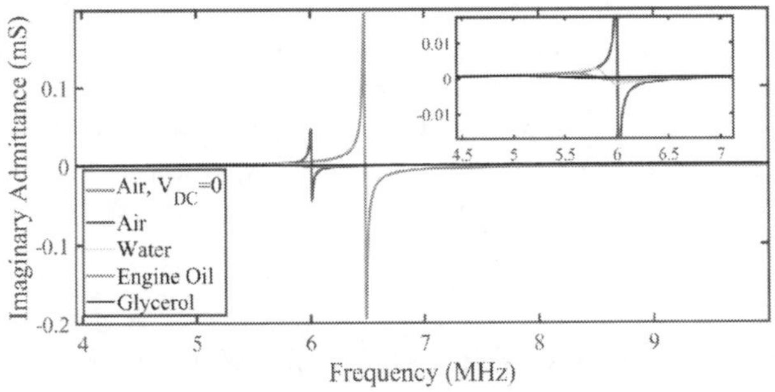

Figure 3. Frequency response of the CMUT cell with bias voltage $V_{DC} = 0.75V_{PI}$ for unloaded (air) and loaded (water, engine oil, glycerol) conditions. (Inset y-axis unit is in µS.)

TABLE I. CMUT MATERIAL PROPERTIES

Material	Young's modulus (GPa)	Poisson's ratio	Density ($kg.m^{-3}$)	Residual stress (MPa)
BCB	2.9	0.34	1050	28
Gold	70	0.44	19300	106
Silicon	165.9	0.26	2329	55

TABLE II. CMUT RESONANT FREQUENCIES IN INVESTIGATED FLUIDS

Fluid type	Fluid Physical Properties		Resonant frequency (MHz)
	Viscosity (mPa/s)	*Density (g/cm3)*	
Air	0.01825	0.001204	6.002
Water	1.0016	0.998	5.783
Engine oil	287.23	0.8787	5.422
Glycerol	1412.8	1.2608	4.975

is further deteriorated by the fluid loading effects contributed by the fluid mass and viscosity as shown in the zoomed-up inset.

B. 3D FEA Based CMUT Resonant Frequency Simulation with Fluid Loading Effects

A 3D FEA of a single CMUT cell was conducted in COMSOL Multiphysics environment to investigate the fluid loading effects on the frequency response of the CMUT cell. The cell was modeled using the electro-mechanical module as shown in Figure 4. The air/fluid column was designed using the pressure acoustics frequency domain physics module.

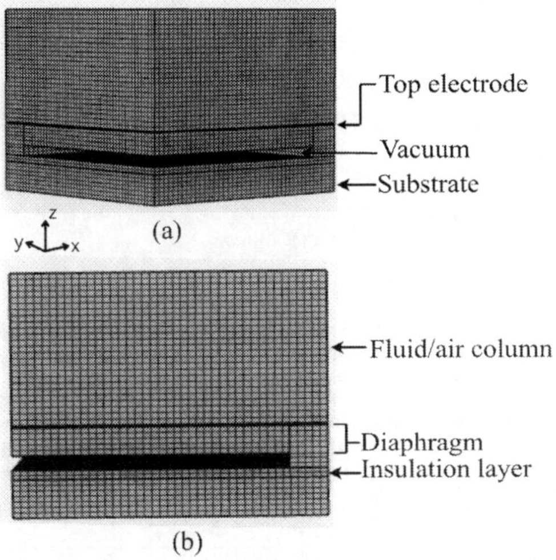

Figure 4. The CMUT model in COMSOL (As the structure is symmetric, only a quarter model of the CMUT was simulated).

The CMUT diaphragm was set as a linear elastic material and necessary boundary conditions were applied. The boundary between the electro-mechanics and pressure acoustics domain was defined as a fluid-solid coupled boundary that acts as a pressure load on the electro-mechanics domain. The maximum element size was set to one-sixth of the smallest wavelength in a frequency sweep while meshing. An AC perturbation signal superimposed with DC bias voltage was applied to the CMUT cell using the default frequency domain modal analysis method in COMSOL.

The COMSOL based 3D FEA generated modal frequency responses of the CMUT model for the fluids listed in Table II are shown in Figure 5.

Table III compares the analytical and 3D FEA results for the resonant frequencies of the CMUT in the investigated fluids. As it can be seen from Table III, the analytical and 3D FEA results are in excellent agreement with a maximum deviation of 2.8% for the liquids that validate the efficacy of the analytical and simulation methods.

IV. Minimizing the Fluid Loading Effects

The resonant frequency drift due to the fluid loading effect as confirmed by the analytical and 3D FEA based analysis can be minimized by adjusting the DC bias voltage following (8) and (10). The spring softening parameter k_{soft} as expressed in (8) needs to be dynamically adjusted by controlling the bias voltage V_{DC}, to offset the fluid loading effect induced resonant frequency drift Δf expressed in (13).

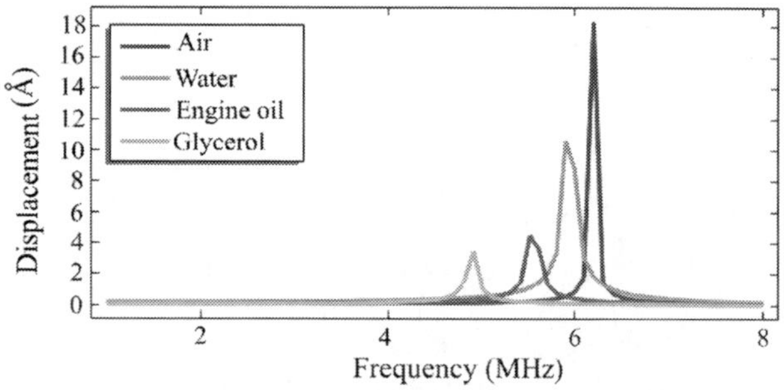

Figure 5. FEA simulation based frequency response of the CMUT cell in different fluids.

TABLE III. Resonant Frequency of the Simulated CMUT in Different Fluids

Medium	Resonant frequency (Analytical) (MHz)	Resonant frequency (FEA) (MHz)	Percentage deviation between analytical and FEA (%)	Drift from the resonant frequency in air (FEA)(%)
Air	6.002	6.19	3.1	-
Water	5.783	5.945	2.8	3.9
Engine oil	5.422	5.545	2.3	10.42
Glycerol	4.975	4.8788	1.9	21.18

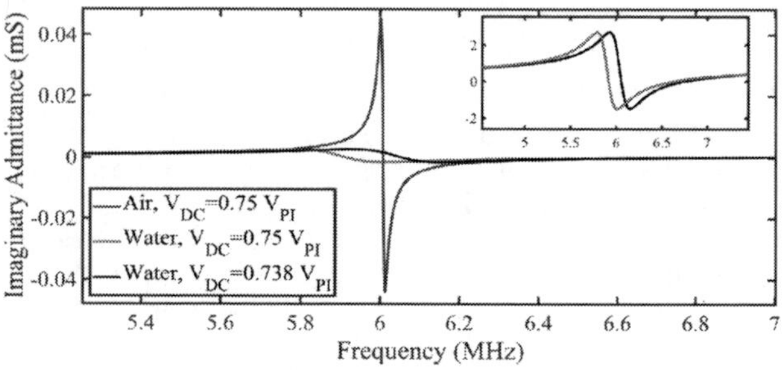

Figure 6. Simulation result of CMUT small-signal analysis for frequency compensation in water. (Inset y-axis unit is in µS.)

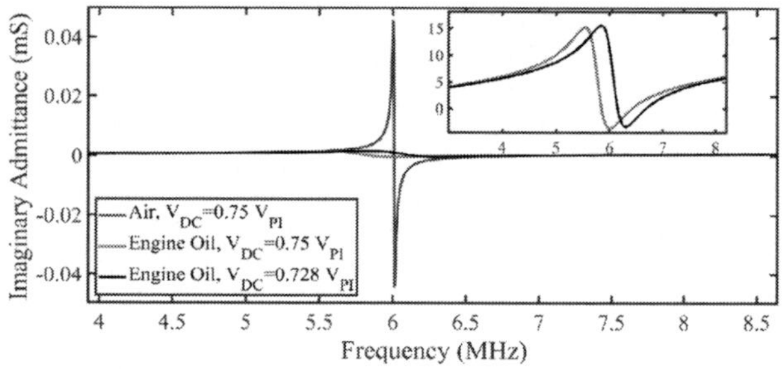

Figure 7. Simulation result of CMUT small-signal analysis for frequency compensation in engine oil. (Inset y-axis unit is in µS.)

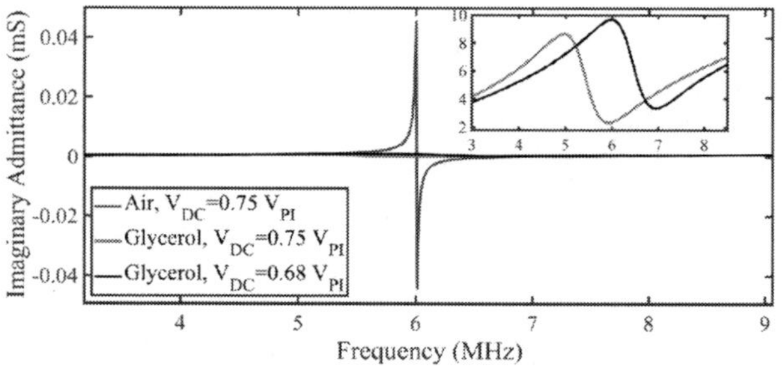

Figure 8. Simulation result of CMUT small-signal analysis for frequency compensation in glycerol. (Inset y-axis unit is in µS.)

$$\Delta f = f_{res} - f_{res\text{-}ss\text{-}fl} \quad (13)$$

COMSOL based 3D FEA simulation results after adjusting the bias voltage to offset the resonant frequency drift Δf for water, engine oil, and glycerol are shown in Figures 6–8. The reference bias voltage was kept at 75% of the pull-in voltage V_{PI} of the CMUT structure as in the previous section. When the CMUT was operated in water, engine oil, and glycerol, the change in bias voltage applied was 2%, 4.2%, and 9% respectively (Figures 6–8). The simulation results confirm that the drift Δf in the resonant frequency can effectively be compensated by a small change in the DC bias V_{DC} to validate the hypothesis.

The improvement in the lateral and axial resolution that could be achieved with the proposed method is 4%, 10.78%, 20.74% when operated in water, engine oil, or glycerol, respectively. Thus, the proposed method will help to achieve the expected resolution even when the array is operated in different fluidic mediums, thereby improving the imaging accuracy of a CMUT array.

V. CONCLUSION AND FUTURE WORK

This paper presented a method to minimize the fluid loading induced resonant frequency drift of a CMUT by dynamically adjusting the bias voltage. Analytical and 3D FEA based simulation studies revealed that the amount of change in DC bias voltage necessary to offset the resonant frequency drift is small and is not expected to affect the acoustic power/pressure output of a CMUT array. The investigation shows that the method can improve the lateral and axial resolutions in water by approximately 4% to improve the accuracy of CMUT based biomedical diagnostic imaging. For NDE applications, the axial and lateral resolution improvements can be as high as 20.74% when glycerol is used as the coupling agent.

The design of a high-speed microelectronic control circuit necessary to implement the proposed scheme is in progress. In the currently investigated scheme, the received signal is signal-conditioned first to remove noise and other high frequency components. A high-speed data converter with a desired sampling rate is used to digitize the actuating AC signal and the received signal. Fast Fourier Transform (FFT) of the transmit and the processed received signal provides the frequency components necessary to calculate Δf. Thus, the frequency drift Δf is measured in real time to determine the DC bias voltage necessary to be adjusted to offset the resonant frequency drift.

ACKNOWLEDGMENT

This research work was supported by the Natural Science and Engineering Research Council of Canada (NSERC)'s discovery grant number RGPIN 293218. The authors also acknowledge the collaborative research support provided by the IntelliSense Corporation, Lynnfield, MA, Angstrom Engineering, ON, and the CMC Microsystems, Canada.

REFERENCES

[1] J. Song et al. "Capacitive Micromachined Ultrasonic Transducers (CMUTs) for Underwater Imaging Applications," *Sensors*, vol. 15, no. 9, pp. 23205–23217, Sep. 2015.

[2] D. Zhao, S. Zhuang, and R. Daigle, "A Commercialized High Frequency CMUT Probe for Medical Ultrasound Imaging," in *Proc. of 2015 IEEE International Ultrasonics Symposium (IUS)*, Oct. 21-24, Taipei, Taiwan, 2015, pp. 1-4.

[3] A. S. Ergun, G. G. Yaralioglu, O. Oralkan, and B. T. Khuri-Yakub, "Chapter 7: Techniques & Applications of Capacitive Micromachined Ultrasonic Transducer," in *MEMS/ NEMS Handbook[Techniques and Applications*; Leondes, C.T., Ed.; Springer Science + Business Media Inc.: Los Angeles, CA, USA, 2006; Volume 2, pp. 222–332.

[4] A. S. Ergun, G. G. Yaralioglu, and B. T. Khuri-Yakub, "Capacitive Micromachined Ultrasonic Transducers: Theory and Technology." *Journal of Aerospace Engineering,* vol 16, no. 2, pp. 76-84, 2003.

[5] Y. Huang, A. S. Ergun, E. Haeggstrom, M. H. Badi, and B. T. Khuri-Yakub, "Fabricating Capacitive Micromachined Ultrasonic Transducers with Wafer-bonding Technology," *Journal of Microelectromechanical Systems*, vol. 12, no. 2, pp. 128-137, April 2003.

[6] B. Azmy, M. El-Gamal, A. El-Henawy, and H. Ragai, "An Accurate Model for Fluid Loading on Circular CMUTs," in *Proc. of 2011 IEEE International Ultrasonics Symposium*, Orlando, Florida, Oct. 18-24, 2011, pp. 584-587.

[7] A. Lohfink, P. -. Eccardt, W. Benecke, and H. Meixner, "Derivation of a 1D CMUT Model from FEM Results for Linear and Nonlinear Equivalent Circuit Simulation," in *Proc. of 2003 IEEE UltrasonicsSymposium*, Honolulu, Hawaii, Oct. 5-8, 2003 pp. 465-468.

[8] M. Tsai and J. Jeng, "Development of a Generalized Model for Analyzing Phase Characteristics of SAW Devices Under Mass and Fluid Loading," in *IEEE Trans. on Ultrasonics, Ferroelectrics, and Frequency Control*, vol. 57, no. 11, pp. 2550-2563, November 2010.

[9] E. K. Reichel, M. Heinisch, B. Jakoby, and T. Voglhuber-Brunnmaier, "Efficient Numerical Modeling of Oscillatory Fluid-Structure Interaction," in *Proc. of IEEE SENSORS 2014*, Valencia, Spain, Nov. 2-5, 2014, pp. 958-961,

[10] M. Thränhardt, P. Eccardt, H. Mooshofer, P. Hauptmann, and L. Degertekin, "A Resonant CMUT Sensor for Fluid Applications," in *Proc. of IEEE SENSORS 2009,* Christchurch, New Zealand, 25-28 October, 2009, pp. 878-883.

[11] H. Wang, X. Wang, C. He, and C. Xue, Design and Performance Analysis of Capacitive Micromachined Ultrasonic Transducer Linear Array. *Micromachines*, vol. 5, no. 3, pp.420-431, 2014.

[12] T. Zure, "Characterization of a CMUT Array," Master's Thesis, Dept. of Electrical and Computer Engineering, Univ. of Windsor, Windsor, ON, Canada, 2012.

[13] V. Yashvanth, "CMUT Crosstalk Reduction Using Crosslinked Silica Aerogel," Master's Thesis, Dept. of Electrical and Computer Engineering, Univ. of Windsor, Windsor, ON Canada, 2018.

[14] R. Zhang et al. "Design and Performance Analysis of Capacitive Micromachined Ultrasonic Transducer (CMUT) Array for Underwater Imaging." *Microsystem Technologies,* vol. 22, no. 12, pp. 2939-2947, 2016.

[15] D. S. Ballantine Jr et al. *Acoustic wave sensors: theory, design and physico-chemical applications.* San Diego, CA, USA: Elsevier; 1996.

[16] M. Rahman and S. Chowdhury, "A New Deflection Shape Function for Square Membrane CMUT Design," in *Proc. of 2010 IEEE International Symposium on Circuits and Systems (ISCAS2010)*, Paris, France, 2010, pp. 2019-2022.

[17] S. J. Martin, Gregory C. Frye, Antonio J. Ricco, and Stephen D. Senturia, "Effect of Surface Roughness on the Response of Thickness-shear Mode Resonators in liquids," *Analytical Chemistry*, vol. *65*, pp. 2910-2922, 1993.

[18] E. Ashley, J. Niebauer, Cardiology Explained. London: Remedica; 2004. Chapter 4, Understanding the Echocardiogram. [Online]. Available: https://www.ncbi.nlm.nih.gov/books/NBK2215/ [retreived: August, 2021].

[19] M. Rahman, J. Hernandez, and S. Chowdhury, "An Improved Analytical Method to Design CMUTs with Square Diaphragms," in *IEEE Transactions on Ultrasonics, Ferroelectrics, and Frequency Control*, vol. 60, no. 4, pp. 834-845, April 2013.

[20] R. Manwar, "A BCB Diaphragm Based Adhesive Wafer Bonded CMUT Probe for Biomedical Application," Ph.D. dissertation, Dept. of Electrical and Computer Engineering, Univ. of Windsor, Windsor, ON, Canada, 2017.

[21] F. Pavlo, "Capacitive Micromachined Ultrasonic Transducer (cMUT) for Biometric Applications," Master's Thesis, Dept. of Nanoscience and Technology, Chalmers University of Technology, Göteborg, Sweden, 2012.

[22] R. Manwar, L. Arjunan, M. Ahmadi, and S. Chowdhury, "Resonant Frequency Calculation of Square Diaphragms: A Comparison," in *Proc of IEEE 6th Latin American Symposium on Circuits & Systems (LASCAS)*, Montevideo, Uruguay, Feb. 24-27, 2015, pp. 1-4.

Footprint Model in a Navigation System Based on Visible Light Communication

Paula Louro, Manuela Vieira, Manuel Augusto Vieira
DEETC/ISEL/IPL,
R. Conselheiro Emídio Navarro, 1959-007
Lisboa, Portugal
CTS-UNINOVA
Quinta da Torre, Monte da Caparica, 2829-516,
Caparica, Portugal
e-mail: plouro@deetc.isel.pt, mv@isel.ipl.pt,
mvieira@deetc.isel.pt

Mirtes de Lima, João Rodrigues, Pedro Vieira
DEETC/ISEL/IPL,
R. Conselheiro Emídio Navarro, 1959-007
Lisboa, Portugal
Instituto das Telecomunicações
Instituto Superior Técnico, 1049-001,
Lisboa, Portugal
e-mail: A43891@alunos.isel.pt; A42101@alunos.isel.pt,
pedro.vieira@isel.pt

***Abstract*— Indoor navigation is hardly managed by the usual Global Positioning System (GPS) due to the strong attenuation of signals inside the buildings. Alternative based on RF optical, magnetic or acoustic signals can be used. Among the optical technologies, Visible Light Communication (VLC) provides good position accuracy. The proposed system uses commercial RGB white LEDs for the generation of the light, which is simultaneously coded and modulated to transmit information. The receiver includes a multilayered photodetector based on a-SiC:H operating in the visible spectrum. The positioning system includes multiple, identical navigation cells. Inside each cell, the optical pattern defined by the VLC transmitters establishes specific spatial regions assigned each to different optical excitations, which configures the footprint of the navigation cell. Demodulation and decoding procedures of the photocurrent signal measured by the photodetector are used to identify the input optical excitations and enable position recognition inside the cell. The footprint model is characterized using geometrical and optical assumptions, namely the Lambertian model for the LEDs and the evaluation of the channel gain of the VLC link. An algorithm to decode the information is established and the positioning accuracy is discussed. The experimental results confirmed that the proposed VLC architecture is suitable for the intended application.**

Keywords- Visible Light Communication; Indoor navigation; White LEDs; Lambertian model; navigation cell.

I. INTRODUCTION

Indoor positioning can be addressed by several techniques, such as Wi-Fi, Assisted GPS (A-GPS), Infrared, Radio Frequency Identification (RFID), and many other technologies [1][2]. The ubiquitous presence of indoor Light Emitting Diodes (LED) based lighting systems enabled Visible Light communication (VLC) as an attractive technology to perform such task. Furthermore, enhanced accuracy is an additional added value to this solution. VLC is a technology based on the use of visible light in the THz range, extending from 400 nm up to 750 nm [3][4]. VLC systems use modulated LEDs to transmit information taking advantage of ubiquitous, energy efficient white LED infra-structures, designed primarily for lighting purposes [5]. Due to its characteristics, LEDs [6] can be switched very fast to produce modulated light in high frequencies, allowing data transmission in high speed. Consequently, this free-space, wireless optical communication technology is attractive to address the growing need for energy saving and speed network data transmission [7][8]. As the technology is mainly related to energy saving lighting sources it uses mostly white LEDs [9][10], either based on blue emitter coated with a phosphor layer or based on tri-chromatic emitters. The phosphor-based LED typically consists of a blue LED chip covered by a yellow phosphor layer. However, when this phosphor-based LED is used for VLC, the modulation bandwidth is limited by the long relaxation time of the phosphor; hence limiting the transmission capacity of the VLC. The increase of the LED modulation bandwidth, can be achieved using a blue filter before the receiver unit to eliminate the slow-response of the yellow light component [11][12]. The tri-chromatic LEDs are more expensive but provide additional bandwidth as three communication channels can be used by independent modulation of each chip of the monolithic device.

The receiver unit of VLC systems usually include based silicon photodiodes, as these devices operate in the visible region of the spectrum. Several applications of VLC systems are currently being developed, spanning from low data rate applications such as indoor positioning and navigation to more demanding bandwidth applications like multimedia streaming or internet access points [13][14].

In this paper we propose the use of a multilayered a:SiC:H [15] device to perform the photodetection of the optical signals generated by white trichromatic RGB LEDs [16], [17]. The system was designed for navigation [18][19], and the emitters of each white LED were specifically modulated at precise frequencies and coding bit sequences [20][21].

The proposed lighting and positioning/navigation system involves wireless communication, computer based algorithms, smart sensor and optical sources network, which constitutes a transdisciplinary approach framed in cyber-physical systems.

The paper is organized as follows. After the introduction (Section I), the VLC system architecture is presented in Section II. In Section III, models for the footprint characterization using both geometrical and propagation assumptions are analyzed. In Section IV, the communication protocol and the encoding/decoding techniques are analyzed and discussed. At last, conclusions are addressed in Section V.

II. VLC SYSTEM ARCHITECTURE

In the proposed VLC system, the transmitter is composed of white RGB LEDs that code the information and modulate the emitted light and of a receiver with a photodiode that measures the modulated signal from the transmitted light and decodes information through a dedicated algorithm for data analysis. The transmitter and the receiver are physically separated from each other, but connected through the VLC channel. In this solution we work in line of sight conditions using the atmosphere as transmission channel.

A. *VLC Transmitter*

The transmitter proposed in this VLC system uses ceiling lamps based on commercial white LEDs. with red, green and blue emitters (w-RGB LEDs). Each ceiling lamp is composed of four white LEDs framed at the corners of a square (Figure 1).

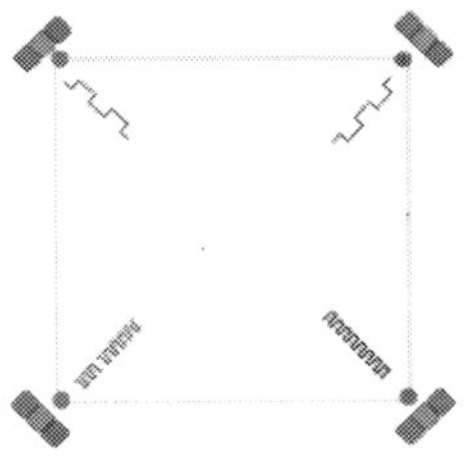

Figure 1. Configuration of the VLC emitter with 4 RGB white LEDs.

The luminous intensity of each emitter is regulated by the driving current for white perception by the human eye and the divergence angle is around 120°.

On each corner only one chip of each white LED is modulated for data transmission carrying useful information. The other emitters of the LED are only supplied with DC to maintain white color illumination. Red (R; 626 nm), Green (G; 530 nm), Blue (B; 470 nm) and violet (V; 390 nm) LEDs, are used [22].

B. *VLC Receiver*

The receiver is a pinpin photodiode that transduces the light into an electrical signal able to be demodulated and decoded. This device is a monolithic heterojunction composed of two pin structures based on a-Si:H and a-SiC:H built on a glass substrate and sandwiched between two transparent electrical contacts. The intrinsic absorber materials of both pin structures of the photodiode were designed to enable separate detection of short and long visible wavelengths. The front, thin pin structure made of a-SiC:H exhibits high absorption to short wavelengths (blue, and green light in this case) and high transparency to the long wavelength (red light). In opposition, the back, thicker pin structure based on a-Si:H absorbs only long wavelengths (green and red). The device selectivity is tuned externally using reverse bias (-8 V) and optical steady state illumination of short wavelength (400 nm).

III. FOOTPRINT, ARCHITECTURE AND BUILDING MODEL

The lamp configuration at the ceiling constitutes a basic unit illumination infrastructure and defines a communication cell, which coverage will be discussed in next sections.

A. *Footprint definition and geometrical characterization*

Each lamp with this configuration constitutes a navigation unit cell) inside which the coverage of the modulated light allows the characterization of different spatial regions assigned to specific illumination patterns. This provides higher accuracy inside the cell for the position determination, and enables the concept of footprint inside the navigation cell (Figure 2). To provide wider illumination and communication signal coverage, several VLC emitters must be placed in adjacent positions, defining thus adjacent, independent navigation cells. To provide wider illumination and communication signal coverage, several VLC emitters must be placed in adjacent positions, defining thus adjacent, independent navigation cells.

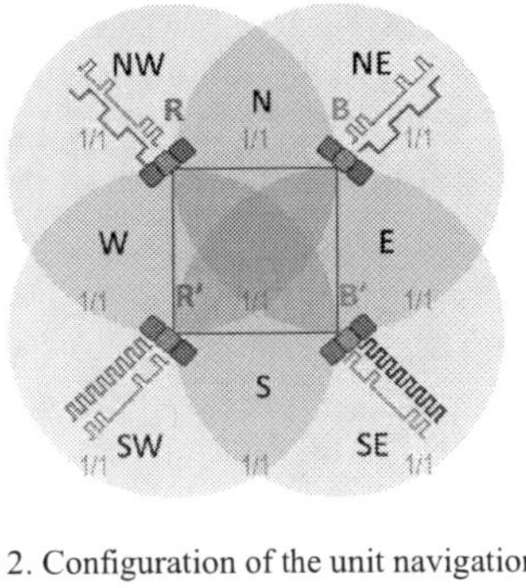

Figure 2. Configuration of the unit navigation cell.

In this model, we will assume that each white LED cone of light overlaps in the central region of the square. In the lateral and corner parts, this intersection is partial due to the radiation patterns superposition of the closest two or three LEDs [23]. Outside the square, distinct optical regions correspond also to different spatial regions, with the presence of a single red or blue signal or of two signals (red and blue, or two red or two blue signals). Consequently, the area covered by the different optical excitations will vary along the navigation unit cell (Figure 3).

The central region, labeled β results from the overlap of the emitted light from the two red emitters, two blue emitters and four green emitters, while the α region at the corners holds the optical excitation of three green emitters and two blue and one red, or two red and one blue emitter. At the γ and γ' regions the optical pattern is due to two emitters (two green emitters and two blue or two red emitters or one red and one blue emitter). Regions δ and Δ include the irradiation pattern from one single white-LED, i.e., light from one green emitter and from one red or blue emitter. Regions of the navigation cell not covered by any irradiation pattern, correspond to "dark" regions, where the photodetector will not be able the perceive the position.

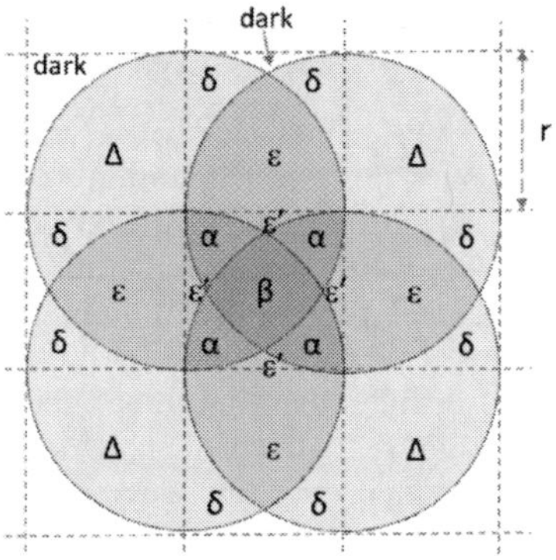

Figure 3. Diagram of the radiation patterns within each navigation unit cell.

As can be depicted from Figure 3, the area covered by each irradiation pattern can be evaluated using simple geometrical considerations. This was computed integrating the shadowed area of each region, assuming a circular irradiation flux for each emitter of radius r.

Thus,

$$A_\varepsilon = 2 \times \int_{r/2}^{r} \sqrt{r^2 - x^2} \cdot dx \qquad (1)$$

$$A_\beta = 4\left[\int_{r/2}^{\sqrt{3}r/2} \sqrt{r^2 - x^2} dx - r^2\left(\frac{\sqrt{3}}{2} - \frac{1}{2}\right)^2\right] \qquad (2)$$

Using polar coordinates equations (1) and (2) can be written as:

$$A_\varepsilon = 2 \times \int_{0}^{\pi/3} r^2 \sin^2\theta \cdot d\theta \qquad (3)$$

$$A_\beta = 4\left(\int_{\pi/6}^{\pi/3} r^2 sin^2\theta \cdot d\theta + r^2\left(1 - \frac{\sqrt{3}}{2}\right)\right) \qquad (4)$$

The solution of equations (3) and (4) is:

$$A_\varepsilon = r^2\left(\frac{\pi}{3} - \frac{\sqrt{3}}{4}\right) \qquad (5)$$

$$A_\beta = r^2\left(\frac{\pi}{12} - 1 + \frac{\sqrt{3}}{2}\right) = 0.315147 \cdot r^2 \qquad (6)$$

The evaluation of adjacent areas is given by:

$$A_\delta = \frac{\pi r^2}{4} - A_\varepsilon = 0.171213 \cdot r^2 \qquad (7)$$

$$A_{\varepsilon'} = r^2 - A_\varepsilon - 2 \cdot A_\delta = 0.043389 \cdot r^2 \qquad (8)$$

$$A_\alpha = \frac{1}{4}\left(r^2 - A_\beta - 4 \times A_{\varepsilon'}\right) = 0.337418 r^2 \qquad (9)$$

Table I summarizes the numerical values of the normalized area of each footprint inside the navigation cell inside (assuming an area 3r×3r for the navigation unit cell).

TABLE I. RELATIVE AREA OF THE IRRADIATION PATTERNS WITHIN THE NAVIGATION UNIT CELL.

Spatial region	**Area**	**Number of regions**	**Normalized area (navigation unit cell)**
ε	$0{,}614 \cdot r^2$	4	0,273
δ	$0{,}171 \cdot r^2$	8	0,152
ε'	$0{,}043 \cdot r^2$	4	0,019
β	$0{,}511 \cdot r^2$	1	0,057
α	$0{,}079 \cdot r^2$	4	0,035
Δ	$0{,}785 \cdot r^2$	4	0,349
Δ+ δ	$0{,}957 \cdot r^2$	4	0,501
ε + ε'	$0{,}658 \cdot r^2$	4	0,292
Dark	$0{,}215 \cdot r^2$	4	0,095

These values allow the evaluation of the accuracy on the determination on the spatial resolution of the positioning system. The dark zones of the navigation unit cell correspond to nearly 10% of the covered area. The region confined to a narrower area is the α region, resultant from the irradiation pattern of three LEDs, followed by the central region (β) where the four LEDs contribute. Regions with poorer resolution are ε + ε' and Δ+ δ, assigned respectively, to optical signals from two and one LEDs.

B. *Footprint characterization based on the LED propagation model*

LEDs are modeled as Lambertian source where the luminance is distributed uniformly in all directions, whereas the luminous intensity is different in all directions. The luminous intensity for a Lambertian source is given by the following equation [24]:

$$I(\phi) = I_N \cos^m(\phi) \qquad (10)$$

where m is the order derived from a Lambertian pattern, I_N is the maximum luminous intensity in the axial direction and , ϕ is the angle of irradiance. The Lambertian order m is given by:

$$m = -\frac{\ln(2)}{\ln(\cos(\phi_{1/2}))} \quad (11)$$

As the half intensity angle ($\phi_{1/2}$) is of 60º, the Lambertian order m is 1.

The light signal is received by the WDM photodetector that detects the on/off states of the LEDs, generates a binary sequence of the received signals and convert data into the original format. For simplicity, we will consider a line of sight (LoS) connection for both VLC links, which corresponds to the existence of straight visibility between the transmitter and the receiver. In Figure 4 it is plotted the geometry of the transmitter and receiver relative position, with emphasis to the main parameters used for characterization of the LED source and the photodiode receiver (angles of irradiance and illumination, transmitter's semi-angle at half-power and field of view). The Lambertian model is used for LED light distribution and MatLab simulations are used to infer the signal coverage of the LED in the illuminated indoors space [25].

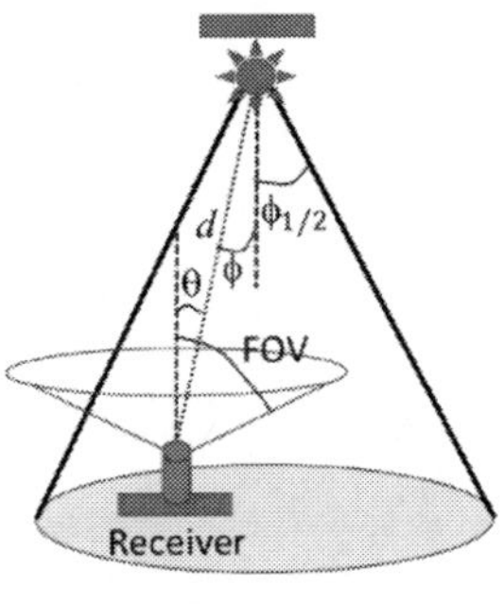

Figure 4. Transmitter and receiver relative position.

The link budget of the VLC link is evaluated computing the gains and losses along the propagation path of the light. It uses the channel gain of the link, which includes the losses due to the path and to wavelength in free space, as well as the spatial delivered power distribution by each emitter. The channel gain (G) is given by equation [26]:

$$G = \frac{(m+1)A}{2\pi D_{t-r}^2} I_N \cos^m(\phi)\cos(\theta) \quad (12)$$

where A is the area of the photodetector.

The evaluation of the channel gain allowed the establishment of the coverage map, that is illustrated in Figure 5. Only high accuracy footprints of the navigation cell are displayed. Each footprint region labelled as #1, #2, ..., #9 are assigned to the correspondent optical excitation illustrated on the right side of Figure 5.

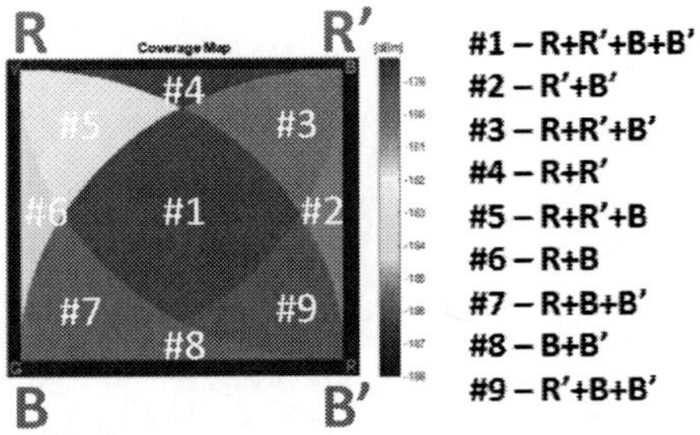

Figure 5. Coverage map of the fine-grain footprint inside the navigation cell, considering as VLC optical sources the top red and bottom blue emitters.

The use of the propagation model confirmed the theoretical prediction (Figure 3) and demonstrated the existence of distinct regions inside the navigation cell, that are assigned to the footprint [27], [28].

C. *Coding and modulation*

Data is converted into an intermediate data representation, byte format, and converted into light signals emitted by the VLC transmitter. The data bit stream is directed into a modulator that uses an ON–OFF Keying (OOK) modulation. Here, a bit assigned to one (1) is represented by an optical pulse that occupies the entire bit duration, while a bit set to zero (0) is represented by the absence of an optical pulse. The data format used to transmit information, namely, the length of the frame, the blocks that make part of the word in each frame and its contents must be known by the transmitter and receiver to ensure proper coding and decoding. In order to ensure synchronization between frames, two blocks labelled as Start of Text (SoT) and End of Text (EoT), are placed respectively, at the beginning and end of the word. The SoT is composed of two idle bits (logical value 1) and two start bits (logical value 0), which corresponds to the 4-bits word 1100. The EoT block is composed of two stop bits (logical value 0) and two idle bits (logical value 1), which corresponds to the 4-bits word 0011.

D. *Decoding strategy*

Based on the measured photocurrent signal by the photodetector, it is necessary to infer the correspondent footprint. For this purpose a calibration curve is previously defined in order to establish this assignment. In Figure 6 it is plotted the calibration curve that uses 16 distinct photocurrent thresholds resultant from the combination of the 4 modulated signals from the white VLC emitter. The driving current of each LED emitter was adjusted to provide different levels of photocurrent.

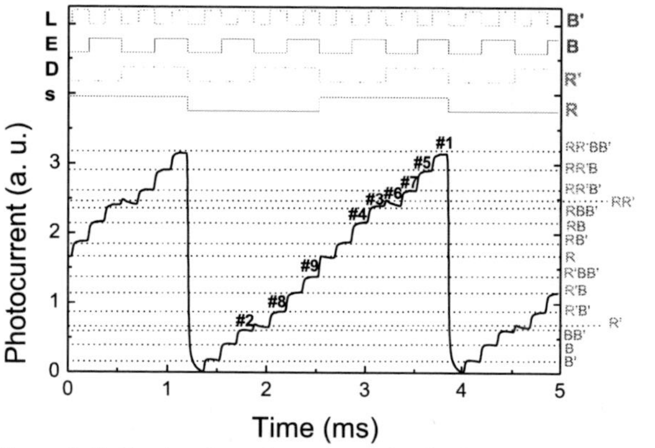

Figure 6. Calibration front photocurrent signal using two red and two blue optical signals modulated with multiple frequencies (on the top it is displayed the waveform of the emitters modulation state).

The correspondence between each footprint and the photocurrent level is highlighted on the right side of Figure 6. The correct use of this calibration curve demands a periodic retransmission of curve to ensure a accurate correspondence to the output signal and an accurate decoding of the transmitted information.

IV. RESULTS AND DISCUSSION

In Figure 7, it is displayed the photocurrent signal acquired by the mobile receiver unit at two different spatial positions inside the navigation cell covered by RR'BB' and R'BB' optical signals, which corresponds, respectively, to the footprints labelled as #1 and #9. The calibration curve is also displayed.

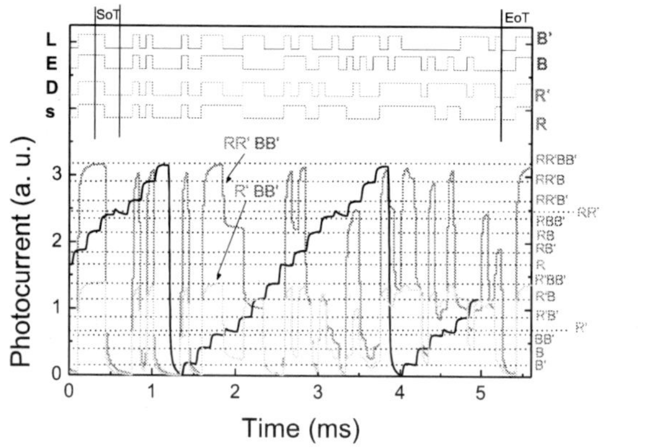

Figure 7. Photocurrent signal acquired by the mobile receiver unit at footprints #1 and #9 inside the navigation cell (RR'BB' and R'BB'). The calibration curve is also displayed.

Synchronization between frames is detected by the blocks SoT and EoT. In both measurements, either inside footprints #1 and #9 (RR'BB' and R'BB'), the presence of these blocks corresponds to maximum values of the photocurrent, because all emitters are simultaneously ON. The decoding of the photocurrent levels uses the calibration curve to identify which emitters are active in the duration period of each bit. On the right side of the graph it is stated the optical state assigned to each step of the calibration curve. The observed correspondence between the different thresholds of the measured signal and the steps of the calibration provide the decoding of the input optical signals.

V. CONCLUSIONS

In this paper, a VLC system for indoor navigation was presented. A theoretical study on the irradiation patterns is presented to support the position resolution of the proposed system and establish the footprint of each navigation cell. The optical signals transmitted by the RGB white LEDs were fully characterized using the Lambertian model. The footprint was predicted using the channel gain model of the transmitter-receiver link. Experimental results demonstrate the capability of the system. Future work will comprise a more detailed and complete description of the decoding methodology.

ACKNOWLEDGEMENTS

This work was sponsored by FCT – Fundação para a Ciência e a Tecnologia, within the Research Unit CTS – Center of Technology and systems, reference UID/EEA/00066/2019 and by project IPL/2020/Geo-Loc/ISEL.

REFERENCES

[1] R. Mautz, "Overview of Current Indoor Positioning Systems", Geodesy Cartogr., vol. 35, pp. 18–22, 2009.

[2] Y. Gu, A. Lo, and I. Niemegeers, "A Survey of Indoor Positioning Systems for Wireless Personal Networks," IEEE Commun. Surv. Tutor., vol. 11, pp. 13–32, 2009.

[3] A. M. Căilean and M. Dimian, "Current Challenges for Visible Light Communications Usage in Vehicle Applications: A Survey", IEEE Communications Surveys & Tutorials, vol. 19, no. 4, pp. 2681-2703, 2017.

[4] M. Z. Chowdhury, M. T. Hossan, A. Islam, and Y. M Jang, "A Comparative Survey of Optical Wireless Technologies: Architectures and Applications", IEEE Access, vol. 6, pp. 9819-9840, 2018.

[5] G. Cossu, A. M. Khalid, P. Choudhury, R. Corsini, and E. Ciaramella, "3.4 Gbit/s Visible Optical Wireless Transmission Based on RGB LED," Optics Express, vol. 20, pp. B501–B506, 2012.

[6] M. Kavehrad, "Sustainable Energy-Efficient Wireless Applications Using Light", IEEE Communications Magazine, vol. 48, no. 12, pp. 66-73, 2010.

[7] E. Ozgur, E. Dinc, and O. B. Akan, "Communicate to illuminate: State-of-the-art and research challenges for visible light communications", Physical Communication, vol. 17, pp. 72–85, 2015.

[8] C. Yang and H. R. Shao, "WiFi-based indoor positioning", IEEE Commun. Mag., vol. 53, no. 3, pp. 150–157, 2015.

[9] E. F. Schubert and J. K. Kim, "Solid-state light sources getting smart", Science, vol. 308, no. 5726, pp. 1274-1278, 2005.

[10] J.-Y. Sung, C.-W. Chow, and C.-H Yeh, "Is blue optical filters necessary in high speed phosphor-based white light LED visible light communications?", Optics Express, vol. 22, no. 17, pp. 20646-20651, 2014.

[11] H. Le Minh et al, "High-speed visible light communications using multiple-resonant equalization," IEEE Photon. Technol. Lett., vol. 20, no. 14, pp. 1243–1245, 2008.

[12] A. M. Khalid, G. Cossu, R. Corsini, P. Choudhury, and E. Ciaramella, "1-Gb/s transmission over a phosphorescent white LED by using rate-adaptive discrete multitone modulation", IEEE Photon. J., vol. 4, no. 5, pp. 1465–1473, 2012.

[13] Z. Zhou, M. Kavehrad, and P. Deng, "Energy efficient lighting and communications", Proc. SPIE 8282, Broadband Access Communication Technologies VI, vol. 8282, pp. 82820J-1-82820J-15, 2012.

[14] A. Jovicic, J. Li, and T. Richardson, "Visible Light Communication: Opportunities, Challenges and the Path to Market", IEEE Communications Magazine, vol. 51, no. 12, pp. 26-32, 2013.

[15] P. Louro, et al, "Optical demultiplexer based on an a-SiC:H voltage controlled device", Phys. Status Solidi C, vol. 7, no. 3–4, pp. 1188–1191, 2010.

[16] M. Vieira, M. A. Vieira, P. Louro, V. Silva, and P. Vieira, "Optical signal processing for indoor positioning using a-SiC:H technology", Opt. Eng., vol 55, no. 10, pp. 107105-1-107105-6, 2016.

[17] M. A. Vieira, M. Vieira, P. Louro, and P. Vieira, "Cooperative vehicular communication systems based on visible light communication," Opt. Eng., vol. 57, no. 7, pp. 076101-, 2018.

[18] P. Louro; V. Silva; M. A. Vieira, and M. Vieira, "Viability of the use of an a-SiC:H multilayer device in a domestic VLC application", Phys. Status Solidi C, vol, 11, no. 11–12, pp. 1703–1706, 2014.

[19] P. Louro, J. Costa, M. Vieira, M. A. Vieira, and Y. Vygranenko, "Use of VLC for indoors navigation with RGB LEDs and a-SiC:H photodetector", Proc. of SPIE, Optical sensors, vol. 10231, pp. 102310F-1-102310F-10, 2017.

[20] P. Louro, J. Costa, M. A. Vieira, and M. Vieira, "Optical Communication Applications based on white LEDs", J. Luminescence, vol. 191, pp. 122-125, 2017.

[21] M. Vieira, M. A. Vieira, I. Rodrigues, V. Silva, and P. Louro, "Photonic Amorphous Pi'n/pin SiC Optical Filter Under Controlled Near UV Irradiation", Sensors & Transducers, vol. 184, no. 1, pp. 123-129, 2015.

[22] P. Louro, M. Vieira, and M. A. Vieira, "Indoors Geolocation Based on Visible Light Communication", Sensors & Transducers, vol. 245, no. 6, pp. 57-64, 2020.

[23] P. Louro, M. Vieira, M. A. Vieira, and J. Costa, "Photodetection of modulated light of white RGB LEDs with a-SiC:H device", Advanced Materials Proceedings, vol. 3, no. 5, pp. 366-371, 2018.

[24] Y. Zhu, W. Liang, J. Zhang, and Y. Zhang, "Space-Collaborative Constellation Designs for MIMO Indoor Visible Light Communications," IEEE Photonics Technology Letters, vol. 27, no. 15, pp. 1667–1670, 2015.

[25] S. I. Raza, et al, "Optical Wireless Channel Characterization For Indoor Visible Light Communications", Indian Journal of Science and Technology, vol 8, no. 22, pp. 1 – 9, 2015.

[26] Y. Qiu, H.-H. Chen, and W.-X. Meng, "Channel modeling for visible light communications - a survey", Wirel. Commun. and Mob. Comput., vol. 16, pp. 2016–2034, 2016.

[27] P. Louro, M. Vieira, and M. A. Vieira, "Bidirectional visible light communication," Opt. Eng., vol. 59, no. 12, pp. 127109-1, 127109-14, 2020.

[28] P. Louro, M. Vieira, P. Vieira, J. Rodrigues, and M. de Lima, "Geo-localization using indoor visible light communication", Proc. SPIE, Optical Sensors, vol. 11772, pp. 117720J-1-117720J-12, 2021.

High-precision Time Synchronization Digital Sensing Platform Enabling Connection of a Camera Sensor

Narito Kurata
Faculty of Industrial Technology
Tsukuba University of Technology
Tsukuba City, Ibaraki, Japan
e-mail: kurata@home.email.ne.jp

Abstract **- The authors are conducting research and development of different types of sensor systems for the maintenance of civil infrastructures, such as aging bridges and highways, and buildings. Highly accurate time information is added to measurement data, and a set of sensing data that ensures time synchronization is acquired and used for multimodal analysis of risk. In research so far, as a first step, a sensor device was developed that uses a digital high-precision accelerometer to perform highly-accurate time-synchronized sensing of civil infrastructure, such as bridges and highways, and buildings. A vibration table test was performed on the new sensor device, and its time synchronization performance was verified by comparing the measurement results with multiple sensor devices and a servo-type accelerometer. In this paper, a different type of digital sensing platform has been developed that allows a camera sensor to be connected in addition to a digital accelerometer. By adding a unified time stamp synchronized with the absolute time to data from the digital accelerometer and the image from the camera sensor when data is acquired, the vibration and the image can be measured synchronously. First, a Chip-Scale Atomic Clock (CSAC), which is an ultra-high-precision clock, is mounted on the sensor device, and a mechanism is implemented whereby a time stamp is added to the outputs of the digital accelerometer and the camera sensor with timekeeping precision. Since the timekeeping precision of the CSAC is too high, a delay occurs when a time stamp is added by the CPU of the sensor device. Therefore, a Field-Programmable Gate Array (FPGA) dedicated to adding time stamps is prepared. In this paper, the results of a performance verification experiment on a camera sensor mounted on the platform, are described.**

Keywords-Time Synchronization; Chip Scale Atomic Clock; Earthquake Observation; Structural Health Monitoring; Micro Electro Mechanical Systems; Camera Sensor

I. INTRODUCTION

As civil infrastructure, such as bridges and highways, and buildings deteriorate over time, it has become important to automate inspections for maintenance of these structures. In addition, since there are many disasters, such as earthquakes and typhoons in Japan, it is necessary to detect damage to structures immediately after a disaster, and to estimate the damage situation. Data collection and analysis by sensor groups is effective for automating the detection of such abnormalities, but to analyze data sets measured by multiple sensors and evaluate structural safety, time synchronization between sensors is required.

The authors applied wireless sensor network technology to develop sensors for seismic observation and structural health monitoring, and demonstrated their performance in skyscrapers [1][2]. In this system, time synchronization was achieved by sending and receiving wireless packets between sensors [1]. However, it is impossible to target multiple buildings, long structures, such as bridges, and wide-area urban spaces with wireless sensor network technology. On the other hand, if sensors installed in various places can autonomously retain accurate time information, this problem can be resolved. The method of using GPS signals is effective outdoors, but it cannot be used inside buildings, underground, under bridges, or in tunnels, etc.

Therefore, the author developed a sensor device that autonomously retains accurate time information using a Chip-Scale Atomic Clock (CSAC) [3]-[5], which is an ultra-high-precision clock [6]-[8]. In order to apply the developed sensor device to earthquake observation, a logic was implemented that detects the occurrence of an earthquake and saves data on earthquake events, and its function was verified in a vibration table experiment [9]. The developed sensor device was also installed in an actual building and on an actual bridge, and used for seismic observation and evaluation of structural health [10]. However, as the developed sensor device had an analog MEMS accelerometer, it was difficult to measure minute vibrations accurately, and there was a risk of noise being mixed with the analog signal. The risk of noise was therefore eliminated by making the accelerometer mounted on the sensor device a digital type. In this paper, a different type of digital sensor platform is further developed wherein a camera sensor can be connected to the sensor device. The details of the digital sensing platform and a mechanism whereby ultra-high-accuracy time information is added to sensor data by the CSAC, are described. The results of experiments performed to verify the time synchronization performance of the camera sensor are also reported.

In this paper, Section II shows the existing time synchronization methods and describes their problems and achievement of the development of digital sensing platform proposed in this research. Section III describes the configuration of digital sensing platform and the development of the actual sensor device. Further, Section IV describes the performance verification experiments on the time synchronization of developed camera sensor device, and it is confirmed that time synchronization among the developed digital sensor devices with camera is achieved.

II. STATE OF THE ART

A time synchronization function is indispensable for sensor devices used to monitor structural health and make seismic observations of civil infrastructure, such as bridges and highways, and buildings. This is because time series analysis using phase information cannot be performed unless a data set is obtained in which time synchronization is achieved. Regarding time synchronization of sensing, many studies have already been performed, such as the use of GNSS signals from artificial satellites and the Network Time Protocol (NTP) for time synchronization on the Internet [11]. There are also studies where time synchronization is achieved by utilizing the characteristic of wireless sensor networks that propagation delay is small. For example, time synchronization protocols, such as Reference Broadcast Synchronization (RBS), Timing-sync Protocol for Sensor Networks (TPSN), and Flooding Time Synchronization Protocol (FTSP) are being studied [12]-[16].

However, although time synchronization using wireless technology is highly convenient, wireless communication may not always be possible. Particularly, if wireless communication is interrupted during an earthquake, it will not be possible to perform sensing where time synchronization is guaranteed. A technology that realizes highly accurate time synchronization in a room includes IEEE1588 Precision Time Protocol (PTP). PTP uses an Ethernet cable in a general Local Area Network (LAN) as a transmission line, and achieves accurate synchronization within one microsecond using time packets. However, it has many problems. For example, it is difficult to achieve stable synchronization accuracy due to packet delay fluctuation and packet loss due to congestion in the LAN. Moreover, since the delay is corrected by packet switching, the PTP devices that can be connected to the master device are limited, and it cannot be deployed in a Wide Area Network (WAN) environment where the delay amount varies drastically.

To obtain a set of sensor data that guarantees long-term, stable time synchronization even when GPS signals are not available, wireless transmission/reception is unstable, and wired network connection is not possible, it would be ideal if different sensors autonomously retain accurate time information. If accurate time information could be added to the data measured by each sensor, a sensor data set that guarantees time synchronization would be obtained. It was therefore decided to develop a sensing system that autonomously retains accurate time information by employing a CSAC [4]-[6], which is a clock with high timekeeping accuracy. The CSAC is a clock that achieves ultra-high-accuracy time measurement to several tens of picoseconds (5 x 10^{-11} seconds), while having an ultra-small external shape that can be mounted on a board. Development began in 2001 with the support of the US Defense Advanced Research Projects Agency (DARPA), and consumer products were launched in 2011.

Applications include measures against GPS positioning interference by jamming signals, high-precision positioning by installing on smartphones, etc., and high-level assessment of disaster situations, and further price reduction is expected as it becomes more widespread. CSAC has a small error of about 4 to 8 orders of magnitude less than that of timekeeping by a crystal oscillator, and time synchronization by NTP or GPS signals. If this CSAC is installed in each sensor device and a mechanism is implemented that gives a highly accurate time stamp to sampling of the data to be measured, sensor data sets that guarantee time synchronization can be collected even if GPS signals cannot be used, wireless transmission/reception is unstable, and wired network connection is unavailable. In development so far, the sensor device had a MEMS accelerometer, and the system configuration allowed for any analog sensor to be connected via an external input interface.

However, as the accuracy of the analog MEMS accelerometer is not high, noise might still be mixed with the analog signal, and it was desired to be able to connect a camera sensor, which is a type of digital sensor, it was decided to develop a new platform with full digital sensing. Specifically, a technology was developed to mount a digital accelerometer on the sensor device to enable high-precision acceleration measurement without the risk of noise contamination, connect a camera sensor, and assign accurate time stamps by CSAC to both digital outputs. Data sets obtained by the sensor device described in this paper, where time synchronization is guaranteed, can be used to analyze the structural health of civil infrastructure and buildings, and understand seismic phenomena.

III. DIGITAL SENSING PLATFORM AND CIRCUIT CONFIGURATION

An ordinary sensor device consists of a CPU, a sensor, a memory and a network interface, and a crystal oscillator is used for the CPU. If a CSAC is mounted on such a sensor device to correct the time information of the CPU and perform measurement, a delay will occur because the timing accuracy of the CSAC is too high. Therefore, in order to directly add time information by the CSAC to the measurement data of the sensor in terms of hardware, a mechanism utilizing a Field-Programmable Gate Array (FPGA), which is a dedicated integrated circuit, was contrived. As a result, the CPU of the sensor device is not overloaded, and it became possible to save measurement data to which time information is added by the FPGA in a memory, and to collect the data via a network. Moreover, since the FPGA is programmable, it can not only handle CSAC time information, but also incorporate logic, for example to detect abnormalities, etc., using the measurement data. In this paper, a mechanism is developed whereby accurate time stamps by the CSAC are added to the outputs of the digital accelerometer and camera sensor.

3.1 System Configuration

As shown in Figure 1, the sensor device in this research consists of an oscillator board that synchronizes GPS Time (GPST) with the CSAC and supplies a stable reference signal, a sensor board on which a digital accelerometer and external analog sensor input interface are mounted, a signal processing board on which a CPU and FPGA are mounted, and a camera that captures images. A high-precision 10 MHz reference clock and one Pulses Per Second (PPS) signal are supplied by the oscillator board, and a time stamp and trigger signal for acquiring data are generated by the FPGA. The sensor board is provided with the digital accelerometer and external analog sensor input interface. Any analog sensor can be connected to the external analog sensor input interface.

The digital accelerometer outputs data according to the trigger signal via a Universal Asynchronous Receiver/Transmitter (UART). The data of the sensor connected to the external analog sensor input interface is converted by an A/D converter according to the trigger signal, and output as a 16-bit serial value. The camera sensor can release the shutter according to the trigger signal, and outputs it as an RGB value. The data thus acquired is saved in a connected storage (SSD). The sensor device is operated via a wired LAN, Wi-Fi, or USB.

3.2 Oscillator board

The configuration and external appearance of the oscillator board are shown in Figures 2 and 3. The oscillator board has a function to synchronize the CSAC with 1 PPS output by the GPS module or 1 PPS input from outside. When time synchronization is required between multiple sensor devices, all the sensor devices are designated as "master", or one sensor device is designated as a "master" and the other sensor devices are designated as "slave". When the sensor device is a master, GPS and the CSAC are synchronized by receiving GPS signals, and inputting 1 PPS obtained from the GPS module to the CSAC. When the sensor device is a slave, the master and slave are synchronized by inputting 1 PPS output by the master. In addition, commands for setting the CSAC synchronization cycle or resetting the phase value, as well as signal selection commands, are executed by the signal processing board through the connector. The 10MHz and 1 PPS output by this board are clock sources for this system.

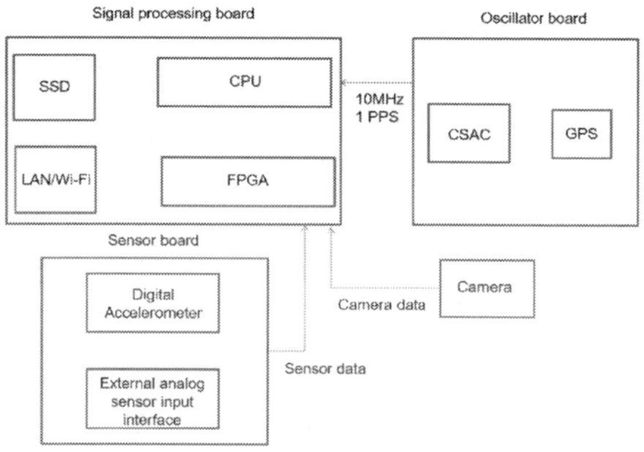

Figure 1. System configuration.

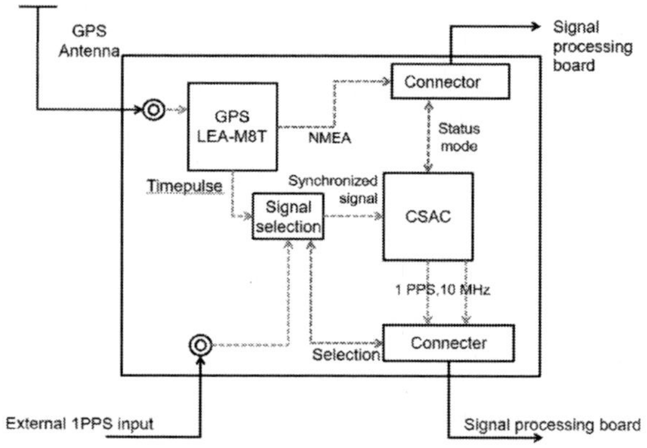

Figure 2. Oscillator board configuration.

Figure 3. External appearance of the oscillator board.

3.3 Sensor board

The configuration and external appearance of the sensor board are shown in Figures 4 and 5. The sensor board is provided with a digital accelerometer and an external analog sensor input interface. The data obtained by the digital accelerometer can be sampled at the timing of the trigger. For the external analog sensor input interface, three channels are provided assuming that a servo-type analog accelerometer is connected for comparison with the digital accelerometer. Depending on the measurement purpose, any analog sensor can be connected in addition to an analog accelerometer.

The signal input from the external analog sensor interface is converted by the A/D converter to output as a 16-bit serial value. Note that the signal is split into two paths, and one of them is amplified 64 times. Therefore, even with an A/D converter having a resolution of 16 bits, a resolution equivalent to 22 bits can be obtained. The data obtained by the digital accelerometer is output by the UART, and the data obtained by the sensor connected to the external analog sensor input interface is output by a Serial Peripheral Interface (SPI), both to the signal processing board.

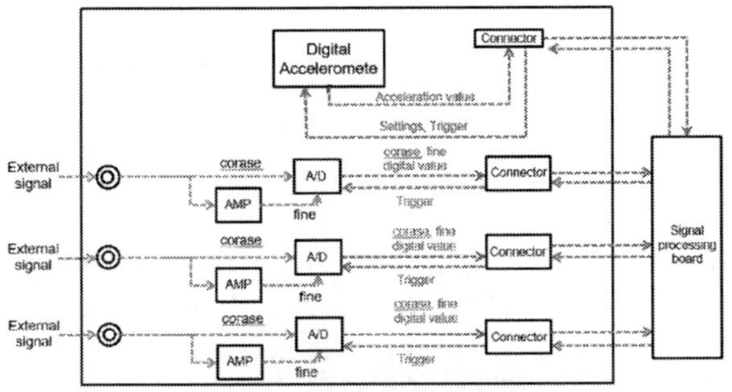

Figure 4. Sensor board configuration.

Figure 5. Sensor board.

3.4 Signal processing board

The configuration and external appearance of the signal processing board are shown in Figures 6 and 7. The FPGA shown in Table 1 is mounted on the signal processing board. As shown in Table 1, Ubuntu is installed as the OS of the CPU and Cyclone V is installed in the FPGA, enabling the use of 1 GB of SDRAM. Also installed is a USB On-The-Go (USB OTG), and it is possible to be connected to an SSD and a Wi-Fi antenna which are extension devices. The Samba function can be used to acquire and browse built-in data via a LAN, and Secure Shell (SSH) allows to perform operations, such as settings and starting measurement. In addition, since it has a USB slave function, it can be operated via USB even when a LAN cannot be used. In addition to the above functions, the CPU mainly performs time setting, sorting of acquired data, format conversion, and filing. The FPGA adjusts the internal RTC (real-time clock), and generates the trigger signal based on the clock obtained from the oscillator. It also constitutes a data acquisition block for the various sensors and camera.

3.5 Digital accelerometer

The external appearance and specifications of the digital accelerometer mounted on the sensor board are shown in Figure 8 and Table 2, respectively. The on-board digital MEMS has a built-in 3-axis crystal accelerometer with high precision and stable performance manufactured by finely processing a crystalline material with superior precision and stability. As shown in Table 2, high-resolution vibration measurement with low noise and low power, is possible.

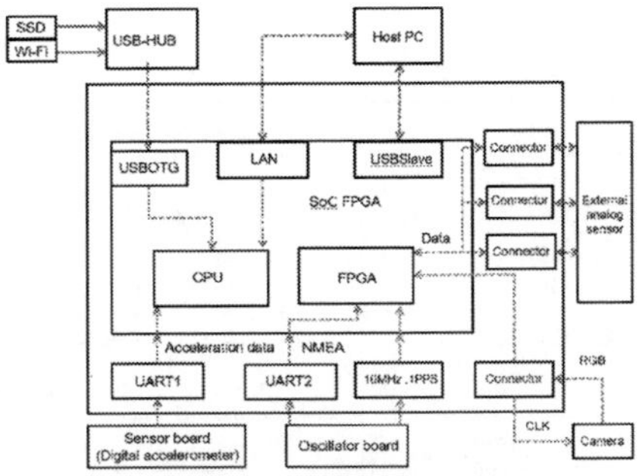

Figure 6. Signal processing board configuration.

Figure 7. Signal processing board.

TABLE I. SPECIFICATIONS OF MAIN FPGA AND DE10-NANO(CPU)

Model	DE10-NANO
OS	Ubuntu 16.04.6 LTS (GNU/Linux 4.5.0-00185-g3bb556b armv7l)
CPU	800MHz Dual-core ARM Cortex-A9
Memory	1GB DDR3 SDRAM
LAN	1 Gigabit Ethernet PHY with RJ45 connector
USB	USBOTG×1, USBUART×1
UART	UART×2
FPGA	CYCLONE V
FPGAROM	EPCS64
Storage	16GB (MicroSD)

Figure 8. Digital Accelerometer.

TABLE II. SPECIFICATIONS OF DIGITAL ACCELEROMETER

Model	EPSON M-A351AS
Range	±5 G
Noise Density	0.5 μG/√Hz (Average)
Resolution	0.06 μG/LSB
Bandwidth	100 Hz (selectable)
Output Range	1000 sps (selectable)
Digital Serial Interface	SPI
Outside Dimensions (mm)	24 × 24 × 18
Weight	12 grams
Operating Temperature	-20 °C to +85 °C
Power Consumption	3.3 V, 66 mW
Output Mode Selection	Acceleration, Tilt Angle, or Tilt Angle Speed

3.6 Camera sensor

The external appearance and specifications of the camera sensor are shown in Figure 9 and Table 3, respectively.

Figure 9. Camera sensor.

TABLE III. SPECIFICATIONS OF CAMERA SENSOR

Model	OmniVision OV5642
Active Array Size	2592 x 1944
Power Supply	core: 1.5VDC±5%, analog: 2.6-3.0 V, I/O: 1.7-3.0 V
Temperature Range	operating: -30 °C to +70 °C stable image: 0 °C to +50 °C
Output Formats (8-bit)	YUV(422/420)/YCbCr422, RGB565/555/444, CCIR656, 8-bit compression data, 8/10-bit raw RGB data
Lenz Size	1/4"
Input Clock Frequency	6-27 MHz
Shutter	rolling shutter
Maximum Image Transfer Rate	5 megapixel (2592x1944): 15 fps 1080p (1920x1080): 30 fps 720p (1280x720):60fps VGA (640x480): 60 fps QVGA (320x240): 120 fps
Scan mode	progressive
Maximum Exposure Interval	1968 x t_{ROW}
Pixel Size	1.4 μm x 1.4 μm
Image Area	3673.6 μm x 2738.4 μm

OmniVision OV5642, which is a CMOS camera module, is used as the camera sensor. It is compact, has low power consumption, supports digital data (YUV422) output, performs very well in poorly lite environments, and can acquire images at the timing of a trigger by inputting an external trigger.

IV. PERFORMANCE VERIFICATION EXPERIMENT ON THE TIME SYNCHRONIZATION FUNCTION OF CAMERA SENSOR

A performance verification experiment was carried out on the time synchronization function of the camera sensor. The experimental system configuration is shown in Figure 10. The trigger signal generated by the signal processing board is transmitted to the camera sensor and the FPGA of the LED control simultaneously. Since the shutter of the camera sensor and the lighting of the LEDs are synchronized, if the image can be acquired when the LEDs light up, it is considered that the image acquired is synchronized with the trigger. The FPGA for LED control shown in Figure 11 is configured to control the lighting of the LEDs at the clock timing of the trigger signal. As shown in Figure 12, 5×5 matrix LEDs light up one by one from upper left to lower right according to the rise of the trigger signal. As shown in Figure 13, the matrix LEDs are photographed with the camera sensor fixed.

Figure 14 shows the result of imaging by the camera sensor. Time elapses from the upper left to the lower right. Since the LEDs in the image light up one by one, images can be acquired according to the signal input to the FPGA for LED control. In the images, the LEDs light up two at a time, and it can be seen that the camera sensor has a certain delay with respect to the trigger. As shown in Fig. 14, it was verified that images could be continuously acquired in synchronization with the trigger.

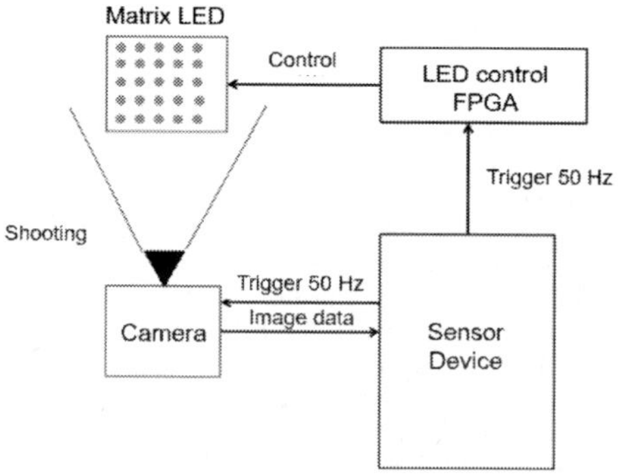

Figure 10. Camera data measurement system.

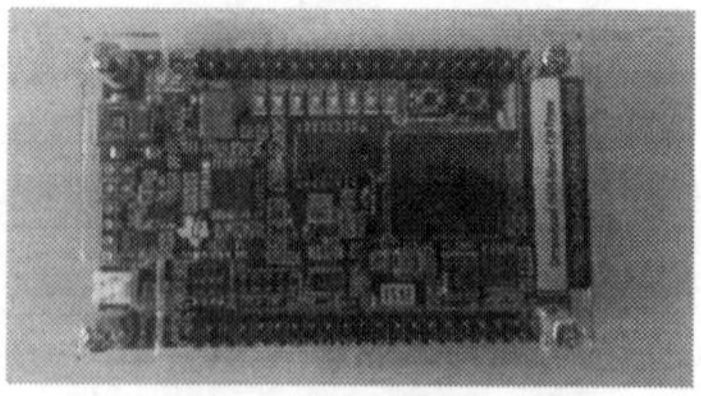

Figure 11. FPGA for LED control.

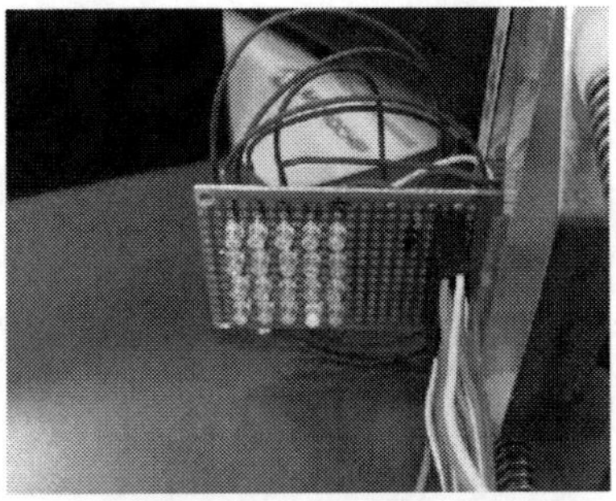

Figure 12. Matrix LEDs.

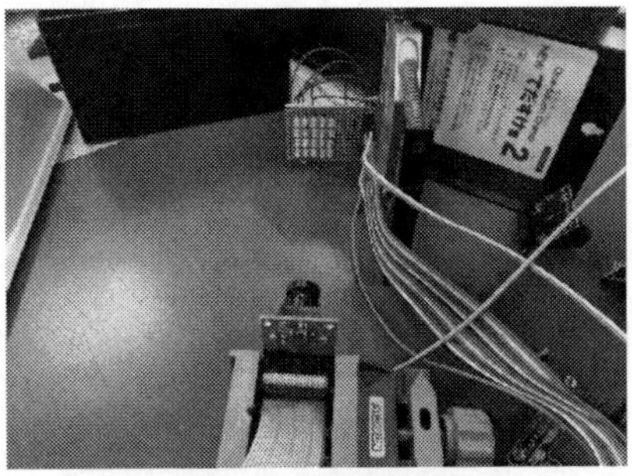

Figure 13. Imaging arrangement.

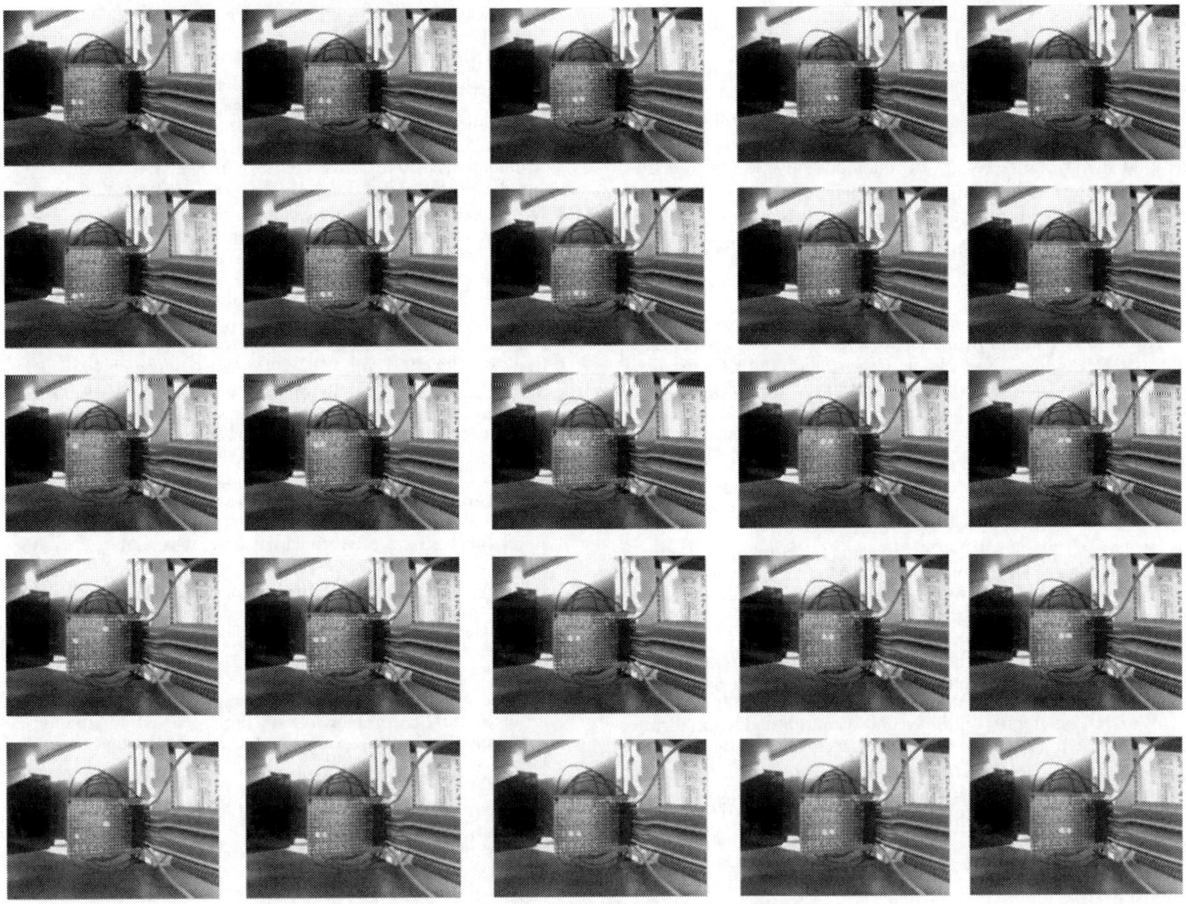

Figure 14. Continuous images from the experimental result.

The performance verification experiment on the time synchronization of developed camera sensor device was carried out as shown above. It is confirmed that time synchronization among the developed digital sensor devices with camera is achieved. The development of this digital sensing platform has enabled time-synchronized measurements between digital accelerometers, camera sensors, and many types of external input analog sensors, as well as multimodal analysis between measurement data.

V. CONCLUSION

In this paper, research and development relating to a digital sensing platform that autonomously retains highly accurate time information by applying a CSAC, was reported. First, a system based on a digital sensor and autonomous time synchronization by a CSAC was described, in which the development of a mechanism and a sensor device that add ultra-high-accuracy time information to sensor data using the CSAC were explained in detail. A function was added to assign the same time stamp as that of the output of the built-in digital accelerometer, to the output of the camera sensor.

The results of an experiment carried out to verify the time synchronization performance of the camera sensor were also reported. In the future, the author plan to apply this new, different type of digital sensing platform to actual structures to acquire acceleration and video data that retain accurate time information. One possible problem is that although the timing accuracy of the CSAC is high, aging will occur in the long term, so it may be necessary to consider how to operate the sensing system according to the purpose and object of measurement. Further, as CSAC are currently expensive, it is hoped that they will be used more extensively in many fields.

ACKNOWLEDGMENT

This research was partially supported by the New Energy and Industrial Technology Development Organization (NEDO) through the Project of Technology for Maintenance, Replacement and Management of Civil Infrastructure, Cross-ministerial Strategic Innovation Promotion Program (SIP). This research was also partially supported by JSPS KAKENHI Grant Number JP19K04963.

REFERENCES

[1] N. Kurata, M. Suzuki, S. Saruwatari, H. Morikawa, "Actual Application of Ubiquitous Structural Monitoring System using Wireless Sensor Networks," 14th World Conference on Earthquake Engineering (14WCEE) IAEE, Oct. 2008, Paper ID:11-0037, pp. 1-8.

[2] N. Kurata, M. Suzuki, S. Saruwatari, H. Morikawa, "Application of Ubiquitous Structural Monitoring System by Wireless Sensor Networks to Actual High-rise Building," Fifth World Conference on Structural Control and Monitoring (5WCSCM) IASCM, July 2010, Paper No. 013, pp. 1-9.

[3] N. Kurata, "Disaster Big Data Infrastructure using Sensing Technology with a Chip Scale Atomic Clock," World Engineering Conference and Convention (WECC2015) WFEO, Dec. 2015, pp. 1-5.

[4] N. Kurata, "Basic Study of Autonomous Time Synchronization Sensing Technology Using Chip Scale Atomic Clock," 16th International Conference on Computing in Civil and Building Engineering (ICCCBE2016) ISCCBE, July 2016, pp. 67-74.

[5] N. Kurata, "An Autonomous Time Synchronization Sensor Device Using a Chip Scale Atomic Clock for Earthquake Observation and Structural Health Monitoring" The Eighth International Conference on Sensor Device Technologies and Applications (SENSORDEVICES 2017) IARIA, Sep. 2017, pp.31-36, ISSN: 2308-3514, ISBN: 978-1-61208-581-4

[6] S. Knappe, et al., "A Microfabricated Atomic Clock," Applied Physics Letters, vol. 85, Issue 9, pp. 1460-1462, Aug. 2004, doi:10.1063/1.1787942.

[7] Q. Li and D. Rus, "Global Clock Synchronization in Sensor Networks," IEEE Transactions on Computers, vol. 55, Issue 2, pp. 214-226, Jan. 2006, ISSN: 0018-9340.

[8] R. Lutwak, et al., "The Chip-Scale Atomic Clock - Prototype Evaluation," 39th Annual Precise Time and Time Interval (PTTI) Meeting, Nov. 2007, pp. 269-290.

[9] N. Kurata, "Improvement and Application of Sensor Device Capable of Autonomously Keeping Accurate Time Information for Buildings and Civil Infrastructures," The Ninth International Conference on Sensor Device Technologies and Applications (SENSORDEVICES 2018) IARIA, Sep. 2018, pp. 114-120, ISSN: 2308-3514, ISBN: 978-1-61208-660-6

[10] N. Kurata, "A Sensing System with High Accurate Time Synchronization for Earthquake Observation and Structural Health Monitoring of Structures," 17th World Conference on Earthquake Engineering (17WCEE) IAEE, Oct. 2021, Paper No. 9a-0008, pp. 1-9.

[11] D. Mills, "Internet Time Synchronization: the Network Time Protocol," IEEE Transactions on Communications, vol. 39, Issue 10, Oct. 1991, pp. 1482-1493, doi:10.1109/26.103043.

[12] M. Maroti, B. Kusy, G. Simon, and A. Ledeczi, "The Flooding Time Synchronization Protocol," Proc. the 2nd International Conference on Embedded Networked Sensor Systems (SenSys '04) ACM, Nov. 2004, pp. 39-49, doi:10.1145/1031495.1031501.

[13] J. Spilker Jr., P. Axelrad, B. Parkinson and P. Enge, "Global Positioning System: Theory and Applications," Vol. I, American Institute of Aeronautics and Astronautics (AIAA), 1996, ISBN: 978-1-56347-106-3.

[14] J. Elson, L. Girod, and D. Estrin, "Fine-Grained Network Time Synchronization using Reference Broadcasts," Proc. 5th Symposium on Operating Systems Design and Implementation (OSDI'02), Dec. 2002, pp. 147-163, doi:10.1145/844128.844143.

[15] S. Ganeriwal, R. Kumar, and M. B. Srivastava, "Timing-sync Protocol for Sensor Networks," Proc. the 1st International Conference on Embedded Networked Sensor Systems (SenSys '03) ACM, Nov. 2003, pp. 138-149, doi:10.1145/958491.958508.

[16] K. Romer, "Time Synchronization in Ad Hoc Networks," Proc. the 2nd ACM International Symp. on Mobile Ad Hoc Networking & Computing (MobiHoc'01) ACM, Oct. 2001, pp. 173-182, doi:10.1145/501436.501440.

Triboelectric-Based Energy Harvesting Face Mask Using Recyclable Materials

Brady Miller, Samantha Barker and Reza Rashidi
Department of Mechanical and Electrical Engineering Technology, State University of New York, Alfred State College
Alfred, NY, USA
e-mail: rashidr@alfredstate.edu

Abstract— **This paper presents the development of a face mask that includes a triboelectric nanogenerator utilizing movements due to pressure changes when speaking to power an embedded temperature sensor. The triboelectric nanogenerator (TENG) produces electricity using common materials including printer papers, ball-point pen inks, and sheets of polytetrafluoroethylene (PTFE). The pen ink is painted onto the paper containing arrays of 2 cm long slots that are 200 µm in width. The paper with holes is placed on the top of a PTFE layer followed by another layer of ink-covered paper without holes. This layer-on-layer device is inserted into the front of the face mask. When the wearer speaks, the acoustic energy travels through the slots and vibrates the PTFE and inked-paper layers. Electrons are transferred from the ink to the plastic through these forms of movement. The electricity generation is due to the transfer of electrons between the negative and positive mediums, which electrically charges each side of the TENG. The electricity generated is transported to a thermistor located near the chin and ear and embedded in the mask band to sense the temperature of the wearer's skin. Testing was conducted using a Bluetooth speaker to create soundwaves that initiated the triboelectric effect. The song that was used to test was "Back in Black" by the band AC/DC. The mask generated a peak-to-peak voltage of 1.72 V and 2.48 V at 70 dB and 80 dB, respectively.**

Keywords-triboelectric nanogenerator; TENG; paper; PTFE; recyclable materials; face mask; thermistor.

I. INTRODUCTION

Sustainability has become an ethical standard in engineering as the world drives towards creating more eco-friendly energy options from sources, such as solar, wind, hydro, geothermal and fuel cells. However, these modern alternative energy sources require high-tech and expensive equipment for effective fabrication. This greatly impacts the widespread availability for such energy sources and therefore prevents the majority of the population from using these types of energy. The high costs of alternative energy sources gatekeeps alternative energy from lower income communities [1], resulting in the continued reliance of current energy sources that are harmful to the environment. Moreover, the size of these alternative energy methods has restricted its applications. Since the use of portable devices has risen so greatly in the past few decades, energy consumption has also greatly increased; therefore, the need for portable-sized energy harvesters is at an all-time high. In recent years, the push for generators on a micro scale has greatly increased [2]. Energy harvesters have been used to power various systems and devices, such as wearable devices [3], wireless sensor networks [4], buildings [5], tactile sensors [6], biomedical devices [7], and roadway applications [8]. Most of these harvesters utilize vibration as the most available energy source in many environments, such as vehicles [9] and human body [10]. This type of energy source can be converted into electrical energy using triboelectric [11], piezoelectric [12], electrostatic [13], and electromagnetic [14] methods. Various energy harvesting devices have been demonstrated by this group [15][16][17].

Triboelectric nanogenerators (TENGs) are a form of energy harvesters that use motion frequency for self-generation. TENGs function through pairs with one side abundant in positive charges and the other being abundant in negative charges. Some positively charged materials include silicon oxide [18], stainless steel and aluminum [19]. Some negatively charged materials include silicon [18], polyvinyl chloride (PVC) [20], and polyvinylidene difluoride (PVDF) [19]. The triboelectric effect occurs when these two sides touch at a high frequency. There are two main motions that are looked at when using the triboelectric effect: sliding motion and tapping motion. At the point of contact, a chemical bond is formed between the two surfaces, called adhesion, and electrons are transferred from the negative half to the positive half to equalize their electrochemical potential. TENGs are effective energy harvesters for applications that require high voltage and low current. This research intends to use a voltage drop across a thermistor to calculate a temperature reading of the wearer. This focus requires the need for higher voltages as opposed to current, making triboelectric a desired choice. The requirement for the nanogenerator to be small enough to fit into a face mask also promotes the decision on the use of triboelectric. TENGs are an effective method of alternative energy harvesting because of their wide variety of applications, such as bicycles [21], clothing [22], and portable power sources [23]; however, these applications are primarily focused on bodily movement. TENGs may also be used to harvest energy through the vibrations of acoustic frequency [19][24].

While the applications of TENGs are still growing, the development of paper-based nanogenerators has allowed for an easily accessible, inexpensive method for alternative energy harvesting [25]. Further research has drifted towards the implementation of other low-cost materials into TENG fabrication, such as papers [20][24], pencil graphite [26], pen ink [27], and PTFE. The combination of these low-cost and easily accessible materials will allow for the wider distribution and use of alternative energy harvesting methods. This is particularly important for applications that demand low-cost, recyclable devices. The implementation of these recyclable materials allows for simple, environmentally friendly, and sustainable applications. Paper is also a flexible material that provides ample movement necessary for TENG applications. This flexibility has allowed for further TENG development in which paper may act as both a structure component of the application and a functioning half of the triboelectric pair [24][27]. Face masks are a disposable supply that require low-cost components. The masks in the market currently focus on protecting others from coming in contact with any germ or virus. In addition, face masks can be designed to trap water droplets produced from respiration [28] in order to control the spread of infected particles.

This paper proposes a face mask that utilizes low-cost, paper-based TENG to generate electricity from the vibrations caused by breath and speech [29] and to power an embedded temperature sensor within the mask itself. To best of our knowledge, this is the first time that a self-sustained, temperature monitoring face mask design using triboelectric nanogenerators fabricated with recyclable materials is demonstrated. In the paper-based TENG, pencil graphite and pen ink can act as conductive electrodes to facilitate the transfer of charges. These materials are thin and easily manageable when being applied to a TENG layer. However, the pencil graphite was determined by sources to be unreliable when deformation occurs to the paper layer [27]; therefore, pen ink is a much more desirable conductive electrode for this TENG application. The paper layer is painted with a layer of pen ink to form one half of the triboelectric pair, and it will be used in an application to address a resultant issue of the current COVID-19 pandemic. The pen ink used in this paper is a more cost-effective solution compared with the silver nanowire [20], evaporated silver [25], or copper [24] coatings used on a soft paper as an electrification layer generating triboelectric charges upon contacting with a mating membrane.

Previous self-powered mask designs were established to deactivate virus-infected particles [30]; however, these claims were only validated through simulation. The proposed TENG design for the face mask in this paper has been developed and tested for the next step of the mask development. The mask design, while keeping people safe from spreading the virus, will be able to read the wearer's temperature. This ability will allow an early detection of a user that may contract the virus. This is particularly more important for the environments where a contagious or deadly virus, such as COVID-19 exists, and mask wearers may want to monitor their body temperature without touching another device. A consideration for this design will be that the addition of the triboelectric generating layers will give the mask an added layer of bulk and protection from the spread of diseased particles. While the temperature sensor, and wiring will give the mask an added weight plus material that could cause a discomfort to the user if not implemented correctly. The added size and weight of the materials have been considered to prioritize user comfort. This paper will focus on only the mask design and its triboelectric energy harvester.

The rest of this paper is organized as follows: Section II describes the design, working principle, flow simulation, and fabrication and assembly of the device. Section III presents the testing method and tools, testing results, the discussion on the results, and the future work. Finally, the conclusions are discussed in Section IV.

II. DESIGN AND FABRICATION

A. Nanogenerator Design

Ballpoint pen ink was determined to be a more stable conductive material than pencil graphite [27]. Therefore, it was the best option to use for easily accessible materials. A layer of ballpoint pen ink was painted onto an A4 style standard sheet of paper. All the ink from seven traditional ballpoint pens was used on the sheet of paper. Once the pen ink was applied, a small painting brush was used to smooth out any uneven spots of the ink and make the layer uniform. This layer acts as the conductive electrode for the paper TENG. The entire sheet of paper being covered in pen ink eases the machining process with the laser cutter itself. Since the laser uses a grid patterned metal as a template for cutting, a full sheet eliminates potential error in cuts that could be off centered or not perfectly symmetrical.

A laser-cutting method was used to create the design with a pattern of slots cut into the ink-painted paper, as shown in Figure 1. The pattern consists of four columns. The two central columns consist of sixty-eight rows each. The column centered in the topmost portion of the shape contains sixteen slots. The column centered in the lower portion of the shape contains eight slots. The placement of the columns is designed to properly utilize available surface area while maintaining uniformity and the ability to catch the vibrations from breath and speech. The distance between each row is evenly distributed.

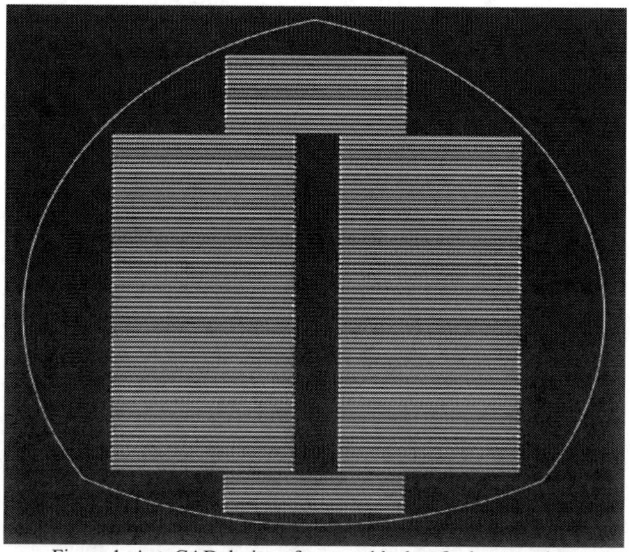

Figure 1. AutoCAD design of paper with slots for laser cutting.

Prior research indicated that the highest output occurs when 20% of the surface area is void and the hole diameter is 200 μm [24]. Through calculation, this design was determined to contain 19.92% void-to-surface area ratio.

The slots are distributed in an evenly spaced pattern to ensure consistent energy harvesting.

B. Working Principle

The diffraction of sound waves is the desired form of energy creation and harvesting. The closeness of the slots directs the acoustic waves through them. The wave interference creates an outbound resultant wave that is of some amplitude compared to the incoming waves. Resultant waves will cause an increase in the number of waves feeding through the two layers of the triboelectric pair. As the number of waves increase between the layers of the pair, vibrations will occur therefore allowing the transfer of electrons to occur. Increasing the frequency and amplitude of the waves will directly increase the resultant waves allowing for more energy to be created. Diagram of sound wave interference is depicted in Figure 2.

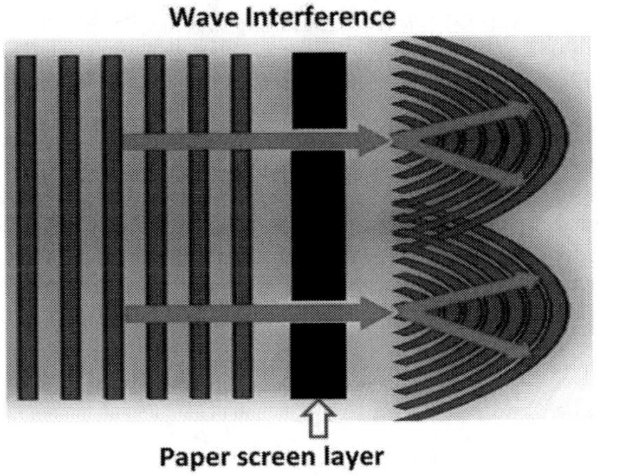

Figure 2. Diagram of sound wave interference.

The triboelectric pair of materials for the TENG design is paper and PTFE [31]. The enlarged view shown in Figure 3 gives the layout layer by layer of the TENG. Printer paper is covered with a layer of ball point pen ink, it is then machined by the laser cuter to create the slits. The layer is placed on the top of a PTFE plastic layer. Directly under this plastic layer is another layer of pen ink spread across paper. These layers are solid and do not contain any slits. The pattern of slots in the paper will allow vibration to move the triboelectric pairs and generate energy to power an indicator LED.

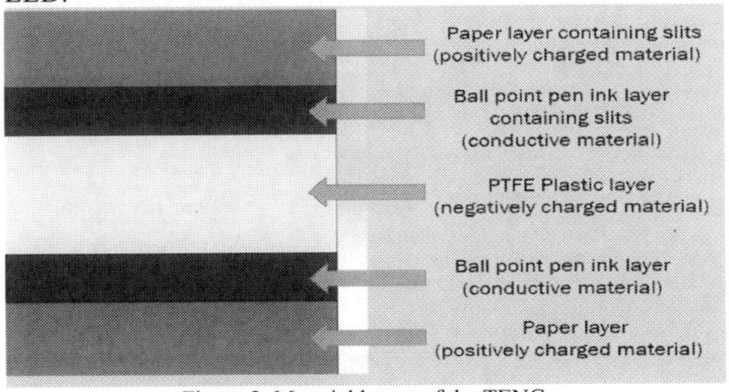

Figure 3. Material layers of the TENG.

C. Flow Simulation

A flow simulation in SolidWorks was performed to determine the pattern of air flow within the TENG. This simulation was used to determine the likelihood of vibration within the TENG to produce optimal transfers of charges. As shown in Figure 4, the velocity contours give a representation of how the air is going to move through the slots of the TENG. As the air flows through the slots, a wave effect is produced within the TENG. This wave effect will allow the layers of the triboelectric pair to vibrate against each other, which will facilitate the triboelectric effect to occur. The figure shows the direction of the voice and breath from the wearer. These two waveforms contact the slits in the paper layer that interferes and creates a resultant wave that vibrates the layers together. The resultant vibrating wave is shown affecting the contours between the layer with slits and the plastic layer. The vibrations continue through the paper layer and affect the contours past the plastic layer into the second layer of paper.

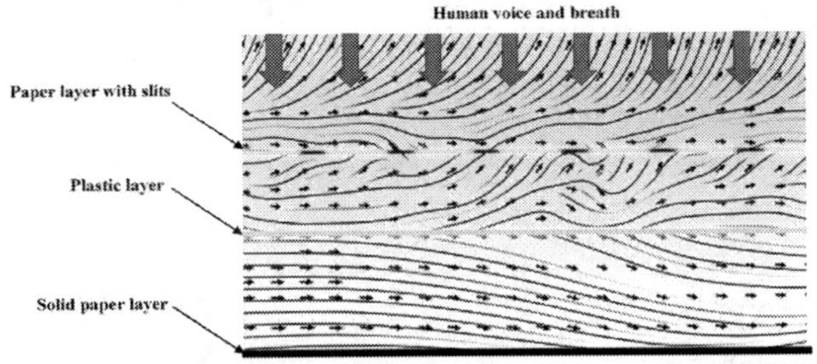

Figure 4. SolidWorks flow simulation of the design with the TENG highlighted in blue. The blue arrows represent the direction of the incoming human voice and breath. The layers of the TENG itself is depicted in a close-up view. The small black arrows in the figure itself represent the movement of the air contours intertwined between the layers of the TENG.

The external velocity representing a human's breath was set as an input of 1.3 m/s. As the contours travel between the layers of the TENG, a wave is created. Since the slots of the material are placed closely together, the waves that travel through will interfere with each other; this interference creates resultant waves, which maximizes the number of waves between the layers. This resultant wave is the main source of movement needed to create the transfer of electrons between the two triboelectric pairs.

D. Fabrication and Assembly

The nanogenerator consists of two sections of paper with measurements of 8 cm width, 6 cm in length, and 0.01 mm thickness. A piece of PTFE plastic was cut to the same measurements as the paper. An evenly distributed layer of ink was spread across an A4 sheet of printer paper. The pen ink cartridge was removed from the barrel of the pen and the ink flowed freely from the cartridge onto the paper. Using a small paint brush, the ink was spread evenly across the surface until the entire sheet was coated. Having a full sheet of paper coated in ink allowed for easier machining with a Fusion 40 carbon dioxide laser cutter. The laser cutter uses a grid system to align and cut material and using a full sheet of paper eliminates potential error in cuts that could be off centered or not perfectly symmetrical. The full sheet of paper promotes stability and accuracy during the cutting procedure. Using AutoCAD, the design template for the slot configuration was uploaded to the laser cutter. This data was uploaded in different cuts; each row of slots was one separate cut; the next cut was the perimeter of the nanogenerator itself. The laser cutter allows the user to change the cutting speed and power of the laser for each job that is uploaded to it. The following job settings are specific to the Fusion M2 40 Epilog Laser only. The jobs associated with the cutting of the slots had a power setting of 15% and a speed of 50%. Cutting time was approximately six minutes for all cuts to be finished. The speed of the process could be lower than six minutes with an increase to the cutter speed, but this setting was utilized to assure the material was cut all the way through. A plastic insert was also cut using the solid configuration of the paper inset. Although PTFE is not harmful to the human respiratory system [30], another layer of normal filter material can be added to the inner side of the face mask to avoid any potential hazard. Figure 5(a) shows different layers of the triboelectric nanogenerator fabricated using common printer paper and PTFE plastic and the laser-cut configuration of the TENG paper inserts.

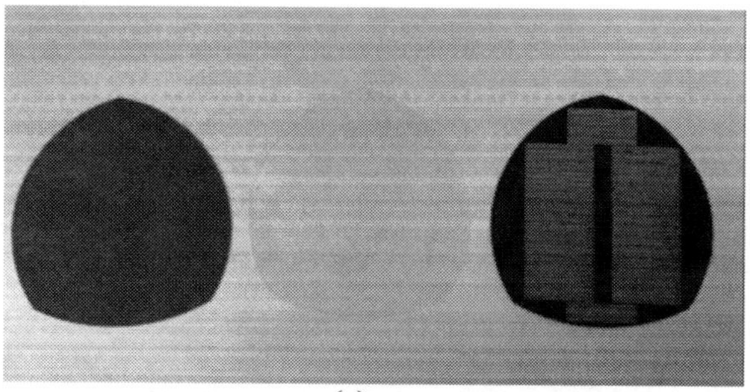

(a)

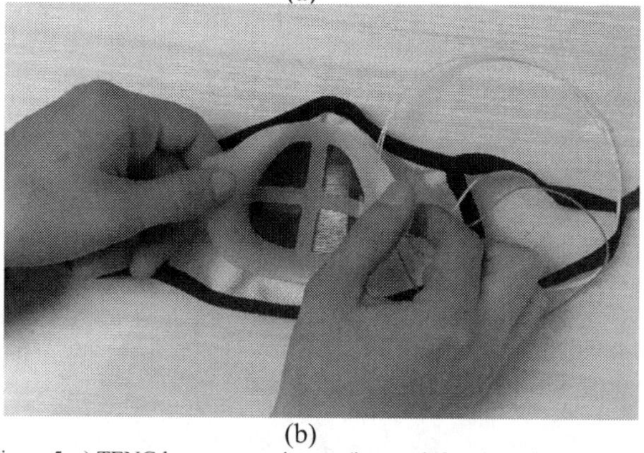

(b)

Figure 5. a) TENG layers: paper inserts (images left and write) with plastic insert (middle image). b) Assembled TENG in mask frame placed into cloth mask with wires for testing purposes.

Six nanogenerators were cut with the laser. These nanogenerator sets were then connected in series to maximize the voltage output of the assembled TENG. The assembled TENG was then placed into the plastic mask frame where it will sit when placed into the mask. Another plastic frame is placed on top of the assembled TENG to hold it in place. When the TENG is layered between the two frames, it can be placed into any cloth mask. Figure 5(b) shows the assembled TENG within the mask frames and the thermistor placed within a cloth mask.

III. RESULTS AND DISCUSSION

The testing procedure involved using a Bluetooth speaker to create acoustic sound waves. Although the type of sound generated by the speaker may not be similar to the one produced by the human, the electronic speaker is the most reliable device generating consistent sound for the proof of concept and testing purposes. The TENG was placed on top of the speaker and music was played from a mobile electronic device. The selected song for this testing process was "Back in Black" by AC/DC. The energy created was recorded using a NI-6003 Data Acquisition Card through the LabVIEW software. The voltage detected directly corresponded to the volume and rhythm of the music.

In order to get the optimum voltage results, different sound intensities were applied to the mask and voltage as a function of time was measured. It was found that sound pressure levels of 70 dB and 80 dB yield the most output. Therefore, these two sound levels were used and the effect was recorded as the voltage outputs. Figure 6 shows the generated voltage as a function of time at two sound pressure levels.

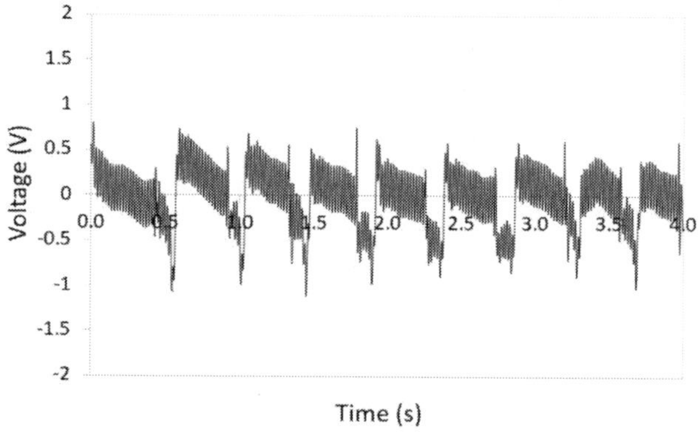

(a)

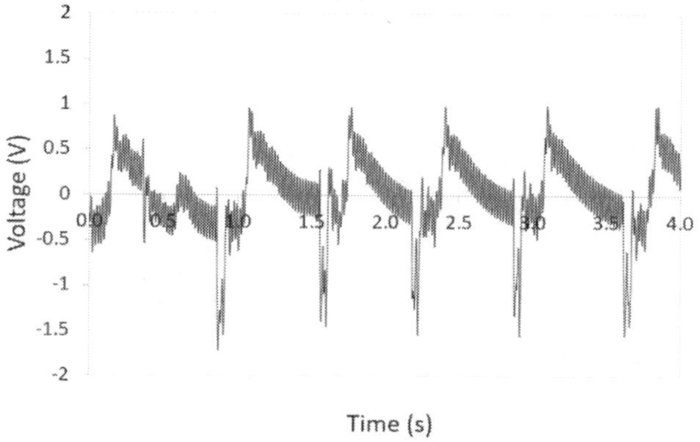

(b)

Figure 6. Generated voltages of the developed TENG as a function of time at two sound pressure levels of 70 dB (a) and 80 dB (b).

The graphs shown illustrate a direct change from an instrumental section back to singing at different decibel levels. It is clear that the graphs contain both major and minor vibrational cycles in both sound pressure levels. The minor cycles are within each major cycle. Comparing the graphs of two sound pressure levels implied that the graph of 70 dB level experienced a higher frequency than that of 80 dB level. This is likely because the layers get a better chance to move against each other in 70 dB case. On the other hand, the graph of 80 dB pressure level shows a higher peak-to-peak voltage amplitude than that of 70 dB level. This is likely because of the longer time that the triboelectric harvester layers take to move against each other, resulting in a more travel between layers and so more voltage amplitude.

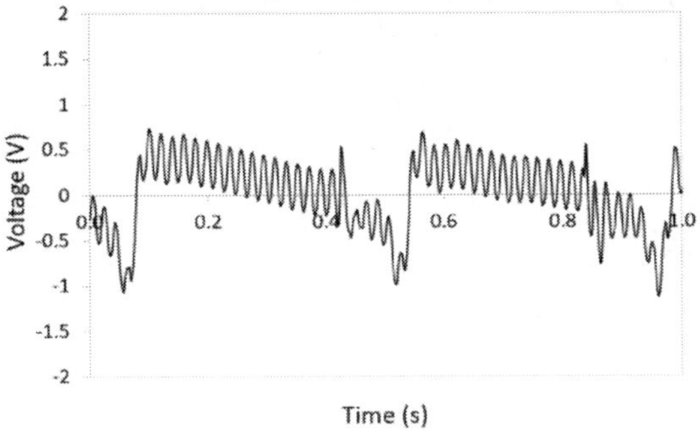

(a)

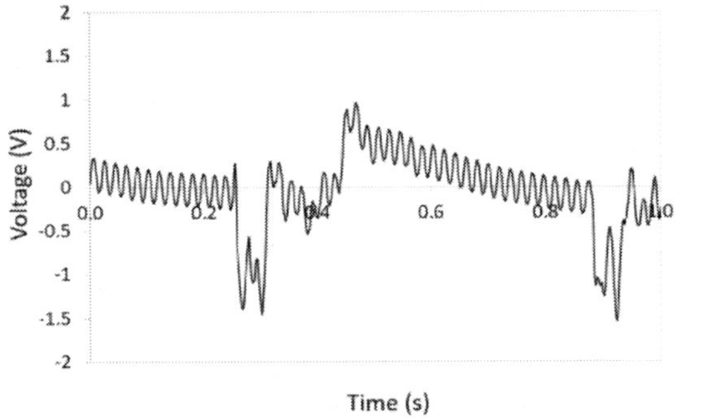

(b)

Figure 7. Zoomed graphs of Figure 6 focusing on individual major cycles (generated voltages as a function of time) at two sound pressure levels of 70 dB (a) and 80 dB (b).

TABLE 1. SUMMARY OF VOLTAGE AND FREQUENCY VALUES OF TESTING RESULTS SHOWN IN FIGURES 6 TO 8.

Cycle Type	Parameter	Sound Pressure Level (SPL)	
		70 dB	80 dB
Major Cycles	Peak-to-Peak Voltage (V)	1.72	2.48
	Frequency (Hz)	2.27	1.61
Minor Cycles	Peak-to-Peak Voltage (V)	0.60	0.38
	Frequency (Hz)	51.3	52.2

In order to analyze cycles in each graph, zoomed graphs focusing on individual major cycles were plotted, as shown in Figure 7. It appears that minor cycles in the two sound pressure levels may have different frequencies and voltage amplitudes. In order to look into this, individual minor cycles were developed for both 70 dB and 80 dB sound pressure levels, as shown in Figure 8.

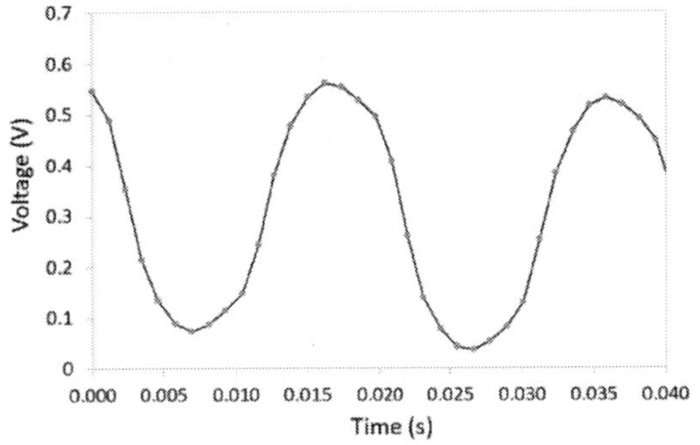

(a)

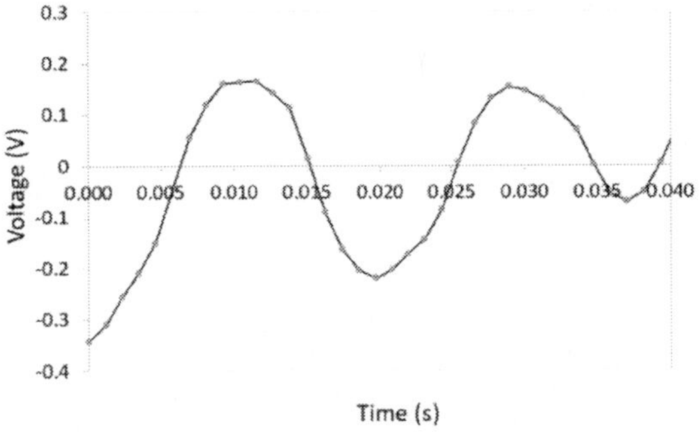

(b)

Figure 8. Zoomed graphs of Figure 8 focusing on individual minor cycles (generated voltages as a function of time) at two sound pressure levels of 70 dB (a) and 80 dB (b).

Comparing the two graphs indicates that peak-to-peak voltage amplitude in 70 dB pressure level is significantly higher that of 80 dB case while frequency of graph of 80 dB pressure level is slightly higher than that of 70 dB case. It is most likely the paper layers vibrate locally in a way that the contact between layers will stay locally longer. Table 1 summaries the voltage and frequency values in all cases. The highest voltage drop recorded resulted in 2.48 PP-V.

In the next research following this work, a thermistor temperature sensor and LED will be used in conjunction with Arduino coding to track body temperature and act as an indicator for feverish temperatures. The major drawback of the triboelectric nanogenerator used in the facemask is the low current harvested which limits a continuous temperature monitoring. This limitation will be overcome using a tiny battery charger used to store the power generated by the nanogenerator and power the thermistor as needed. In addition, further testing will be performed using the sound generated by human respiration.

IV. Conclusions

A novel paper-based triboelectric nanogenerator was used to develop the groundwork of a self-powered face mask. This TENG uses low-cost, easily accessible, and recyclable materials to act as the triboelectric pair. These recyclable materials are paper layered in pen ink and PTFE plastic. The triboelectric effect was facilitated within the mask through the vibrations of acoustic frequency. The purpose of this TENG is to power a temperature sensor to indicate feverish body temperatures on the wearer.

Acoustic energy was used to generate vibrations within the layers of the triboelectric pair. Slots were laser-cut into the paper layer to create a void for sound waves to move through. The slots were also placed closely together to generate wave interference and maximize the number of waves travelling in the TENG to create optimal vibrations. These vibrations allowed for the materials to touch and transfer electrons. The triboelectric effect of this design was also enabled through an up-down-and-around sliding motion to mimic the movement of the mask wearer's jaw. The combination of these two motions was able to generate a voltage within the TENG. The produced TENG generated a maximum peak-to-peak voltage of 2.47 V at the sound pressure level of 80 dB.

REFERENCES

[1] T. Dillahunt, J. Mankoff, E. Paulos, and S. Fussell, "It's not all about 'green': energy use in low-income communities," in Proceedings of the 11th international conference on Ubiquitous computing, pp. 255-264, September 2009.

[2] Z. L. Wang, "On Maxwell's displacement current for energy and sensors: the origin of nanogenerators," in Materials Today, vol. 20, no. 2, pp. 74-82, March 2017.

[3] H. Zheng et al., "Concurrent harvesting of ambient energy by hybrid nanogenerators for wearable self-powered systems and active remote sensing," in ACS Appl. Mater. Interfaces, vol. 10, no. 17, pp. 14708–14715, April 2018.

[4] M. H. Anisi, G. Abdul-Salaam, M. Y. I. Idris, A. W. A. Wahab, and I. Ahmedy, "Energy harvesting and battery power based routing in wireless sensor networks," in Wireless Networks, vol. 23, no. 1, pp. 249–266, Jan. 2017.

[5] X. Yue et al., "Development of an indoor photovoltaic energy harvesting module for autonomous sensors in building air quality applications," in IEEE Internet Things Journal, vol. 4, no. 6, pp. 2092–2103, 20 September 2017.

[6] K. Kim, G. Song, C. Park, and K. S. Yun, "Multifunctional woven structure operating as triboelectric energy harvester, capacitive tactile sensor array, and piezoresistive strain sensor array," in Sensors, vol. 17, no. 11, p. 2582, 9 November 2017.

[7] Q. Shi, T. Wang, and C. Lee, "MEMS based broadband piezoelectric ultrasonic energy harvester (PUEH) for enabling self-powered implantable biomedical devices," in Scientific Reports, vol. 6, no. 24946, pp. 1-10, 26 April 2016.

[8] I. Jung, Y. H. Shin, S. Kim, J. Y. Choi, and C. Y. Kang, "Flexible piezoelectric polymer-based energy harvesting for roadway applications," in Applied Energy, vol. 197, pp. 222-229, 1 July 2017.

[9] M. A. Abdullah and J. F. Jamil, "Harvesting energy from the vibration of suspension of a passenger vehicle," in Proc. Recent Adv. Mech. Mech. Eng., pp. 128–133, 2015.

[10] S. Wu et al., "An electromagnetic wearable 3-DoF resonance human body motion energy harvester using ferrofluid as a lubricant," in Applied Energy, vol. 197, pp. 364–374, 2017.

[11] J. He et al., "Triboelectric-piezoelectric-electromagnetic hybrid nanogenerator for high-efficient vibration energy harvesting and self-powered wireless monitoring system," in Nano Energy, vol. 43, pp. 326–339, January 2018.

[12] Y. Liao and H. Sodano, "Optimal power, power limit and damping of vibration based piezoelectric power harvesters," in Smart Materials and Structures 27, no. 7, p. 075057, 2018.

[13] X. Ma and X. Zhang, "Low cost electrostatic vibration energy harvesters based on negatively-charged polypropylene cellular films with a folded structure," in Smart Materials and Structures, vol. 26, no. 8, p. 085001, 20 June 2017.

[14] M. L. Seol, S. B. Jeon, J. W. Han, and Y. K. Choi, "Ferrofluid-based triboelectric-electromagnetic hybrid generator for sensitive and sustainable vibration energy harvesting," in Nano Energy, vol. 31, pp. 233–238, 2017.

[15] R. Hall and R. Rashidi. "Multi-Directional Universal Energy Harvesting Ball," in Micromachines 12, no. 4, p. 457, 2021.

[16] J. Bianconi, J. Hallett, J. Pealo, and R. Rashidi. "A hybrid piezoelectric and inductive rotational energy harvester," in IOP Conference Series: Materials Science and Engineering, vol. 626, no. 1, p. 012004. 2019.

[17] R. Rashidi, N. Summerville, and M. Nasri. "Magnetically actuated piezoelectric-based rotational energy harvester with enhanced output in wide range of rotating speeds." in IEEE Transactions on Magnetics 55, no. 9, pp. 1-8, 2019.

[18] C. Chen et al., "Micro triboelectric ultrasonic device for acoustic energy transfer and signal communication," in Nature Communications, vol. 11, no. 1, pp. 1-9, 2020.

[19] N. Cui et al., "High performance sound driven triboelectric nanogenerator for harvesting noise energy," in Nano Energy, vol. 15, pp. 321-328, July 2015.

[20] C. Wu, T. W. Kima, S. Sung, J. H. Park, and F. Li, "Ultrasoft and cuttable paper-based triboelectric nanogenerators for mechanical energy harvesting," in Nano Energy, vol. 44, pp. 279-287, February 2018.

[21] S. Khalid, I. Raouf, A. Khan, N. Kim, and H.S. Kim, "A review of human-powered energy harvesting for smart electronics: recent progress and challenges," in International Journal of Precision Engineering and Manufacturing-Green Technology, vol. 6, pp. 1-31, 29 July 2019.

[22] S. Wang, L. Lin, and Z. L. Wang, "Nanoscale triboelectric-effect-enabled energy conversion for sustainably powering portable electronics," in Nano Letters, vol. 12, no. 12, pp. 6339-6346, 6 November 2012.

[23] H. Zhang et al., "Single-electrode-based rotating triboelectric nanogenerator for harvesting energy from tires," in ACS Nano, vol. 8, no. 1, pp. 680-689, 2014.

[24] X. Fan et al., "Ultrathin, rollable, paper-based triboelectric nanogenerator for acoustic energy harvesting and self-powered sound recording," in ACS Nano, vol. 9, no. 4, pp. 4236-4243, 19 March 2015.

[25] Q. Zhong et al., "A paper-based nanogenerator as a power source and active sensor," in Energy & Environmental Science, vol. 6, no. 6, pp. 1779-1784, 28 March 2013.

[26] X. S. Zhang, M. Su, J. Brugger, and B. Kim, "Penciling a triboelectric nanogenerator on paper for autonomous power MEMS applications," in Nano Energy, vol. 33, pp. 393-401, March 2017.

[27] K. Xia et al., "Painting a high-output triboelectric nanogenerator on paper for harvesting energy from human body motion," in Nano Energy, vol. 50, pp. 571-580, 2018.

[28] Centers for Disease Control and Prevention, "Considerations for wearing masks," United States of America, 2020.

[29] R. A. Lester and J. D. Hoit, "Nasal and oral inspiration during natural speech breathing," in Journal of Speech, Language, and Hearing Research, vol.57, no.3, pp.734-742, 1 June 2014.

[30] B. Ghatak et al., "Design of a Self-powered Smart Mask for COVID-19," in arXiv:2005.08305 [physics.med-ph], 2020.

[31] D. W. Kim, S. W. Kim, and U. Jeong, "Lipids: source of static electricity of regenerative natural substances and nondestructive energy harvesting," in Advanced Materials, vol. 30, no. 52, p. 1804949, 2 November 2018.